GULAG BOSS

GULAG BOSS

BOSS

A SOVIET MEMOIR

FYODOR VASILEVICH
MOCHULSKY

TRANSLATED AND EDITED BY

DEBORAH KAPLE

OXFORD
UNIVERSITY PRESS
2011

OXFORD
UNIVERSITY PRESS

Oxford University Press, Inc., publishes works that further
Oxford University's objective of excellence
in research, scholarship, and education.

Oxford   New York
Auckland   Cape Town   Dar es Salaam   Hong Kong   Karachi
Kuala Lumpur   Madrid Melbourne   Mexico City   Nairobi
New Delhi   Shanghai   Taipei   Toronto

With offices in
Argentina   Austria   Brazil   Chile   Czech Republic   France   Greece
Guatemala   Hungary   Italy   Japan   Poland   Portugal   Singapore
South Korea   Switzerland   Thailand   Turkey   Ukraine   Vietnam

Published by Oxford University Press, Inc.
198 Madison Avenue, New York, NY 10016

www.oup.com

Library of Congress Cataloging-in-Publication Data
Mochulsky, Fyodor Vasilevich, 1919–1999.
Gulag boss : a Soviet memoir / by Fyodor Vasilevich Mochulsky ;
translated and edited by Deborah Kaple.
p.   cm.   Includes bibliographical references.
ISBN 978-0-19-974266-0
1. Mochulsky, Fyodor Vasilevich, 1919–1999.   2. Soviet Union. Narodnyï
komissariat vnutrennikh del—Officials and employees—Biography.
3. Prisons—Soviet Union—Officials and employees—Biography.
4. Soviet Union—History—1925–1953—Biography.   5. Glavnoe upravlenie
ispravitel'no-trudovykh lagereĭ OGPU—History.   6. Concentration camps—Russia
(Federation)—Pechora River Region—History—20th century.   7. Political prisoners—
Russia (Federation)—Pechora River Region—History—20th century.
8. Political prisoners—Russia (Federation)—Pechora River Region—
Social conditions—20th century.   9. Forced labor—Russia (Federation)—
Pechora River Region—History—20th century.
10. Pechora River Region (Russia)—History—20th century.
I. Kaple, Deborah A.   II. Title.
DK268.M59A3 2010   365'.45092—dc22   [B]   201[000]7440

1 3 5 7 9 8 6 4 2

Printed in the United States of America
on acid-free paper

Frontispiece: First assignment in the Gulag: Mochulsky as unit boss and foreman in Pernashor,
north of the Arctic Circle, winter 1940–41.

In memory of all who suffered in the Gulag

CONTENTS

GULAG BOSS

INTRODUCTION

Deborah Kaple

This is one man's story of work and survival in Pechorlag, an outpost of Stalin's Gulag situated north of the Arctic Circle. Fyodor Vasilevich Mochulsky (1918–1999) was not a prisoner in a Gulag camp; he was an employee. Unlike the famous accounts by Aleksandr Solzhenitsyn, Evgeniia Ginsberg, Varlam Shalamov,[1] and others, this story is told by an employee of the NKVD (People's Commissariat for Internal Affairs) who worked as a boss in charge of several units of convicts in the 1940s. In the Gulag literature, memoirs written by camp bosses are rare. *Gulag Boss* is the first account of the Gulag from a "management" point of view to be published in English.

In 1940, Mochulsky was a twenty-two-year-old student at a transport engineering institute and a candidate member of the Communist Party of the Soviet Union (CPSU). As a party member, he was recruited as an engineer to work in the Gulag to help construct a 500-kilometer-long railroad line over permafrost. Although he was sent to work as a foreman, upon arrival at the forced labor camp he found himself thrown into the role of boss because of the lack of personnel.[2] In this memoir, he describes the lives and concerns of the Gulag staff, NKVD guards, and Communist Party cadres during the years 1940 to 1946. As a GULAG NKVD[3] employee and not a prisoner, Mochulsky provides a new perspective on the particular evil of the Gulag. His story brings us again to the age-old question of how apparently "ordinary men" can participate in extraordinarily evil actions.[4]

GULAG is an acronym for the words *Glavnoe Upravlenie Lagerei*, or Main Administration of Camps. Although it is extremely difficult to establish how many camps existed, scholars have found evidence in the Russian archives of approximately 478 large and small camps in 1940. This included 53 corrective labor camps, a network of 425 corrective labor colonies, as well as various prisons and "special settlements."[5] Between 1928 and 1953, the Soviet government saw these camps and colonies as a significant labor source for the building of Soviet socialism.[6] Although it is exceedingly difficult to estimate the numbers of victims of the Stalinist repression, scholars estimate that between 20 million and 28.7 million people served time in the Gulag (including special exiles).[7] As to the number of victims, some scholars feel that in the years 1921–1953, as many as 7 million executions took place, others say 2.7 million perished, while documentable executions account for around 1.1 million deaths.[8] We do know from hundreds of disparate accounts, that thousands of people were summarily shot, or died in transit during long treks across the USSR and are therefore not accounted for in any ledgers.[9] And we also know now that during the war years one of every four Gulag prisoners died annually.[10]

Despite the extent of the murder and abuse that Russian survivors documented in innumerable books, memoirs and articles, as well as the excellent academic work starting in the 1940s in the West,[11] Stalin's Gulag nevertheless remains shrouded in mystery for many outside of academia. The Gulag was very much the creature of the secret police that dominated life in the Soviet Union for much of its existence.[12] Shortly after the Bolsheviks took power in 1917, Lenin himself advocated carrying out "merciless mass terror" and forcing the fledgling regime's enemies into concentration camps.[13] Thus the newly created Soviet police apparatus quickly began to oversee the new government's prisons and labor camps. The secret police were crucial to maintaining the Communist Party's tight grip on Soviet society.[14] Both Lenin and Stalin used this organization extensively to eliminate real and perceived enemies. In 1928, when Stalin introduced the massive industrialization and collectivization programs of the First Five-Year Plan, the NKVD expanded its role to ensure fulfillment of his goals.

The secret police not only ran the prisons and the Gulag's system of forced labor, but it carried out extra-legal mass arrests and executions, detained persons believed to be hostile to the government, rounded up thousands of peasants and non-Russians in the USSR and sent them to special settlements in remote areas of the country, guarded state borders, and even made Gulag propaganda films under Stalin.[15]

GULAG NKVD was crucial in the push toward the modernization of the country that was central to Stalin's vision. Forced labor camps were an integral part of the gigantic construction projects that became a hallmark of Stalinism. Many Soviet cities, dams, bridges, canals, rail lines, factories and mines, and even the beautiful Moscow subway system, were all built using slave labor provided and managed by GULAG NKVD.

For decades, the USSR government went to great lengths to conceal the NKVD's involvement in Soviet life. Today, thanks to the opening of the archives of the former Soviet Union in the 1990s, the NKVD's central role has become clearer. Certainly, we better understand the enormity of the human tragedy that was the Gulag. The Soviet Gulag surely ranks as one of the most evil political creations of the twentieth century, along with Hitler's Holocaust in Europe, Pol Pot's slaughter of millions in Cambodia, and Mao Zedong's serial campaigns that killed millions of Chinese citizens. The Gulag stands alone as the longest-running program of state sponsored killing in that very bloody century.[16]

THE SECRET WORLD

Most Soviet citizens knew that there was a "separate country behind barbed wires" in the former USSR. People spoke of the *malenkaia zona,* or "little zone" (the Gulag camps) and the *bolshaia zona,* or the "big zone" (the USSR as one big Gulag camp).[17] The writer and Gulag survivor Varlam Shalamov commented that everyone was "constantly aware of the gaping jaws of the Gulag threatening to devour us."[18] But the Gulag's very enormity and the fear of terror led to a generally understood silence among Soviet citizens. Today some scholars feel that the damage to the Russian national psyche was not limited to the millions who served time in the camps or their families. The Gulag as an institution harmed social relations by normalizing government-sponsored violence, spreading terror, universalizing mutual suspicion, and fostering paranoid secrecy even among close friends and family members.[19]

In the West, survivor memoirs began appearing in the 1930s.[20] Although a number of academic specialists were interested in understanding the scope and importance of the Gulag during the Soviet period, hard data were sketchy, and allegations were not easily proved.

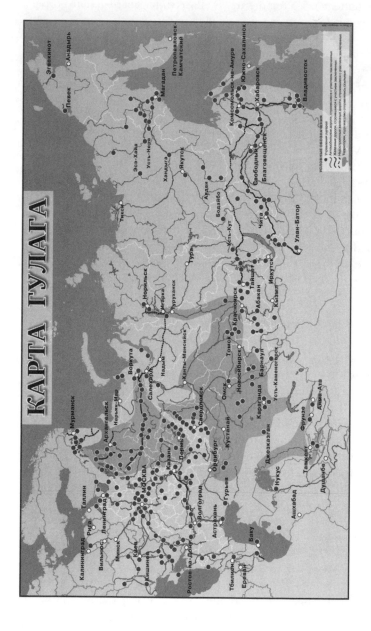

This map shows the most developed Gulag camps of the USSR (many more existed for which we have no data). Courtesy of the Memorial Society, Moscow, 1989.

During Stalin's time, there was an almost complete blackout of real information, and in its place a sophisticated propaganda machine assured many that Soviet socialism was correct and on track. In addition, even official legislation concerning the Gulag was not always publicly known, so neither Soviet citizens nor the international community understood exactly what was happening.[21] It is important also to remember that there were many adherents of socialism in the West in those days.[22] These influential people either believed in Stalin and kept quiet about any real or suspected negative aspects of Soviet life, or simply felt that the idea of socialism was important enough to be supported, no matter the costs.[23] It would be easy to judge these people when we look at events through today's eyes, but we need to keep in mind that the Soviet government was incredibly successful at hiding the truth.[24] Ignorance may be no excuse, but it makes the decades of silence more comprehensible.

This pervasive secrecy made studying even apparently banal aspects of Soviet life very difficult. For example, I worked for a few years as a Soviet transportation specialist at Wharton Econometrics. I published scholarly articles on rail transport in the USSR, and I was surrounded by the best experts in the field. Yet until the 1990s, very little in the available Soviet literature led us to believe that GULAG NKVD had built and maintained the Soviet transportation system. Revisiting the pre-1990s scholarly literature on Soviet transport, I found few references to the NKVD, forced labor, or the Gulag.[25] Yet a recently discovered Soviet government memo dated January 2, 1940, revealed that the Politburo approved the organization of the Chief Administration of Camps for Railroad Construction, within the NKVD. From then on, until Stalin's death in 1953, this division of the NKVD built all the rail lines in the USSR. They did this using Gulag labor.[26] It is now somewhat difficult to recall the extent to which even the most committed scholars of the Soviet system had to work through suppositions, inferences, and guesses to try to understand what was happening in the USSR.[27]

Mochulsky himself, a party member in 1940, had a very sketchy understanding of the Gulag before he arrived at Pechorlag. He writes that he believed what he'd heard and seen in the Soviet press: that the Gulag transformed criminals into honest citizens through hard labor. A high-ranking CPSU apparatchik clarified how the subterfuge was carried out. He explained that every Gulag camp had two names. The real name of his camp was Pechorlag, literally "Pechor" for the Pechora River and "lag" for *lager*, or camp. But if the camp were ever mentioned in the press, it would always be called Pechorstroi, "stroi" being the word for construction site. To anyone outside of the Gulag system, Mochulsky needed to say that he was stationed at a construction site. There would be little reason to associate his job with a prison labor camp.

WHO WAS FYODOR MOCHULSKY?

I first met Fyodor Mochulsky in 1992. I had gone to Moscow to take advantage of the opening of the Communist Party archives for a book I was researching about the Soviet Advisors Program.[28] My work in the archives did not go well, mostly because the archivists were reluctant to let me tell a story that ended badly, in their eyes, with the Sino-Soviet split in 1959. In desperation, I did a very American thing: I placed an advertisement in two daily newspapers, *Pravda* and *Moskovskaia Pravda* (*Moscow Pravda*), asking to interview people who had been sent as advisors to China in the 1950s. My Russian friends warned me that no one would answer such an advertisement, but actually, a few hundred citizens called to offer their stories.[29]

Mochulsky was one of these respondents, and I chose to interview him because of his work advising the Chinese on ideological and Communist Party matters. After his job at GULAG NKVD, he served as a diplomat in China. He later took another job with the NKVD, by then called the KGB, to work at the CPSU Central Committee. He was intelligent and knowledgeable, and in the course of our many meetings, we became friendly. Our friendship was largely based on a mutual interest in China. Not until nearly the end of my year in Moscow did he tell me about his Gulag memoir. He had written the memoir after he had retired from the USSR Foreign Ministry in 1988. His family says that he often spoke about the Gulag and his work there because the experience deeply troubled him all his life.[30] During the late 1990s, the years that might be called the "repentance/confessional" glasnost years, he sat down and wrote out his reminiscences.[31]

In the early 1990s, Mochulsky attempted to publish his memoir in Russia, but he never found a publisher. This was a time of great change in Russia, and everyone was looking forward to the new, post-Communist future, so his story detailing how the NKVD ran the Gulag camps found no takers. In the end, he brought the manuscript to me, along with photos he had taken, and asked me to translate and publish it in English.

I was taken aback to realize that this apparently pleasant and affable man had been part of a system I already associated with terror, but I accepted the manuscript. For many years it sat on a shelf, as other professional and personal obligations claimed my attention. But with time, and in the face of an apparent rehabilitation of Stalin's legacy in Putin's Russia, I realized that this was a story that needed to be told.[32]

THE GULAG RISES: A BRIEF HISTORY

Vladimir Lenin, the founder of the Soviet state and the genius behind the Communist takeover of Russia in 1917, established the first secret police just weeks after the Bolshevik Revolution. Known as the Cheka (which means Extraordinary Commission), its original purpose was to guard the Petrograd site of the Bolshevik Revolution. It was not long before the new regime experienced major opposition, and the Cheka was ordered to pursue all "enemies of Soviet power" and throw them into prisons.[33] As Marxists, the Bolsheviks distinguished the class of a person and used class labels to carry out mass arrests. By 1918, the year Mochulsky was born, these early Soviet prisons already housed a sizable population, mostly opponents of the Bolsheviks, as well as a number of common criminals.[34] By the end of 1920, there were eighty-four camps in forty-three provinces of the RSFSR.[35] In 1923, the OGPU (precursor to the NKVD) founded Solovki, a prison labor camp complex housed in a former monastery on several islands in the White Sea. This was the first camp where the secret police learned to use prison labor for profit.[36]

Several key events in the late 1920s and early 1930s (after Lenin's death and Stalin's rise to absolute power) helped shape the Gulag. Among these were the Bolshevik policy of grain requisition and "dekulakization," which meant the arrest and deportation of the *relatively* prosperous peasants (labeled "kulaks," or fists, in Russian) who resisted the state's forced seizure of their grain; the organization of the first major corrective labor camps and special settlements in remote areas; and a June 27, 1929, law by which the Politburo created a network of self-supporting camps to replace the existing system of prisons. The Politburo stated that task of the camps was to colonize remote areas of the country and "develop mineral deposits using convict labor."[37] Then, in October 1928, Stalin announced the First Five-Year Plan, which included forced collectivization in the countryside and rapid industrial development in the country.

Collectivization of agriculture was accompanied by mass arrests, executions, and the deportation of peasants, primarily the more prosperous ones, village intelligentsia, and priests.[38] In the cities, the secret police sought out all "counterrevolutionary organizations," the intelligentsia, and the so-called bourgeois specialists (the management class that was trained before the Bolshevik Revolution). Those arrested were sent to the Gulag, exiled far from their homes, or shot. Millions were killed and deported in these grand schemes to change Russia overnight, and the resultant ruinous famine in the early 1930s killed millions more.[39]

In the 1930s, Stalin built on the prison system by simultaneously expanding the camp network and exploiting prisoners as slave labor for his gigantic economic programs. State-sponsored NKVD terror led to a huge increase in the number of prisoners in the Gulag.[40] Between 1929 and 1953, a sizable cross-section of the Soviet (and foreign) population passed through the Gulag, as the prison system filled with people arrested on trumped-up charges.[41] Russian estimates are that between 1931 and 1953, about 3.8 million people were arrested for generic "counterrevolutionary" crimes, of whom 786,000 were simply shot. During the Great Terror of 1937–1938, approximately 1.6 million people were arrested, and more than half of them were shot (this would mean roughly fifteen hundred daily executions).[42] We now know that local NKVD officers were given a quota of people to arrest or execute, an order they often proudly overfulfilled.[43]

Mochulsky lived through the Great Terror as a young man. He recalls how the Soviet government justified the witch hunts and mass arrests in his native Belorussia. Excuses for this violence appeared in the press every day: geopolitical "realities," capitalist encirclement, and what the Soviets felt was an international hostility to the building of socialism in the USSR. The relentless propaganda against "Enemies of the People" was enough to lead many to suspect that real opponents to socialism existed and that the NKVD was simply protecting the motherland.

The Gulag continued to grow, coming into its own with enormous, remarkable projects that impressed both Russians and foreign observers with their size and the speed with which they were built. The first prison-labor showcase was the White Sea Canal (called Belomor in Russian), begun in mid-1930. Stalin demanded that the canal be built in twenty months using the most primitive equipment and tools. More than one hundred thousand convicts worked on the canal, and many perished. Although the canal ended up not being very useful, it was immortalized in a propaganda book of vignettes edited by the prominent writer Maxim Gorky.[44] It was a project of which Stalin was enormously proud.[45] By mid-1931, the NKVD was the USSR's largest construction organization.

On the basis of the "success" of Belomor, NKVD slave labor camps began to be built across the nation. For instance, in November 1931 a Politburo directive ordered the NKVD to form a Gulag camp in the far east, in Kolyma; in September 1932, the NKVD took over the construction of the canal linking the Volga and Moscow Rivers; in October 1932, the NKVD moved into the construction of the Baikal-Amur Railroad in the far east. In October 1932, the NKVD also formed the Ukhta-Pechora Trust to organize coal and oil production and develop other resources in the Pechora basin.[46] This was the area that included the camp that Mochulsky describes in his memoir.

During this frightening time of "terror by quota," the Mochulsky family was very lucky. When Fyodor was young, and the family still lived in Minsk, his father worked as a senior research fellow at the Institute of Belorussian Culture. When Fyodor's father sensed that he was about to be purged (because his boss, a prestigious professor, was arrested on bogus charges), the family left their native Belorussia for Moscow. There, young Mochulsky went to work in a factory, after which he entered an institute to study railroad engineering.[47]

In 1939 the Soviet Union, anticipating the coming war in Europe, signed a nonaggression pact with Nazi Germany. This agreement had the incidental effect of adding thousands of new prisoners to the Soviet Union's slave labor camps. As the Soviet government moved in to take over parts of the countries allowed it by the secret protocols of the Nazi-Soviet Pact, the NKVD arrested huge numbers of non-Russian "enemies of Soviet power." The period between September 1939 and the Nazi invasion in June 1941 saw a huge increase in the number of prisoners sent to the Gulag due to these territorial acquisitions as well as to prisoners taken during the Winter War with Finland.[48]

Mochulsky was to see this influx of foreigners into the prison camps for himself in 1940, with the arrival of Polish and Finnish prisoners at Pechorlag.[49] Mochulsky's camp was in the vicinity of Vorkuta in the Pechora Basin, which contained massive coal and other mineral deposits critical to the Soviet war effort. Given fears of the coming war with the Germans, the Soviet government planned to build a new railroad that would provide access to these underground riches far from any possible invasion route. Transporting the coal out of the Pechora Basin and back into the central part of Russia was Stalin's hope for surviving the war. Pechorlag was deemed so important to winning the war that it was designated a "camp of military significance." Later this would be useful to the bosses, who could demand extraordinary sacrifices from the prisoners.

The memory of these sacrifices is still painful today, as Russian scholars now believe that the Gulag was neither economically viable nor very helpful to the economy.[50] From new archival research, we know that Gulag labor was poorly used and sadly mismanaged. Gulag management often risked lives building structures that were not feasible and often later abandoned these projects. The use of "cheap" labor in the form of prisoners encouraged the regime to recklessly build whatever they fancied. Oleg Khlevniuk, one of Russia's most respected Gulag researchers, says it best: "Many prisoner-built projects were difficult, or almost impossible, to build with free workers, but was there a need to build them at all?"[51] In the end, the contribution of Gulag labor to the Soviet economy is questionable, especially given the enormous human costs.

In 1940 Mochulsky and other NKVD "civilians"[52] who were to work in the camp, along with many convicts, made an arduous forty-five-day journey from Moscow. When they arrived to start building the new rail line, they found few settlements and almost no roads. Their camp consisted of nothing but prisoners living outdoors. Despite the lack of facilities, the prisoners continued to arrive. During Mochulsky's time at Pechorlag, the prisoner population ballooned. In January 1940, when he arrived, there were thirty-eight hundred prisoners at Pechorlag. A year later, there were already thirty-five thousand prisoners, and by June 1941 there were ninety-two thousand.[53] Inmates from all over the USSR and eastern Europe flooded in every day.

The war years were horrific for the Soviet Union, particularly so for those in the Gulag. The situation for prisoners deteriorated greatly as the government reduced the amount of food rations and increased the number of hours prisoners worked, and prisoner mortality was high. The Soviet government organized penal battalions to fight at the front, especially in 1942 and 1943, causing the total Gulag camp population to drop by a million.[54] After the war, a new wave of people was repressed (arrested), and the prison population grew again. The NKVD continued work on its own building and construction projects, with the Gulag supplying the necessary convict labor all across the country.

After the war, Stalin pushed the Soviet people to quickly rebuild and help the country recover from the ravages it had suffered. Prison labor was active in mining and infrastructure construction such as railroad building, and large hydraulic-engineering projects, such as the Volga-Don, Volga-Baltic, and Turkmen Canals and the Kuibyshev and Stalingrad hydroelectric stations. All of this work continued until shortly after Stalin's death on March 5, 1953, when NKVD chief Lavrentii Beria proposed dismantling the Gulag.[55] A broad amnesty freed about 1 million prisoners, with the remaining 2.5 million transferred from the NKVD to the Ministry of Justice. Beria himself was arrested in the months following Stalin's death, and executed in December 1953. (The two previous NKVD chiefs, Genrikh Yagoda and Nikolai Yezhov, had suffered similar fates.)

PECHORLAG: THE ZONE

Pechorlag, the camp where Mochulsky worked, was located in the Komi ASSR, situated northeast of St. Petersburg and west of the Ural Mountains. This territory of mostly taiga and tundra reaches, in some parts, above the Arctic Circle.[56] Anne Applebaum has said that Komi was "one vast camp," for prisoners built all of the region's major cities, its railways and roads, and all of its original industrial infrastructure.[57] The indigenous Komi were herders, fishermen, and hunters; indeed Mochulsky's only contacts with them concerned buying a reindeer carcass, and witnessing how they trapped birds for food.

The administrative structure of Pechorlag was situated in a town at the southern end called Abez. The camp was divided into three regions roughly along a North–South axis. Within each region, there were several numbered departments and within these departments were the units, each of which included hundreds of convicts and their living quarters. Mochulsky was first assigned to the Third Region, 6th Department, Unit Pernashor, at the very northern tip of this long administrative structure, above the Arctic Circle.

Each region, department, and unit of every prison labor camp was staffed with NKVD employees. There was also a parallel Communist Party structure of authority to exercise "party control" over the camp. In Mochulsky's unit, the NKVD employees consisted of the members of the security platoon, the boss of the unit, and the unit foreman. The one non-NKVD Communist Party employee worked as the political instructor. Mochulsky, as an NKVD employee and party member, had two bosses: the NKVD and the Communist Party.

At Pechorlag, as in most Gulag camps, the convicts were housed according to their criminal status. Thus, as Mochulsky was transferred from unit to unit within the camp, his labor force changed. Sometimes, his workers were political prisoners; in others they were ordinary criminals. Anyone arrested for a real crime, such as robbery or rape, was known as a "nonpolitical" prisoner. The others, arrested mostly under the catch-all category of Article 58 of the criminal code for "counterrevolutionary crimes," were known as "politicals" or "58ers."[58]

ON THE INSIDE: THE CONVICT EXPERIENCE OF THE GULAG

In this memoir, Mochulsky focuses on the civilian employees who worked in the Gulag. We have no other accounts of "civilian life" in the Gulag, so this is of inherent interest. However, since he relates the civilian story almost exclusively, he does not describe in detail the lives of the prisoners with whom he worked. The difference between Mochulsky's and the convicts' experience, of course, is that the civilian employees went to the Gulag for a job, while the prisoners were mostly arrested on false charges and sentenced via nonlegal means.

For instance, when the CPSU proposed the Gulag job to Mochulsky, he was about to graduate from a transport engineering school in Moscow. He was invited to the CPSU Central Committee's main office, where they spoke to him in grandiose language and treated him with respect. Although he had no choice but to take the job, he was not directly coerced. Contrast this with the experience of one Yelena Sidorkina, a party member and the editor of a local newspaper. She was arrested in 1937, charged with belonging to a "bourgeois nationalist counterrevolutionary organization." She described the experience in her memoir:

> The interrogations started. I was questioned day and night for seventy-two hours. I was forbidden to stand and walk around, let alone sleep. The interrogators changed every five or six hours, and each demanded that I confess my counterrevolutionary activities. Again I denied all the charges: I had never engaged in

counterrevolutionary activities, even in my head. "All enemies of the people say that," they replied, and produced a number of stunning accusations.... I denied all these fabrications.

...I was exhausted and unable to keep my eyes open. But the moment my eyelids started to droop, the guards would shout, "Stand up! Sit down! Stand up! Sit down!" Then it started up again.... Every so often they would offer me something to eat. Some bread, gruel, and tea were brought in, but I could eat nothing. Shoving these slops at me, they would smack their lips over white bread and glasses of cocoa or tea with lemon, then ostentatiously push their plates aside. "What's the matter, Yelena Yemelyanovna?" they would sneer. "Why aren't you eating?" After three days and nights of continuous interrogation, I was virtually unconscious. I suppose I must have signed something, but for the life of me to this day I cannot remember what."[59]

Mochulsky had some difficult moments on his way to Pechorlag, which he details in chapter 4, but his journey was not the same as the convicts' harrowing, often deathly experience. Evgeniia Ginsberg's trip to the gold mines of Kolyma took a month. During the month of July, she and hundreds of other prisoners were crammed into a hot rail car marked "Special Equipment." She recalls, "The roof of the car was red-hot and the nights were not long enough to cool it. While the train was in motion, the car door was left open a hand's breadth, but whenever we slowed down before a stop the guards came along to shut the doors and fix the bars in place."[60]

Often, the convicts in transit were fed very little. In Ginsberg's rail car, they were given salted soup of boiled herring tails, and one small mug of water to drink for the day, so they all nearly went out of their minds with thirst.[61] Janusz Bardach writes of his train journey to Kolyma: "After ten days, everyone and everything is filthy. We only got water to drink twice a day, and all had to drink from a single cup chained to the wall. With no water for washing and no toilet paper, everything we touched caused diarrhea."[62] Soon, people on the train began to die. "The guards removed the corpses in the mornings with the same disinterest and detachment they showed when delivering our rations."[63]

When Mochulsky arrived at Pechorlag, the convicts built him a cozy dugout, which he describes in detail. But barracks life in the camps was very different. The American Gulag survivor John Noble was a prisoner in a Vorkuta coal-mining camp. His bunk was a segment of a two-foot width of long, hard, wooden shelf with no sheets, mattress, pillow, or blanket.

> When the next prisoner lay down, a big Russian peasant who smelled of *makhorka*, their crude tobacco made from the stem of the plant, our shoulders were touching. Later, when new men came in, I had only enough room to sleep on my side flat against the next man....It was a human jungle, smelly, overcrowded. Everyone, including the guards, spat large globs openly on the floor....There was no toilet in the barracks, just an outhouse 150 yards away.[64]

Mochulsky, as a boss of several units of prisoners, focuses on how he and his prisoner-laborers worked to fulfill the government's demands that were enumerated in the Five-Year Plan. He only infrequently mentions that his convict labor force was so sick and ill-fed that often the plan could not be fulfilled. Vladimir Petrov, speaking about gold mining in Kolyma, gives a typical prisoner's perspective on GULAG work: "Even in the early weeks of the brief Kolyma summer, the men revealed a tendency to die at a rate never before known in the region....A man pushing a wheelbarrow up the high runway to the panning apparatus would suddenly halt, sway for a moment, and fall down from a height of twenty-four to thirty feet. And that was the end."[65]

Sometimes there were prisoners who refused to work, or who angered the guards. In Mochulsky's camp, he recounts bargaining and giving them extra incentives to get them out on the job. Although Mochulsky mentions the "punishment cell," called the Isolator, only once, this was actually a common tool in the Gulag (as was the more direct form of oppression—murder). Many prisoner memoirs recall it with horror. A stint in the Isolator could fundamentally harm one's health or lead to death. The Isolator normally consisted of four walls without a roof, and thus was completely exposed to the elements even in extreme temperatures. Sometimes, there would be a hole in the ground where the prisoner stood. Solzhenitsyn tells how one Arnold Rappoport stayed in a hole like that at the Vorkuta-Vom camp in 1937, with rags pulled over his head to shelter himself from the rain and snow.

> Here is how they were fed: The jailer came out of the gatehouse hut with the bread rations and called to the men inside the log frame: "Come out and get your rations!" but no sooner did they

stick their heads out of the log frame then the guard on the watch-tower aimed his rifle: "Stop, I'll shoot!" And the jailer acted aston-ished. "What, you don't want your bread? Well, then, I'll leave." And he simply hurled the bread and fish down into the pit in the rain-soaked clay.[66]

Mochulsky and many other Gulag memoirists mention the strict divi-sion between the political prisoners (the 58ers) and the common crimi-nals. In Mochulsky's camp they appear to inhabit different barracks. Since the Soviet government held that the nonpoliticals were reformable through indoctrination and reeducation, and the politicals were more socially dangerous, the criminal elements were deemed more trustwor-thy than the other convicts. Often the camp administrators employed the criminal prisoners (called *urkas*, or thieves) to help control the other prisoners. As Solzhenitsyn notes, "The thieves were egged on against the 58ers, permitted to plunder them without any obstacles, to beat, to choke....The thieves became just like an internal camp police, camp storm troopers."[67]

John Noble had eight criminal prisoners in his barracks, sharing an area that would otherwise hold more than twenty prisoners. According to Noble, the criminals spent their time stealing, sleeping, sharpening the knives they made, playing homemade balalaikas, and dancing. No boss in the camp would dare ask them to go out and work. "If one of them should as much as lift a shovel, he would be murdered instantly by his comrades."[68]

Noble and Mochulsky both describe the hardened criminals betting on some other prisoner's life in their card games. The loser had to exe-cute the person the others chose. Noble witnessed this scene in his barracks.

A young blond-haired *blatnoi* (criminal) about 18, the loser, pulled a knife out of his belt and calmly approached the lower shelf of bunks about halfway between me and the place where they had been playing cards. He had a padded jacket in one hand and the knife in the other. Sleeping on the shelf was a well-fed prisoner, one of the cooks in the mess hall. The *blatnoi* walked silently, with-out causing a creak in the old flooring, then leaped at the cook. In one swift professional movement he threw the *bushlat* (quilted jacket) over the cook's head, held him down with a viselike grip around the neck, then jabbed the long blade to the hilt some twelve times in the victim's chest and stomach. The cook screeched through the *bushlat.* Dripping blood from his chest, he pushed the *blatnoi* off him. He got off the shelf and started to run down the barracks aisle toward the door. He got about fifteen feet then collapsed and died in a pool of his own blood.[69]

Hunger plagued everyone in the camps, and Mochulsky writes about how he struggled to feed the staff and prisoners by trapping birds for them. Later he leaves the camp to buy himself a reindeer to live on. What he does not write about is the number of prisoners who slowly and painfully starved to death, or who contracted diseases that killed them. In Lev Kopelev's camp, everyone suffered from pellagra, a disease caused by a lack of Vitamin B3. Its symptoms are diarrhea, dermatitis, dementia, and death. "Sometimes," Kopelev wrote, "in addition to the usual gruel for dinner, we were given rations of coagulated blood, said to be very good for pellagra. Many of us refused to touch it, hungry as we were; it stank too much of carrion. So a lot of it was left over."[70]

Nadezhda Surovtseva writes about an outbreak of typhoid in her camp.

> Every night we would hear the male prisoners howling "Water...," yet apart from occasionally firing warning shots from the watchtowers, the camp authorities did nothing. The prisoners were also starving. Later, throughout July and August, when the epidemic was at its height but was still not acknowledged, prisoners would conceal the death of a neighbor on their bunk and lie beside the decomposing body so as to continue receiving the few extra grams of the dead man's bread ration. The guards, growing suspicious that a prisoner had not gotten up for a long time, would twitch his leg, and their hand would sink into a soft porridge of flesh. Prisoners were not treated but only carted away to the morgue.[71]

Dmitri Panin describes how his camp, Viatlag, in northern Russia, turned into a "house of death."

> Men in the prime of life were stretched out half-frozen and totally exhausted on their bunks, capable only of scratching flea bites and fighting off bedbugs. By the spring of 1942, the death rate in this camp of a thousand men had climbed to a rate of eighteen a day. Thousands of excellent men had gone to their graves. I will never

forget how they were carried out of the barbed-wire zone in specially-made made crates with lids, and how at the sentry post a bayonet was run through their heads—just to make sure that none of them was merely feigning death with the intention of trying to escape once they were outside.[72]

Starving to death was such a common occurrence that the other prisoners called the starving inmates "goners." Evgeniia Ginsberg describes one female doctor, who before prison had been married to a former chairman of the RSFSR Council of People's Commissars. Now she was just a "goner."

She was never parted from her quilted jacket, which had become stiff as a board with dirt; she hid away from the communal bath routine; and she went around the canteen carrying a bucket into which she slopped all the dregs of the soup from other people's bowls. Then she sat down on the step and greedily gobbled up the slop straight from the bucket, like a sea gull.[73]

When Mochulsky first arrives at Pechorlag, he mentions seeing carpenters building coffins for the many dead prisoners. Varlam Shalamov's character describes a mass grave he saw while working on a gang opening up a new road to a mountain. "A grave, a mass prisoner grave, a stone pit stuffed full with undecaying corpses from 1938 was sliding down the side of the hill, revealing the secret of Kolyma."[74]

He continues:

The permafrost keeps and reveals secrets. All of our loved ones who died in Kolyma, all those who were shot, beaten to death, sucked dry by starvation, can still be recognized even after tens of years. There were no gas furnaces in Kolyma. The corpses wait in stone, in the permafrost....The earth opened, baring its subterranean storerooms, for they contained not only gold and lead, tungsten and uranium, but also undecaying human bodies. These human bodies slid down the slope, perhaps attempting to arise.[75]

Then, as the prisoners stood watching, "The bulldozer scraped up the frozen bodies, thousands of bodies of thousands of skeleton-like corpses. Nothing had decayed: the twisted fingers, the pus-filled toes which were reduced to mere stumps after frostbite, the dry skin scratched bloody and the eyes burning with a hungry gleam."[76]

Why was this evil perpetrated? Why the Gulag? Was it for economic, political, or ideological reasons? There has been no definitive answer to this question. At a 2006 conference at Harvard University, several scholars put forth various possible explanations.[77] Some feel that the Gulag existed for economic reasons, that is, to provide free labor. It was much easier to send prisoners to the least inhabitable parts of the USSR than to entice free laborers. In this way, the Soviets could fully exploit the underground riches of the country. And once held in these remote areas, the prisoners could be kept indefinitely in exile, thus helping to colonize remote, inhospitable regions like Komi, where Mochulsky's camp was located. Others feel that the purpose of the Gulag was political. The use of terror intimidated people from opposing the regime, or simply isolated any potential "enemies to Soviet power." The Gulag could also weaken those parts of society that previously were large and powerful as a block (such as the farmers before collectivization, the church, entire ethnic groups). Still others feel that the reeducation component of the Gulag was important; that convicts, by doing time at a forced labor camp, could be "reforged," that is, shaped into genuine Soviet citizens.

The Gulag as it existed in the Soviet Union from 1917 to 1953 was an unimaginable place, a world inside a world, with its own rules, rulers, and ruled. It involved millions of people, including staff and prisoners. The Gulag was one of those quintessentially Soviet institutions that bound together victims and perpetrators, bureaucrats and ordinary workers, the Communist Party and the NKVD, foreigners and Soviet citizens. Mochulsky's memoir of his jobs as a camp boss in the Gulag forces us to recognize that a large number of Soviet citizens worked in this horrendous institution.

More than a million Soviet citizens staffed the Gulag during its existence.[78] No matter what kind of job a Gulag staffer had, and no matter how hard an NKVD employee worked to fulfill the plan, we cannot forget that these Soviet citizens formed a solid column of support for the crimes committed in the name of "building socialism" in the USSR. Their jobs depended on the existence of an institution that arrested people on bogus charges, then starved, mistreated, exploited, manipulated, worked to death, and ruined them.

Presumably, many Gulag staffers went on to have different jobs, to have families and to carry on with the "building of socialism." Mochulsky later became a diplomat and had a very prominent international career in the most prestigious and comfortable wing of the bureaucracy. He was an elite member of the system. He remained a Communist Party member his entire life. And yet, as a thinking person, he carried an uneasiness about the great disjunction between theory and reality. Like millions of Soviets, he somehow had to square his belief in the dream of building communism with the reality of maintaining an enormous system of slave labor.

This memoir allows us to examine the thoughts and actions of a man on the largely unknown side of this massive human tragedy. We should not forget that this is one person's memoir, with all the promise and dangers of the genre. But for now, we need to listen to Mochulsky. This is his story.

TRANSLATOR'S NOTE

I am hoping that this book will be widely read both inside and outside the formal academic world, and I have tried to balance scholarly depth with broad accessibility. I have used the Library of Congress transliteration system, with the exception of hard and soft sign indicators, to make the text easy to read (hence, the town of Abez' is written simply as Abez). Some already familiar names are spelled as is conventional, such as Gorky (and not Gorkii) or Mochulsky (as opposed to Mochulskii). In addition, although in Russian the word Gulag is an acronym and is generally written in all caps, in this book it generally appears as Gulag. The one exception is when the author refers to the actual organization, as in GULAG NKVD.

In the body of the memoir, the text as presented is largely the same as the original. Where required for flow of the narrative, I have moved some small sections. Occasionally, I have cut some redundant paragraphs. I have preserved Mochulsky's chapter structure and titles, but in a few cases I divided long chapters and named new ones myself.

All notes to the text are mine. Because this book is intended for a general readership, I have focused on English-language sources. There is a small Russian-language reading list at the back for specialists.

Fyodor Vasilevich Mochulsky

In 1956, at the 20th Communist Party Congress, Stalin's cult of personality was openly criticized for the first time in the Soviet Union. Since that first denunciation, a tremendous number of publications have appeared year after year, detailing the horrific handiwork of the Stalinist system, especially the Gulag. Tens of millions of Soviet citizens passed through the Gulag, which was formally known as The Main Camp Administration NKVD USSR.[1] Of course there were Gulag prisoners who actually had committed some type of real crime, but the majority of the repressed were honest, innocent people from cities and villages of every republic in the Soviet Union.

In the camps, there were veteran Communists, many of whom had served the Communist Party during the prerevolutionary period, as well as people who had been honored with prestigious Soviet awards, such as Heroes of the Civil War and Heroes of the First Five-Year Plan. There were also well-known scholars and cultural figures, folks who had distinguished themselves by their work in industry and agriculture. There were also countless Soviet patriots who had fought with distinction in Republican Spain, and various soldiers and commanders of the Red Army who had been taken as prisoners during the war with Finland in 1939–1940.

A great number of the prisoners were simple farmers, the so-called "dekulakized" people,[2] whose only fault was that they loved the land and were able to produce food on it. In many cases, these were families in which every member, from the youngest to the oldest, worked from midnight to morning, and had become prosperous relative to their less hardworking neighbors. These successful farmers were denounced as "kulaks" and were sent to the Gulag. Even so, it is well known that the real enemies of Soviet power in the countryside had fled en masse behind the lines with the remnants of the White Army.

As a rule, the people who ended up in the Gulag were given long sentences (many from ten to twenty-five years), and frequently, after they had served their time, their prison sentence was for some reason extended. Prisoners in the Gulag worked twelve-hour shifts (on a day or night shift) and were fed meager, unvarying food. The quantity a prisoner was fed each day depended on his work that day: in other words, he was fed an amount that corresponded to whether or not he had worked up to the norm that was set for him by the Gulag authorities.[3] In the Gulag camps, there was almost no appropriate medical care, which was sorely needed because most of the Gulag camps were located in the Far North or the Far East, in regions with very severe climate. Millions of our unfortunate fellow countrymen never got out of the Gulag, never saw their homes again, and will languish forever in unknown graves.

Various eyewitnesses of these horrifying years have written books, articles, and other accounts documenting this dark side of our history.[4] These people spent many years living "in the zone" as prisoners deprived of rights, where they were known simply as "zeks."[5] They themselves experienced the absolute horror and theatrics that Stalin and his surrounding repressive system unleashed on them.

I, Fyodor Vasilevich Mochulsky, as fate would have it, found myself in a different situation. I was sent to work by mandatory work assignment[6] to the Gulag camp called Pechorlag GULAG NKVD after graduating from my training at a railroad engineering school in Moscow.[7]

I was born in 1918 in the city of Slutsk, in Belorussia.[8] In 1933, I finished the seventh grade, which at the time was still taught in Belorussian, in Minsk. That same year, my family and I moved to Moscow, where I started working, at the age of fifteen, as a lathe operator in a factory called Borets [fighter]. In 1935, I graduated from the Komsomol Middle School at the factory,[9] and started my studies at the Moscow Institute of Railroad Transport Engineering (known as MIIT). I graduated from MIIT in 1940.

Until 1946, I worked at two prison labor camps in the GULAG NKVD system. The first was called Pechorlag, which was a railroad building camp above the Arctic Circle, and the second was called Camp No. 3, which was part of the Main Administration of Highways GULAG NKVD.[10] This camp existed to restore the highway that went from Moscow to Kharkhov, since it had been destroyed during World War II.

At the highways labor camp, I worked as the deputy director of the Political Department for Komsomol Work. In 1946, the government abolished the Political Departments in the Main Administration of Highways GULAG NKVD, so I was re-assigned. In 1947, the Moscow City Committee of the CPSU[11] sent me to study at the Higher Diplomatic School of the USSR Ministry of Foreign Affairs (MID USSR).[12] After graduating from the Higher Diplomatic School, I worked for some years as a MID USSR employee at the United Nations, then for fourteen years in the USSR's embassy in the People's Republic of China. There I went from being a low-level diplomat to advisor/envoy and the chargé d'affaires in charge of Sino-Soviet relations. Upon returning to the Soviet Union, I worked for the Central Committee of the CPSU as the head of the China Sector in the Department of Socialist Countries. When the chief of that department, Yuri Andropov,[13] was chosen to be chairman of the KGB USSR in 1967, the CPSU Central Committee sent me to work in the Intelligence Services run by the First Chief Administration[14] of KGB USSR. I worked there until 1988.

I spent more than twenty years in Asia. Besides my work in China, I also was advisor/envoy in Indonesia and Vietnam, and I traveled to all the governments of Southeast and Southern Asia. In those days, I was conversant in English and Chinese. In my career, I held the military rank of major general[15] and the rank of envoy with emergency powers. I retired in 1988.

This memoir begins in 1940, a year before the outbreak of the Great Patriotic War,[16] when I began working as foreman and boss of a unit of prisoners at Pechorlag GULAG NKVD.[17] This prison camp was located in the village of Abez, in the Komi ASSR, in the most northern part of the camp. This book is a collection of reminiscences and observations from the point of view of a civilian employee of the Gulag.[18] It focuses on the lives of the Gulag prisoners, as well as on the lives of the Gulag's various civilian employees. At that time, there were at least one hundred thousand civilian employees working in the GULAG NKVD system. In many ways, the daily lives, and even the fate of the prisoners depended on these civilian employees in the Gulag.

PART I

GULAG FROM THE OUTSIDE

CHAPTER I

The NKVD

Villain or Protector?

My friends and I, who were born around 1918, were all exposed our whole lives to Soviet propaganda, which portrayed the GPU-NKVD as a necessary part of our government. This propaganda surrounded us as I studied in school in Minsk in the 1930s, as I worked as a lathe operator at a Moscow factory, and as I spent five years at the Moscow Institute of Railroad Transport Engineering. We all believed that the NKVD was an organization that vigilantly guarded the interests of the country from external and internal enemies. Even the press and radio reports detailing the conspiracies and the sensational trials of the "enemies of the motherland" did not cause us to doubt this.[1] Nevertheless, some odd things that happened forced us to start thinking about what was really going on.

In the seventh grade in Minsk, I remember my friend Yura Loiko, whose father was a prominent specialist. In those days, I spent a lot of time in their luxurious apartment. His father deeply impressed me with his education, erudition, and intellect. And suddenly, one day: arrest, open trial, and the order to be shot. His last words, shouted out in despair in the hall as he was leaving the court, were: "Son, I am not guilty."[2]

At that time, my father was a successful young scholar in Belorussia. He worked at the Institute of Belorussian Culture as a Senior Research Fellow under the leadership of Academician I. I. Zamotin at the

Belorussian Academy of Sciences. While there, my father wrote and published a separate book on the Belorussian roots of the famous ancient poem "The Lay of Igorev's Campaign."[3]

Then one day in 1933, out of the blue, Academician Zamotin was arrested. The newspapers covering this incident stated that the authorities also intended to expose and rip out the roots left behind by the arrested man. My father did not stop and wonder when his turn would come: we left his beloved Belorussia forever. Before we left, he had a talk with me, the eldest son (there were three children, I was the oldest), that made me start to think about the real crux of the matter. Our father was physically strong, he did sports, and suddenly he was telling me that his heart was bad and that he could not rule out an early death. He wanted to be sure that if something happened to him, that I, as the oldest son, would take care of our mother and my younger brother and sister. I gave my word (I was already fifteen then) but I was deeply alarmed.[4]

This made me wonder about the facts behind the notices that were read out at nearly every Komsomol meeting at the Institute, the denunciations and arrests of "enemies of the people" from among the students. We knew these students, many of them very well. For instance, the son of a master road-builder on a small railway station in Siberia. How was he an "enemy of the people"?[5]

These sorts of thoughts surfaced from time to time, but then faded away as we concentrated on our daily lives and other things that kept us busy. We never doubted the course of the Communist Party or that of those organizations that protected our rights. You could find reasons to doubt just about anything, if you thought about it hard enough.

To us, the work of the NKVD was shrouded in mystery, in which was hidden something inexplicable and extraordinarily important for the security of our motherland. And we looked at the people who worked at the NKVD with a feeling of respect, and somehow, with a tinge of reverence mixed with fear. But still, at the same time, we knew very little about the Gulag. We had heard of Solovki[6] and about the construction of the Belomor-Baltic Canal,[7] which were built using prison labor. There was even a popular ditty then:

> Without swindling the boss, and ammonal
> We could not have built the Canal.

Or another:

I don't want to drink tea
From an empty teapot
But I'd like to fall in love with
A chief from the GPU.

I also remember seeing a 1930s film from the life of convicts called *Aristocrats*, about the fate of thieves and bandits.[8] In general, though, for me and my friends, the Gulag was an unfamiliar world. None of us ever tried to look into this world, nor did we ever think of working there.

In 1940, I finished my studies at the Railroad Transport Engineering Institute and received my diploma "with honors." My favorite professor in the Department of Railroad Survey and Design then proposed that I stay on as a graduate student. He promised that if I did want to stay on and study more, he would get the permissions from the institute as well as from the People's Commissariat.[9] I was sorely tempted by the chance to continue at the institute as a graduate student. But at the same time, I was still working at the factory and I had seen how the workers treated the specialists there. The specialists knew theory, of course, but the workers did not respect them at my factory, because most of the time they lacked practical experience.

I could imagine what kind of a scholar they would produce from me if I had strong theoretical knowledge but no practical experience. I would be like a blind kitten. So I asked the department leadership if I could defer my graduate studies for five or six years. And I told the institute that as one of their graduates, I was ready for my mandatory work assignment. I felt ready to take on any practical work they had for me in any region of our huge country.

At first, they proposed to send me to one of two places. I could either be sent to work in the bureaucracy of the People's Commissariat of Railroad Transport, the NKPS, or to work as an engineer in, as we said in those days, the "liberated region of the Western Ukraine," in the town of Stanislav.[10]

But as it turned out, I didn't have time to think about either of these proposals. Instead, I received instructions from the institute telling me that I needed to go to one of the buildings of the Communist Party's Central Committee to meet with some official. At that time, I already was a candidate member of the CPSU.

CHAPTER 2

FIRST ACQUAINTANCE
WITH GULAG NKVD

Meeting at the Central Committee of the CPSU

AN ELDERLY GREY-HAIRED MAN WITH A WEARY, PREOCCUPIED face welcomed me. He sat alone in a small, light room, with only a clean desk and two chairs. Behind him on the wall was something hidden behind blinds. From what was said during the meeting, it was clear that he knew all about me. After a short chat on that theme (about me), he went on to talk about the international situation.

Here is what he said, in short. As a result of the perfidious attack of Hitler's Germany on Poland,[1] the Polish army had been quickly defeated, and the Fascist troops had made their way to our borders. He said that we could not rule out that their next step would be an attack on the Soviet Union. He explained that in order to gain some time to prepare for war, if Hitler dared to take this step, as well as to try to avoid all-out war with Nazi Germany, the Soviet government had signed a pact of friendship with Germany.[2] With this pact, our government had agreed to the division of Poland, which had extended our western borders far to the west.[3] The official emphasized that we could not trust the Fascists, and that we could not waste any time because this would only give them more time to prepare themselves and strengthen their defenses.

If Hitler begins a war with us, he pointed out, then the Fascists could take the Donbas and Krivoi Rog out of commission.[4] Then our military factories, including the ones that produce tanks and aviation equipment, would be deprived of coal and steel. At this point, the official reached behind his chair for a cord and pulled open the blind that hung on the wall. This revealed a map of the USSR's railroads and other roads. Without coal, he continued, our military factories in Kirov and Nizhnii Novgorod will grind to a halt.

However, he said, pointing at the map, we in the USSR have a wealth of coking coal deposits, which are as good as those in the Donbas, around Vorkuta, in the far North. And over here, on the road to Vorkuta, in a town called Ukhta, the oil is so plentiful that it comes to the surface on its own. But these places are remote, almost devoid of people. The region north of the Pechora River is what I'm talking about, he said, but it is a very bleak spot, way north, beyond the Arctic Circle. During the winter, it is always nighttime, and during the summer, it is always daytime.

Right now, he said, we only have rail connections from Kirov to Kotlas. And from Kotlas to Vorkuta, you have to travel about 600 kilometers (372 miles) up the Pechora River, but at least there you will see forests, and now and then, some towns. However, to get from the Pechora River to Vorkuta it is another 500 kilometers (310 miles). And along that path, it is just solid tundra and impassible bogs and midges[5] during the summer, and deep snow and blizzards during the winter. Not to mention, intense cold.

As to war, the official continued, we can expect it to break out at any moment. The Authority[6] has decided to immediately set up two construction sites,[7] one that will stretch from Kotlas to Pechora and another from Pechora to Vorkuta. Both sites are designated as military, considering their importance, urgency, and complexity, and will be administered by the NKVD. The first one will be called Sevzheldorlag, or Northern Railroad Corrective Labor Camp. In the press, it will be referred to as Sevzheldorstroi, Northern Railroad Construction Site. The second one will be called Pechorlag, or Pechora Corrective Labor Camp, but will be known in the press as Pechorstroi, or Pechora Construction Site.[8] GULAG NKVD USSR will oversee these camps. They are already moving thousands of prisoners there, as well as transferring civilian specialists from other Gulag camps.

Don't forget, he said, if war begins, the Fascists will be very interested in these prison camps. At any time, they might drop landing forces and weapons down onto the prisoners, and use them against us in the war. And, since Pechorlag is surrounded by hundreds of kilometers of empty

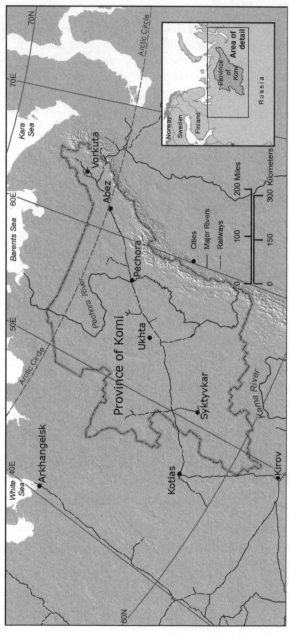

This map of Komi Province shows the finished rail lines built by prison laborers at Pechorlag. Komi is situated in northern Russia to the west of the Ural Mountains. Some sections of the Gulag camp was located in the Arctic section of the province. Courtesy of Tsering Wangyal Shawa.

land, devoid of cities or military garrisons, this is a huge danger for our country, from our northern frontier.

And one more thing, he continued. A large number of the Gulag's civilian employees are former prisoners who have served their time and now work for GULAG NKVD. If war breaks out, we do not feel that we can fully trust these former prisoners. This is especially dangerous, if, as I noted, the Fascists were to land there at the camp. They could free the prisoners, give them weapons, ammunition, and rations, and provoke them into an insurrection.[9] This is why the CPSU Central Committee has decided to strengthen the staff at both prison labor camps, especially Pechorlag. We need people to be working there who are devoted to the motherland, ideologically stable, and physically hardy and strong.

I will say this right now: during the first winter there you may be living in tents when the temperature dips to minus fifty degrees. There may be interruptions of food supply. There will be little contact with the center, and for long periods, you will not have normal communications with family and friends. But Pechorlag is important to the military effort, and someone has to do this job. Your institute and the institute's Communist Party Committee both recommended you. What do you say to this?

This was the gist of the conversation that took place in a small room in one of the CPSU CC buildings. What could I say? Wasn't I that young, strong, citizen of our motherland, a kid who had been brought up in the Komsomol and Pioneers all those years? Of course, I said "yes," and then I said that I was grateful to be trusted by so many people. I also assured him that I would do everything that was expected of me, so as to warrant that trust.

He told me then that he had been counting on this answer since before our meeting, ever since he had read my dossier[10] from the Institute. He added that in the unlikely event that there was no outbreak of war, I would still work at the labor camp for two years without leave.

At this, we parted. But before I left, he told me that my next visit would be with the Cadres Department[11] of GULAG NKVD.

CHAPTER 3

MEETING IN THE CADRES
DEPARTMENT OF GULAG NKVD

AT PECHORLAG, MY CLOSEST FRIENDS FROM THE MOSCOW
Railroad Transport Engineering Institute were Nikolai Gradov and
Volodia Kravstov.[1] Nikolai and I had gone downhill skiing together many
times, just for fun, in the beautiful Caucasus. Volodia had finished technical college training at the institute and had a little construction
experience.

On the appointed day, we three met the deputy director of cadres at
GULAG NKVD in an NKVD building. To outside appearances, this man
was an attractive, intelligent, and attentive person. He was also very skilled
at listening and he could speak very persuasively. We talked a long time
with him. Obviously trying to win us over so that we would be honest with
him, he began by telling us about himself. He explained that before he
took this job, he had worked for a long time in the Kremlin as the secretary of the Kremlin's Communist Youth League, or Komsomol
organization.

When he was working as a young Komsomol secretary, he told us, he
had met Stalin himself several times. One day, the Komsomol Bureau
sent him to Stalin, to ask him to speak to the Kremlin's Komsomol members. Stalin answered that he would be glad to do this, and that he had
something to say to the young members. But then he said that since he
was "Stalin," and not just an ordinary Communist, he would have to
really work on the speech. And he said that he did not have the time.

Finally, he told them that he would do it "somehow or another, at another time."

Just from that little snippet of conversation, we got the impression that already back then, in the 1930s, Stalin wanted all of his utterances as leader to have deep meaning. Each word had to be so deeply meaningful that we could carve them into stone for our descendents, and for their descendents, as well. And, because there were not very many opportunities for such words, and the preparation for such a talk was so great, Stalin rarely spoke in public. He also avoided all meetings and contacts with ordinary people, especially ones that might be spontaneous or accidental encounters. He kept a closed life.[2]

Next, the deputy director of cadres at GULAG NKVD asked us to each speak about ourselves. From our short speeches, he could tell that we knew practically nothing about the Gulag. That is when he launched into a persuasive lecture about the great and honorable mission the party and government had placed on the Gulag.

In capitalist countries, the official continued, prisoners just rot in jail. No matter what their sentences were, they were never given the possibility to be reeducated, because this kind of retraining could only be done through honest labor. The capitalist prisoners simply sit in their jail cells for several years, and then they are let out when their time is up, and they go back into society being the same criminals they were when they were arrested. It is an absolutely different matter here, he said, in the country with the first socialist government in the world. Our laws are humane. The Soviet government sets itself the goal of giving each convicted person the opportunity to atone for his guilt to society by letting him do some honest labor for the common good.

That is to say, he continued, in the USSR we do not let our prisoners languish in prisons. We send them to special camps that we have created, so that they can be reformed through productive labor. While in the camps, many of the prisoners master new professions and specialties. And when they finish their terms and get out of prison, they often choose to work in their new specialties, which they only have thanks to their time in the camps. And the responsibility for all of this prisoner reeducation work, he emphasized, has been placed on GULAG NKVD.

The deputy director of cadres at GULAG NKVD then acknowledged that once we, the three young men sitting in his office, arrived at the camp for our jobs, we would begin to have daily contact with the convicts.

He cautioned us against being too friendly with the prisoners. Do not forget, he warned, that above all, these are criminals, and some of them are very smart. They will all insist that they are not guilty. Many will ask you to help them qualify for early release. Do not engage in these kinds of conversations.

Your answer to them is that you believe in the Soviet court system and the organizations that are in charge of taking care of these kinds of questions. Make sure that they know that you are on site as engineers. This Gulag camp, Pechorlag, has been deemed important to the military, and your job consists only of successfully fulfilling your construction plans.

But remember, he cautioned us, that although these workers in the camp are prisoners, they are also still Soviet people. And when they have done their time, they get back all their rights as Soviet citizens. Therefore, you can count on their patriotism and their high level of awareness.

We three young men, with no work experience behind us yet, listened with great attention and trust to everything the deputy director of cadres told us that day. At that time, we believed beyond a shadow of a doubt that when we arrived at the prison labor camp, all would be as he said. We would see with our own eyes just how humane socialist treatment of prisoners was compared to that in the capitalist countries.

CHAPTER 4

FORTY-FIVE DAYS TO PECHORLAG

PECHORLAG NKVD'S HEADQUARTERS WERE SITUATED IN the village of Abez on the small Usa River, which originated in the northern spurs of the Ural Mountains and flowed from the east into the Pechora River. The trip to Abez was long and complicated. Everyone who went to Pechorlag in those days followed the same route. First, they had to take a train from Moscow to the city of Arkhangelsk, where they then boarded a steamship on the White Sea. From the White Sea, they passed into the choppy Barents Sea, and traveled past Kolguev Island. Then they would arrive in the city of Narian-Mar, which was the capital of the Nenets Autonomous Okrug. In Narian-Mar, they had to board a smaller steamboat on the Pechora River, on which they traveled until they reached the Usa River.

At the Usa River, they had to again change to a smaller steamship that could navigate this shallow, wide river, up to the place where the water became deeper. Sometimes the steamships could make it all the way to the village of Abez. If not, then the passengers had to disembark along the way, and make the rest of the trip on foot or on horseback. (That is, if there were any horses available where the ship let them off.)

When we three went to Pechorlag, we left Moscow at the beginning of September 1940, on the train to Arkhangelsk. Once in Arkhangelsk, we were given padded jackets, quilted pants, "Kersey boots" (made from a leather substitute),[1] cloth for binding feet and socks, in other words, everything that we Gulag employees would need for working outdoors on the railroad tracks. In Arkhangelsk, we waited a long time for the

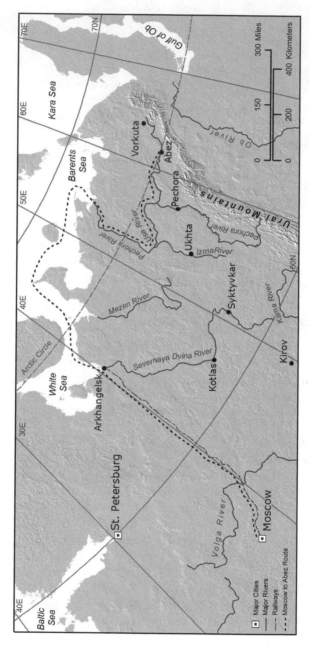

In September 1940, Mochulsky and his two classmates take off from Moscow by train to Arkhangelsk. There they board a steamship, The Vologda, and sail to Kanin Nos. From Kanin Nos, it takes five days on the White Sea and the Barents Sea to get to Naryan Mar, where they get on a passenger ship down the Pechora River to the Usa River. Once the barge freezes in the Usa River, they all disembark and walk (with horses and luggage) for 18 days to Abez, the headquarters of Pechorlag. The men arrive in Abez on November 7, 1940. Courtesy of Tsering Wangyal Shawa.

seagoing steamship to Narian-Mar. A dry-freight ship, The *Vologda*, which was carrying large construction materials, finally arrived. The *Vologda* had some passenger cabins on it, even several first-class cabins, where they settled our threesome.

There were no prisoners on the steamship. We coasted peacefully to Kanin Nos, where the White Sea leads out to the ocean. As soon as we left Kanin Nos and headed into the Barents Sea, though, a terrible storm began. The captain of the ship told us that we had experienced force 12 winds.[2] My friends and I had never traveled on a seaship, and we had never been in a storm like this. We also did not know what seasickness was, and how the ship could rock so hard that everything inside you would wrench free and shoot out of the body. The storm lasted for five days, and it was so strong that waves thundered up onto the decks. All three of us sighed audibly when we arrived in Narian-Mar and stepped onto solid ground.

In Narian-Mar, we boarded a large passenger river steamship on the Pechora River. This river flowed directly up to the mouth of the Usa River, which was to be our next stop. Here is what sticks in my mind about the Pechora River. It was a very wide river with narrow banks that were covered by thick forests with almost no sign of life in them. Above us the whole time, lead-colored storm clouds opened frequently and for long periods with a fine cold rain.

At the mouth of the Usa River, we switched to a smaller steamship. The civilian employees of the Gulag, like our group of three, who were all headed for Pechorlag, were settled into cabins. Down below, in the hold, there were prisoners who were headed for the same place. The prisoners were not allowed on deck. Even to visit the bathroom, the prisoners had to be accompanied by an armed guard. This was the first time we saw prisoners close-up.

From time to time we heard the prisoners singing their criminal songs from the hold. Some of them were sad, like "Taganka,"[3] or just bawdy. We heard "Hello, My Murka, Hello, Dear" many times.[4]

One day, I happened to see a prisoner escape from this ship. He had locked himself in the bathroom, and while in there, he had managed to squeeze himself out through the toilet opening, which simply hung over the river. When the guard on watch who had been waiting for him outside the bathroom door saw that he had escaped, he opened fire recklessly, shooting crazily at the prisoner in the river. The convict swam quickly away from the ship as if he were on his life's mission.

We all watched the fugitive, who dove and swam very well. He would swim for quite a long time under water, and then his head would appear above water briefly for a breath of air, and then he would disappear underwater again for a long time. The armed guard demanded that the boat stop so he could catch the prisoner, but the captain refused him, and we, the civilian passengers, watched the fugitive as he climbed out onto the northern bank of the river.

But what awaited him next? There were no signs of life along the river except the rare little hovels that belonged to the buoy-keepers. Farther to the north lay the Arctic Ocean, but otherwise, not a soul. It was October and the river was just about to freeze over.

Halfway from the Pechora River to Abez, there came an unexpected, early heavy snowfall, and the cold really set in. The Usa River became locked in ice, and would not be navigable until next fall. It was the middle of October 1940.

Pechorlag was only accessible by river for two months a year. And every nail and every sack of flour had to make this trip by sea, by river, and by marshy roadlessness over many hundreds of kilometers. Everything had to be sent during this very short navigation period. Now, all the things we would need to survive the Arctic winter were trapped in barges that were frozen in the river. The barges held basic foods, winter clothing, above all padded jackets, quilted pants, boots (outer and felt), winter hats, gloves, sheepskin coats for the nonprisoner civilians, and also timber, wooden planks with which to build barracks, axes, saws, nails, trolleys, and other things.

At the same time, the government was also sending huge numbers of people to Pechorlag, mostly prisoners. With the barges stuck in ice, the prisoners were sent off walking for weeks to reach the prison camp. But at the camp, the future building site for the railroad tracks, there were almost no barracks in which to house them and barely any food. There was only one thing we all could count on—the quickly approaching severe winter beyond the Arctic Circle.

They let the passengers off the boat on the northern bank of the river. Like everyone there, we prepared to make the rest of the trip on dry land.

The civilian employees created a staging base where we collected the cargo and the horses, which were all wild from the long ride in the hold. A temporary camp was formed to hold a large number of prisoners who were put ashore under armed guard. The rest of the prisoners immediately set off under armed guard to walk the rest of the way to Abez. They had to stomp down a path (sometimes this meant brutally hacking at the foliage) along the Usa River. The Usa's marshy floodlands were covered with thickets of dense shrubbery, stunted northern forests of dwarf birches and low spruce trees.

These northern creations of nature were many years old. Due to the permafrost that lay only a meter below the surface, the trees never matured. Before the onset of frost, all you had to do was to put a bit of pressure on these saplings, and the small tree along with its weak roots would topple over. Where we were, there were no roads or bridges, nor were there any of the Usa's many tributaries in the area. And because the banks of these northern rivers are low and very swampy, every path across to the other side presented problems. The prisoners and the armed guards who had already set off along the banks of the Usa River spent the night out in the open on the frozen ground in the bitter cold. At that time, mid-October, this meant that the temperatures dipped to -20 Celsius (-4 Fahrenheit).

For several days we three stayed at the staging camp, where we saw some unforgettable things. Another barge dropped off a large group of prisoners who had come from the western parts of the Ukraine and Belorussia, which had been part of Poland before it was divided between Germany and the USSR in 1939. The prisoners were still dressed in their civilian clothes, many in stylish coats, suits, and boots.[5] Once on shore, they were ordered to unload bricks from the barge. Each pair of prisoners was given a wheelbarrow for the task. Right in front of our eyes, one pair of fancy Polish men who had not yet lost their arrogant air of "distinguished Polish gentlemen," pushed their wheelbarrow to the pile of bricks on the barge. Then each of these "gentlemen" pulled out some creased pages of a newspaper from their pockets and unfolded them. They used the newspapers as gloves, so as not to soil their hands. In this way, each of them picked up one single brick and placed it into the wheelbarrow. Then they hoisted the wheelbarrow with the two bricks in it down the gangway from the barge to the riverbank.

There, again with the help of the newspaper pages, they removed the bricks from the wheelbarrow, blew the brick dust from the newspapers, folded them again and stuck them back into their coat pockets. Then they slowly and decorously set off for another load. You could see their haughtiness as they looked at the others around them, including our trio, as they did this. They did not realize yet that the amount of food they would get every day at the camp would depend on how much work they did.[6] Later, when they were given 300 grams (about 10 ounces) of black bread and a bowl of thin gruel for their "work," I saw these "workers" shaking from cold and hunger as they circled around the mobile kitchen saying "Pane, zupy" ("Sir, give me soup"). The harsh conditions of camp life quickly dislodged their noble Polish conceits. It did not take long for most prisoners to adapt to the physical labor that was given them and begin to work up to the required norms.

In all my years at Pechorlag, I never had any other experiences like I had with the prisoners who came from divided Poland. There were many Poles in the camps, but not in the camp units where I worked. However, I do know that when the Great Patriotic War began, the Polish prisoners were ordered to volunteer in the newly forming Polish Army on Soviet territory, known as the Polish Army of Anders, which was created by the Provisional migr Government of Poland in London.[7]

But let's return to the trip to Abez. When our steamship froze in the ice after the unexpected snowstorm and all the passengers were put ashore, several tens of civilian employees bound for Pechorlag were gathered on the banks of the Usa River. Most of these civilians were people with previous experience with Gulag life and how the Gulag ran things. For the most part, they were engineers and managers who had spent many years already working at other forced labor camps. The three of us joined a group of about twenty of these civilian specialists.

Someone from the group proposed that each of us choose two horses from the bunch we had brought, and that we make ourselves harnesses, which we would need, out of some thick rope that lay on the ground in a big skein. We were also supposed to fashion a saddle girth and stirrups from the same rope, and make saddles by sewing hay into some sacks we had collected.

So each of us was assigned two horses, because someone had to get these horses to Abez. They made us sign a receipt stating that we had received the horses and that we understood our obligation to deliver the horses to the labor camp. What they had in mind was we would each ride one horse, and the other horse would carry the things we had to bring.

Nikolai and I had never ridden horses before. We had never even been around horses before this. Volodia had once worked at a construction site where there were horses, so we held him up as our expert. But then, this happened: We walked over to the fence where our horses were tied up, and Volodia walked around one of them to untie it. The horse spotted him, pulled back its ears, and suddenly snapped its teeth at his padded jacket and ripped out a tuft of the cotton batting. Volodia barely got away. In any case, none of the other specialists cared a bit whether or not we had an experience with horses.

What to do? We did not know how to ride the horses, we could not make the cart, we did not know how to harness the horses, and actually, we could not even make the harnesses. The others in our group advised us to go back to the temporary camp on the banks of the Usa River where all the prisoners were waiting with their armed guards. In that group, there were several prisoner-specialists who were allowed to travel outside the prison camp without an escort guard, if they stayed within the boundaries of the base. This was our first personal contact with prisoners.

In any case, the prisoners helped us to get some experience riding the horses, and how to saddle, harness, and unharness the horses. We also worked on learning the art of riding a horse that had a second horse tied to its tail (while the second one dragged a cart of freight). They coached us on how to get ourselves back up when the whole cart toppled over on sharp turns. While we were still learning our skills in the temporary camp, our original group of civilian employees took to the road. They tossed us off with the farewell words "Just catch up!" We never saw them again in the two weeks it took us to get to the camp headquarters.

Then we went to a nearby forest, where we cut wood for building the horse-carts. The carts consisted of two long shafts of wood. We hung one end of the wood from the horse's collar, and the other end, fastened together with crosspoles, dragged on the ground behind the horse. On this we tied our load, and added our modest personal items. Along with our most essential things, Nikolai and I also carried our skis and ski boots on our backs. Once we were ready to go, we did not linger. We headed down the path, knowing that we were still 150 kilometers (93 miles) from Abez.

We three guys were on our own with our six horses, which we had to tie up at nights and feed. We let them graze in the grass that still poked up above the snow. In the mornings, we had to catch the horses, saddle them and load up, give them water (but not immediately after the road) and repair our pathetic harnesses. At the same time, we somehow had to get used to sleeping out in the open on frozen ground in subzero temperatures, and learn how to fix food and dry our soaking wet clothes.

The first day we traveled only about 7 kilometers (4.3 miles) because we had to cross a fairly wide and deep tributary of the Usa River. Its banks were very muddy and covered over with a crust of ice. It was the kind of ice that could hold a person, but not a horse. Moreover, the river in the middle was deep enough for the horses to swim. We rode our horses into the frozen water, while dragging the second horse with a rope. After that we had to build a raft to carry the horse-carts across the river. We spent that whole night drying out next to the fire. And the next day, back on the road.

The horse-carts totally exhausted us. They stuck to the trees and shrubs, and often toppled over. Remember, we were each riding a horse, and leading a second horse behind us. That second horse was tied to the tail of the first one, and was also dragging the awkward horse-cart. So when the cart toppled over, the second horse would snort, and sometimes fall down, since its legs would get stuck up to the knees in the marshy earth. We would have to get off and unharness the horses. And right at these moments, the horses somehow managed to bite their torturers. And then, once we got the cart and its load back into a horizontal position, saddled them, the horses resisted us in every way possible.

We deliberated, and decided at the first buoy-keeper's to throw out the carts and leave part of our stuff until winter, when we could go come back in sleighs that could travel on the frozen river. Instead of the carts, we made crude packs from the backpacks that we carried, and tied them to the second horses. Then it was easier to move. We spent the nights either at a buoy-keeper's place, or in the rare stacks of hay (we wondered who had made them). We cut down branches from spruce trees, placed them on the ground we had cleared of snow next to the fire and lay down to sleep. We had to take turns watching the fire while periodically turning our freezing side to the fire. We exerted a huge amount of time and energy just on crossing the rivers that flowed into the Usa.

Then something happened that scared us very much. If it had not happened at the very moment when a unit of prisoners was walking by, then who knows how it would have turned out, especially for me. On our path along the banks of the Usa River, we tried to cross a very muddy ravine. The legs of the horses became stuck up to their knees in the thick mud. We were trying to hurry past this dangerous spot on horseback. My horse was carrying the largest and of course, the heaviest, load. She crossed last on the already thinning path, and at the very bottom of the ravine, she suddenly began to sink deeper into the watery slime. We took the pack off of her, but she kept struggling. And the more she struggled trying to get out of the mud, the deeper she sank. We cut down some poles and tried to shove them in under the horse's stomach, and using the poles as levers, help her get out of the marsh that was swallowing her alive.

But it was all in vain. The horse was thrashing around, and sinking even deeper into the marsh. And that horse was so sad. Her eyes looked at us with fear and begged us to save her. Her eyes made us feel our own impotence even more. At the same time, we all shared a very worrisome thought: How will we explain that our horse disappeared when we arrive at the Gulag Camp Administration? It was a fact that we had all signed a form saying that we had taken two horses each and that we were obligated to get them to their destination. Losing a horse—by the rules of the day—qualified as "plundering of socialist property."[8] And this crime, we all knew, had a corresponding legal statute: ten years imprisonment in the camps. By now, we had worked so hard to get that horse out of the quagmire that we were losing our strength. We were in total despair.

Aside from the horse slopping in the mud, we were surrounded by total quiet. There was not a soul in the area. And suddenly, we heard a group approaching. We could hear their voices. It was a convoy of prisoners and their armed guards. We threw ourselves onto the commander of the convoy. He looked over the entire scene, and commiserated with us. Then he commanded his convoy to halt, and picked out a group of prisoners to drag the horse out. With great difficulty, they pulled the horse out of the mud. The horse had barely stood back up on its legs again before it started shaking all over with cold. The convoy of prisoners went on. We stayed as long as it took for the horse to recover herself. We split her load between two other horses that were pulling carts, and we trudged on.

On the very eve of the celebration of the twenty-third anniversary of the Great October Socialist Revolution, we arrived at the Camp Administration headquarters, in the village of Abez. It was November 7, 1940.

PART II

GULAG FROM THE INSIDE

CHAPTER 5

AT THE CAMP ADMINISTRATION

AT THE GULAG CAMP ADMINISTRATION, THEY PUT US UP IN a "hotel," which was a large army tent with individual wooden planks, as bunks, built in. Every plank had two spaces for sleeping on the bottom, and two on the top. They gave us each a bunk. Inside the tent, a large iron stove pumped heat into the tent. It was always on, making the tent very warm. The other lodgers had placed their clothes out to dry all around it.

The Camp Administration's top staff welcomed us. They took us to the Cadres Department, where we were given specific work assignments. They explained that the entire prison camp of Pechorlag was divided into three regions. The southern part was called the First Region, the middle one was called the Second Region, and the most northern, the Third Region. Each region was then divided into departments, and each department contained various units of prisoners. Each unit of prisoners worked on one section of future railroad track. The sections of track they worked on were relatively large, measuring between 10 and 20 kilometers (6.2–12.4 miles), depending on the difficulty of the work.

They assigned the three of us to the Third Region, specifically, to its most northern department, the Sixth, known as the "Sivaia Maska" (Grey Mask). Nikolai Gradov, as the oldest of the three, was assigned to be an engineer in the department headquarters of "Sivaia Maska." Volodia and I were assigned to be unit foremen in the two northernmost units of the region. I was sent to the unit known as "Pernashor," just below Volodia's unit. Volodia was given the one next to mine, the most northern unit of the department.

The village of Abez, where the Camp Administration was located, sat on the right bank of the Usa River. All the houses in the town of Abez were wooden. Many of them had been built using various high-quality pine logs that floated along the Usa River from the spurs of the Northern Ural River. The Camp Administration occupied the main buildings, which included its offices and housing. The Camp Administration had a large staff of employees. On the whole, these were engineers and technical people, and also a service staff that looked after the prisoners and civilians. The Camp Administration also had a high number of subunits of armed guards, called the VOKhR[1] and Chekists,[2] as well as employees of the Political Department.[3]

The prison camp itself sat on the edge of the village. Known as "the zone," its tall watch towers on each corner were manned by armed VOKhR guards. Besides housing the regular convicts, the camp also included a large staff unit of prisoners who could go to work and move around the village without needing armed guards. They worked in various jobs serving the Camp Administration's civilian employees. The convicts who had technical expertise before being sent to the Gulag were called "specialists," and many of them had permanent staff positions (as prisoners) in the Camp Administration.[4]

We hardly had the chance to properly investigate the administration's complex structure at the camp when we were taken to our work site out on the tracks.

During the three week or so stay at the Camp Administration, we made some friends with whom we stayed in contact after going out to our jobs on the tracks. Later on, when we had to go back to Abez for some reason, to meet with people at the Camp Administration, we could stay with friends in their warm apartments, and not in the tent "hotel." As a rule, we had to go to Abez once or twice a month, sometimes more. The inevitable "payback" for this hospitality was playing cards at night, either "proferanc" or poker, and sometimes "ochko."[5] These card games always included a liberal amount of diluted liquor. I say diluted because the civilian employees received only one bottle of straight liquor once a month, and it had to last. We civilian workers were well paid, compared to other places in the country, but in the Far North, there were no stores and no other places to spend our money. And at the time, playing cards was prohibited, but almost everyone did it. The civilians were not the only ones playing "illegal" cards, the prisoners played them as well. They liked to play "ochko."

Speaking of salaries, we three young engineers each earned a base salary of 120 rubles a month. As compensation for doing work located above the Arctic Circle, they paid us a double salary for the first six months. After the first six months, they took away the double salary and replaced it with a 10 percent bonus of our regular salary, which was added on every six months. In this way, your salary would be double what you originally made after working for five years. After that, you could earn more only by getting a promotion at work.

Anyway, we were a bunch of lonely guys with nowhere to spend our money, so playing cards was our main distraction. Sometimes we played cards for big money, too. I especially remember one of our acquaintances in the Camp Administration, the head of the Department of Technical Supplies for the camp. At that time, this man was around forty years old. He was a lively, energetic, cheerful guy, he loved to joke around, and at heart, he was an optimist. In contrast to his young face, his thick head of hair was completely grey. One day he told me how his hair had gone grey at such a young age.

It seems that he had worked in Moscow once, at a job where he had been promoted to the position of big boss before he was even forty years old. He was a party member, and at the time, it seemed that he had a brilliant career ahead of him. But in 1937, the mass arrests hit his office, and he was arrested.[6] They kicked him out of the party in absentia. A "troika" sentenced him, without any legal examination, without any meetings with other officials, and without any lawyers present.[7] They sentenced him to death by firing squad. He could not believe this, but when they read him the sentence and put him on death row (in the cell with other prisoners who had been also sentenced to death), then he finally believed it.

In prison, they allowed him to write an appeal for pardon. They said that they would consider it within seventy-two hours. He was one of four men in his cell who had been condemned to death. In the prison, the authorities would appear around 4:00 AM, to call out the prisoners with the NKVD's response to their petitions and appeals. His corridor was lined with other cells full of condemned men. This meant that toward dawn, everyone else in all the other cells was awake, waiting. Each prisoner was listening and trying to figure out whether the echoing sounds they heard down the hall were the jailers' footsteps, and whether they were coming to his cell. In other words, if the footsteps passed by your cell, it meant that you had another twenty-four hours to live.

One day, though, the footsteps stopped outside his cell. They called his name and told him to come out with his belongings. (Bringing one's personal things meant that the prisoner was not being taken again to the interrogator.) They led him to some sort of prison boss, who told him that his appeal for pardon had been accepted. Instead of the death sentence, they said, his sentence had been commuted to a twenty-five-year term in a Gulag labor camp. He served more than a year in a Gulag camp, and out of the blue, in 1939, they pardoned him. He was reinstated in the party, all of his orders and medals that he had earned were returned, he was paid his wages for the last prearrest period of work and his wages for the his entire term of incarceration. Then they suggested that he stay on at the Gulag and work as a civilian. He agreed to stay.

A year after I met him, this man literally saved me from ending up in prison as a convict with my own long sentence. But more on that later.

In all the years I worked in the Gulag, I met many people who had been former prisoners, who served some time, and then suddenly, were rehabilitated and given back full rights. But most of them had not, like this man, walked away from it all with his optimism intact and with a cheerful soul. Most of them were broken morally and physically for their rest of their lives.

During that three-week period we spent at the Camp Administration before going to our jobs out on the tracks, something happened that shocked us and made us worry about where we had landed and what lay ahead of us. At the Camp Administration, one person always worked as a night watchman. One of the nights we spent there, the night watchman happened to be a young, highly educated specialist (like us), who had been at Pechorlag for a while, and already had his job out on the tracks. The morning after his shift as night watchman, they discovered that this young specialist had hanged himself. The way he did it was very unusual. He tied one end of a rope to the handle of a window frame, and on the other end he made a noose, placed it around his neck and lay on the floor. The length of the rope was such that if he lay on the floor, the noose would tighten. If he stood up, the noose would loosen. We understood that he preferred to die an excruciating death just to get away from all that he had seen in the Gulag.

It is important to understand that once a person went to work in the Gulag, there was no possibility of exiting the Gulag system freely. In order to leave a job in the Gulag, you had to get permission from GULAG NKVD's head of the Department of Cadres. Since GULAG NKVD was always short of people, getting permission to leave a Gulag job was nearly impossible. (The exceptions were, of course, bribery or just crazy luck.)

Getting back to the Camp Administration at Pechorlag, I wanted to speak about how difficult it was for the administrators to manage the camp from Abez. As I mentioned above, Pechorlag stretched along a future railway line that was 500 kilometers (310 miles) long. It was located near the Arctic Circle, where there were no normal roads or any sort of developed communications system. The units of prisoners lived and worked in an area that stretched along this 500-kilometer distance. Therefore, the Camp Administration and its regions and departments could communicate with these prisoners' units only by using a device called a "Selektor." It was a kind of a telephone with a button on the handle that, when you pressed it, allowed you to speak to the other party but not to hear them.[8]

The departments could communicate with the administration only by letter or Selektor. Since there was no track built yet, only temporary track, they sent freight to the prisoners' units mostly by sleigh in the winter, and by horse in the summer. In those few areas of camp that were located near the Usa or Pechora rivers, they could use boats. Letters from the units to the administration took weeks to arrive, and beyond the boundaries of the camp, they took months. There were no books, except those that a few people had brought with them when they came, and propaganda literature that arrived from the administration. There was no electricity, so on those long nights we had "oil lamps," which were empty tin cans that we poured "fuel" onto and they shot out a wick. I am not talking about lamps with light bulbs.

This meant that the daily leadership over the units took place by Selektor. And most of the time, when you picked up the receiver, you heard a slew of bad words and curses, and also threats to imprison you in the camp if you did not fulfill the daily, weekly, or monthly plans. Rarely, and as a rule unexpectedly, the leadership from the regional or departmental administration would appear for a short time at the unit. Once a month the camp unit's foreman and boss (if there was one, because at many camp units there was no boss, and his job was filled by the foreman) were called in to the department to confirm the monthly plan and give a briefing. The Camp Administration, that is, the headquarters of the site, called very rarely.

Generally, there were no other civilian employees in the prisoners' units other than the foreman, and sometimes the unit boss, or the commander of the security platoon. Sometimes they sent a nurse for a short visit, but usually we used some prisoner who had some medical expertise when we needed help. A very large percent of the prisoners were chronically ill. This was due to the harsh climate, substandard food, poor clothing, twelve-hour work days out in the open, the absence of most necessary medicines, boredom in the barracks, a continual morally depressing situation, and many other reasons. The really sick patients were sent to a hospital, but the others stayed on their feet, looked after by that chance medically trained prisoner. The absence of civilian doctors at the units had an extremely negative impact on the prisoners' productivity on the job.

CHAPTER 6

UNIT FOREMAN, FIRST
CONTINGENT OF PRISONERS

Soviet Volunteer Ski Troops from the Finnish War

A FEW WEEKS AFTER CELEBRATING THE TWENTY-THIRD anniversary of the October Revolution,[1] we three left the Camp Administration offices in a sleigh for our new jobs in the "Sivaia Maska." As I said before, this was the northernmost section, also known as the 6th Department of the 3rd Region of the labor camp. We rode the sleigh on the frozen Usa River to the buoy-keeper's house, where we had stored some of our belongings on our way in to Abez. All our things were there as we had left them, including our skis and ski boots.

Before we left, they gave us army-issue short sheepskin coats, padded boots, and fur hats. On the advice of those who had lived in the Far North longer than we had, we wore quilted pants and padded jackets under the sheepskins, and we shoved hay into our felt boots. Then we buried ourselves in hay on the sleigh. Prisoners who could freely travel in the camp without armed escorts drove the sleighs.[2] These men were also bundled up in padded clothing and felt boots. Our sleigh carefully headed down the banks of the frozen Usa River, and started off toward the north along smooth tracks. We were on our way to meet our new fate.

As we rode in the sleigh, we noticed that our cheeks were starting to freeze from the snow and icy wind. First we would see a light redness from the snow and wind on the cheeks, and then, suddenly a white spot would appear and quickly spread. Our driver had warned us that if the redness faded and the cheek no longer had any feeling, then we had to immediately rub snow on the cheek. The severity of the polar climate was rapidly becoming clear. After that, we always wrapped scarves over our faces when we rode on horses or in sleighs.

When we arrived at the "Sivaia Maska," Nikolai was dropped off at his part of the camp, and Volodia and I then stayed the night in a tent "hotel." Early the next day, the two of us set out again. As we traveled, we could see, off to the right, a spur of the Ural Mountains covered in dense forest. The tundra was buried under a thick layer of snow. Here and there shrubs stuck up. After traveling 14 kilometers northward from "Sivaia Maska," I finally saw the prison camp watch-towers of my unit, "Pernashor," where my new life awaited me.

I will never forget our approach to that place. The road went alongside the prison camp. A heavy snow was falling. Just ahead, I saw a group of prisoners, about six of them, in padded jackets covered with army-issue greatcoats, walking out from a thin stand of trees. They wore army boots, and on their heads they had on army caps without the star.[3] They were bent low, pulling the straps of a sleigh loaded with wood. Behind them, in a fur hat, felt boots, and a sheepskin coat with its collar upturned, paced a VOKhR guard carrying a bayoneted rifle under his arm. The whole group made its way to the camp gates. The gates opened, the prisoners and the sleigh disappeared into the zone. The gates closed.

The guard with the rifle walked to the long, snow-covered barracks that were located next to the camp, which, I was to find out later, was where the security platoon was located. Next to those barracks sat two dugouts. One belonged to the commander of the platoon, who on the day of my arrival, was not in the zone. The other dugout housed the political instructor and his wife. He had been notified by Selektor that I was arriving. As he helped bring my things into his dugout, he seemed surprised that I had brought my skis from Moscow. Volodia traveled on to his new job in the camp unit further north.

One of the first things the political instructor did for me was to choose a group of prisoners to build me my own dugout. While this was happening, I asked him to show me around "Pernashor." When we entered the prison camp, I was gripped with horror at what I saw.

There was not one barrack in our camp. Instead, the prisoners were lying on spots they had cleared off on the bare ground. They had scraped the snow off of several meters of frozen ground in the shape of squares, and had placed crudely-cut branches down as make-shift beds. On top of these branches lay the prisoners, dressed in their greatcoats and army boots, "resting" after their twelve-hour workday.

Under their greatcoats the prisoners wore padded pants and padded jackets. On their heads were their forage caps. Several of them had wrapped their heads up in towels. Some of them had stuck fir branches into the snow around their heads, which they seemed to think would protect them a little from the icy wind. Each brigade had its own quadrant for sleeping, but depending on which way the wind was blowing, they switched places constantly to try to avoid the freezing air. Several prisoners were moving about the territory of the camp like shadows.

Near the gates at the end of the camp, a brigade of carpenters was building coffins.[4]

All the while, the Camp Administration officials continually screamed over the Selektor at the unit bosses, demanding an accounting of how many prisoners had worked, and how many had fulfilled their norms for the twenty-four-hour period. All they cared about was how much each prisoner needed to be fed, which was tied to how much work he had done that day. And to show how serious their demands were, they constantly cursed at us and threatened to slam us into prison, unless "by tomorrow all the prisoners went to work and fulfilled 100 percent of the plan." As I mentioned earlier, those who did not fulfill their work norms received 300 grams (about 10 ounces) of bread, and soup.

It was clear that winter had already arrived in full force, and the building of living quarters for the prisoners had not been included in the work plan. I immediately turned to the political instructor and asked him what was going on. Weren't we simply condemning all of these prisoners to an early death with such terrible conditions? To my questions, the political instructor only raised his hands, saying that it was not up to him, and that he himself could not understand what was happening. There was nobody to turn to, but we had to do something quickly to fix this. But what to do?

One morning shortly thereafter, Volodia came to see me from the neighboring camp unit, and told me that it was the same dreadful situation in his camp. He said: "Fedia, what will we do? This is a nightmare! When they were sending us off in Moscow, they told us something absolutely different than this. What kind of labor reeducation is going on with these prisoners if they are all just dying during the winter?"

He spoke to me to as a close friend, with full awareness that I was at the time a candidate member of the Communist Party. (Volodia never had joined the Komsomol, and did not belong to the party.)[5]

But what could two young specialists who had just arrived at the Gulag—which was a state within the state—what could we actually do? We were far from Moscow and we had no way to get in touch with anyone there. Formally, we answered for our positions at Pechorlag both to Moscow and to the Party Obkom (Regional Communist Party) of Komi, ASSR, which was located in the capital of the republic, in Syktyvkar. But there were no roads to Syktyvkar, and neither the prison camp nor the department had any kind of connections with them. But still, the leadership of Pechorlag had to be aware of the actual situation at the camp, because every day, each camp unit had to report to Pechorlag headquarters, via the Selektor. Every boss of a unit of prisoners gave a summary of what the unit had managed to build during the preceding 24-hour period. In this report, we always included the number of sick prisoners, how many had died, the situation with food, and so on. We did this every day.

Volodia waited for an answer from me. I agreed with his thinking. We discussed this terribly difficult situation for a long time, without coming up with a solution within the confines of the camp. Then, finally, we came to the following conclusions:

— According to what the Gulag officials had told us in Moscow, the prisoners were being held in the camps so that the Soviet State could reeducate them through labor. And after the prisoners had finished their sentences, they would return to a normal life.

— What clashed with this, though, was that in our camp, the living conditions were dangerous, and were, in fact, just leading the prisoners straight to a quick death. With the onset of winter, we felt that, more than anything, we had to do what was necessary to save their lives, even if it meant stopping work on railroad building.

— Insofar as we had neither the opportunity nor the time to convince the leadership in our camp department and above in the Gulag hierarchy, and people were dying already right now, we decided that we had to act fast and work with the quickest methods available to save lives.

— At the same time, since the Soviet government had designated our camp as having importance to the war effort, and war could break out at any moment, we also had to fulfill the monthly construction plan.

Once we said all this to each other, we figured out what to do.

When we had first traveled to our units in Pechorlag from Abez, both of us remembered noticing the number of good-quality pine logs that were trapped in the banks of the Usa River. These logs were supposed to float from the Ural Mountains to another destination, but many of them had gotten stuck in the mud. Volodia and I decided that our two camp units could go and get those logs, bring them back, and do some building. We drew up plans up for some solid barracks, a mess house, a bathhouse, a "lice-fighter" (which was a place where you could turn up the temperature to 100 degrees Centigrade [212 degrees Fahrenheit] in order to kill lice), and other buildings we thought we might need.

In one night, then, we put together plans for all these buildings from our available materials. We did not even have one nail. There were none in either of our camp units.

In order to construct stoves in the barracks, I took the risk of damaging "socialist property."[6] Someone at some time had thrown out several mining carts in my unit. I thought that we could turn these carts upside down and cut a hole in the bottom for pipes (we had tin plate). Then we could cut a door in the end of the cart for fuel, and line the whole thing with a base of stone and clay (bricks were not available). Then we only had to add the pipe and the stove was ready.

Volodia and I agreed to call a meeting with the prisoners in each of our camp units, and explain the situation to them. We planned our words carefully. We told them that their camp had been designated as significant to the war effort, and that war could break out any day. And because of this, the Gulag headquarters demanded that the prisoners fulfill their twenty-four-hour plans. However, the Arctic winter was just beginning, and it would only get much worse. It was a huge problem that we did not have proper barracks and other buildings in our camp unit.

We proposed to the prisoners that we all take two weeks from railroad building and devote the time to constructing our camp. We told them honestly that during these two weeks, we (the unit bosses) would be feeding the leadership "tufta," or made-up numbers,[7] that would show all the prisoners fulfilling the daily plan by 100 percent. In this way, we would ensure that every prisoner received a normal amount of food during this two-week period.

We needed to be protected, so we made all of the prisoners promise not to tell the authorities anything. During these two weeks, we told them that we would build warm barracks, a mess hall, a bathhouse, the lice-killer, through which we would immediately run all the linens, and supply the new camp. Then, after the two weeks spent on constructing our camp, we would work to fulfill the norms on track-building by 200 percent for the next two weeks. In this way, we would still fulfill GULAG NKVD's monthly plan of construction. We told the prisoners that the security platoon had also agreed to go along with our plan. The VOKhR armed guards themselves had been suffering, like the prisoners, with no housing and little food, so they too were ready to support us.

Volodia left for his own camp unit, fully ready to implement all that we had agreed on. Between shifts, I gathered all the prisoners in my camp unit together. By this time, I already had a good idea of who was in my unit. For instance, I knew I had many excellent skiers from Leningrad. In 1939, these men had volunteered to go to the Finnish front after the government had recruited them to join battalions of skiers that were sent to the enemy's rear.[8] At the time, Nikolai and I also had volunteered for these battalions, but the recruiters had explained to us that for the time being, they were only taking men from Leningrad. We were told that we would be called if they decided to take volunteers from other cities. We did not get our turn. The war with Finland ended at the beginning of 1940.

In practice, when these battalions were thrown across the front line, they inevitably left ski trails. The Finnish aviators then cut off the trails, found the battalions by following their tracks, and destroyed them. They took as prisoners all the men who were left alive, which were mostly the wounded ones. Then the war ended, and our countries exchanged prisoners. But the Soviet Union, instead of sending our soldiers home, sent them to do forced labor at Pechorlag.[9]

In November 1940, these men still did not know their ultimate fates, since they had not been officially sentenced. In the meantime, they were being kept as convicts, and treated as such. Several of these former soldiers were students, many of them my age. There are no words that could convey their suffering. When any of these unfortunate young people complained about their fate, I looked at them and could not find any way to comfort them.

Jumping ahead, I'll say that in all my time at this camp, the usual sentence that most had been given was "betrayal of the Motherland." With this sentence, those workers who had middle school education were given five years, high school students were given seven to eight years, and graduate students and other sportsmen with higher education were given ten years.

At my meeting with the prisoners, under the open sky inside the camp, I explained my understanding of our situation and how Volodia and I had decided to try and resolve it. I asked them to listen to me, and I said I hoped they would agree with my proposal. In the dimming eyes of the worn-out men, hope lit up. They became animated, and as a chorus might, they all agreed to the plan I proposed.

I told them that they all knew best who was good at what. I proposed that we nominate candidates for deputy foreman and the section foremen, so we could form brigades of carpenters, joiners, stove men, and snow-stompers. The groups would be divided into those men who would stomp down the path in the snow from the camp to the Usa River to where the pine logs were lodged in its banks, those men who would saw the logs into boards (we had saws), and those men who would make the sleds for getting the wood to camp. We also needed men to cut stakes in the nearby small woods. We would need many of these small sticks, since we could build only the skeleton of the barracks and other structures from the pine logs, and the walls would have be built from boards covered with turf.

My meeting with the prisoners was very friendly. At that gathering, we chose a deputy foreman. He was a tall, strongly built, intelligent, highly educated, and very likable young man, who, judging from his speech, was a Leningrad native. With his help, we quickly tackled all the organizational problems, and soon we were in full swing.

After two weeks, we had the warm barracks we needed on camp territory. Each prisoner had his own berth on a two-plank bunk (two berths below and two above). We also built our mess hall, a bathhouse with a steam room, the "lice-fighter," and a laundry house. We had established a new, sturdy camp. Along the paths of scattered gravel that led from building to building, we planted fir trees.

Then, as we had planned, we spent the next two weeks fulfilling the monthly plan of railroad building. Now, it seemed that we had every right to be happy.

During this time, I became more familiar with the other civilians, that is, the people in my social circle, at my new job. The political instructor turned out to be an affable young man, barely thirty years old. I had a nice, friendly relationship with him. I came to see that he had a sharp, observant mind, and was a bold thinker. Many people felt that he was not well educated, though, because he had completed only four grades at a rural school.

Likewise, the Gulag's security platoon (the VOKhR guards) were usually country boys with elementary education. And sometimes, they were absolutely illiterate. Most often these men had previously served in the army, and then had signed up for a few years to work as VOKhR guards. This was seen as a good way to earn a bit of money. After the army and then the security job, they would return to their villages as "men of substance," find a wife, and start life with something in hand. As to their intellectual level, though, this story that circulated in the camps says everything. It went like this:

One morning, a VOKhR guard receives his group of prisoners that he has to escort to the job sites. He gives the command to the group: "Line up by fours!" And the answer he receives is: "Citizen VOKhR, there are only two of us." Upon hearing this, the guard gets angry, and repeats: "Line up by fours anyway, the VOKhR knows best!"

The political instructor suggested that I get acquainted with the guys in the security platoon, so from time to time, we met for informal discussions. We would talk about things that had happened recently in our country, both at home and in the international arena. Or we simply discussed Soviet history and culture. Sometimes I told them about novels and books I'd read. I tried to answer all the questions these plain country boys had. These meetings helped us get to know each other better, and in the end, it helped me in my work.

The security platoon's commanding officer did not come back to the zone for a long time. When he did arrive, he turned out not to be a shining intellect either. He did not hang around and make friends. He and his wife lived in their dugout, and he carried out his platoon duties. Once, he asked me to build a new camp since the existing one was made of decrepit deciduous wood, and was from his point of view not secure. There was no use in talking to him.[10]

On the work front, I found that I had ended up in a place where I was not just the foreman, but the boss as well. Before I had left the Camp Administration in Abez for my job in the unit, they had warned me that the unit boss would not be on site for quite a while. Evidently he had left some months earlier, but the Camp Administration had not yet found a replacement for him. All of this was by way of telling me that in the meantime, I was to do his job. How this would work they did not clearly say.

Well, once I became acclimated and came to terms with doing both the boss and foreman jobs, I saw that I had to start from scratch, and choose people to work with from among the prisoners in my unit. I had to put together an entire new staff of essential administrative and technical employees, including a deputy foreman, some section foremen, an economist, a norm-setter, an accountant, some medical personnel, and others.

The prisoners in the unit (and in the entire prison camp), worked, as I mentioned above, in two shifts. The first shift went from 6:00 AM until 6:00 PM, and the second shift went from 6 PM until 6:00 AM. Having two shifts was a big strain, and meant that we had to increase the number of guards.[11] Our main work took place on both sides of the proposed rail tracks, so the area was quite large. However, just to get up to speed where we could actually begin constructing a rail line, there were many things we had to do first.

Our job was to raise embankments, collect the excavated soil, and dig drains along the lines. So every day I sent different groups of prisoners off to work on related tasks. Because the local soil as a rule was not good as fill, we had to bring in suitable material by using carts harnessed to horses or wheelbarrows, from the closest quarry. We had to build bridges or pipelines for the numerous little rivers and rivulets that crossed the tracks because during the day these always flooded with melting snow. In all, my good relationship with the VOKhR platoon made this work go a bit more smoothly.

Anyway, while we were busy building the prisoners' barracks, the political instructor's chosen group of prisoners built me a dugout. They constructed it in one night, while working under armed guard, and using spades, saws, and axes. It was the same kind of dugout that the platoon commander and the political instructor had; in fact, it was located right next to theirs.

The prisoners first dug a hole about three by four meters (13 feet) and a meter (3.3 feet) deep, out of the frozen soil. The walls were reinforced with local, poor-quality wood, and they stood out from the ground around 1.5 meters (4 feet 11 inches). The floor, ceiling, and roof were also made of wood. The parts of the walls and the roof that stood above ground they covered with sod. The sod came right off the frozen ground next to my dugout. First they had had to clear snow off of it, and then they cut it.

Inside the dugout they created a kind of entrance hall, where on the right wall they made a wooden bench to hold two buckets of water. Along the wall of the entrance in the living quarters, there was a door on the left, and on the right they placed an iron stove, the main part of which was in the living quarters but had to be lit from the hallway. The pipe from the stove went up through the roof to the outside.

On the back wall of the dugout they created a small window. Near it was a table. On the left and right walls were two wide "ottomans" of mattresses, filled with hay and covered with wool blankets. I slept on one of the ottomans, and on the other one, I rested while still dressed. If ever a person from the Camp Administration came to my camp unit to check on us, he slept on this one.

This was the simple place that became my first home in the Gulag.

When the dugout was ready, the political instructor recommended that a nonpolitical prisoner orderly come to work for me. He turned out to be an old Uzbek, balding, with gray hair, who spoke Russian very poorly. He had been sentenced to ten years' imprisonment in the Gulag for "plundering socialist property." It turned out that he (like other Uzbeks) had many children at home. When his family got to the point of not having enough food, and the children were starving, he stole a sack of corn from the collective farm warehouse.[12] Someone noticed it. They tried him in court, then sent him away for a term at the Arctic Circle at Pechorlag, in my unit. His name was Mamarisut Oglyi Ishankl.

In the mornings, they sent him outside the camp without the armed guard to my dugout, and in the evenings he went back to sleep in the camp. In his duties as my orderly, he had to chop wood, light the stove, fill the buckets with water, and fix food. He was very skillful at fixing plov,[13] when we managed to get hold of rice and meat.

Speaking of food, there was a real problem with supplies in our camp unit at that time. We had plenty of water and wood, but little food. As I already mentioned, the State had planned well in advance for the huge increase in the number of prisoners at Pechorlag, and had intended that all prisoners would have enough basic foodstuffs, clothing, and building materials. As I mentioned earlier, because of the horrendous northern climate and unanticipated early freezing of the rivers, the steamships and barges that were carrying our supplies were frozen in the iced-over rivers far from Abez. This meant that all the things we needed to survive on had not made it to our camp. But the people—prisoners and camp administrators—had appeared.[14]

When I arrived at my camp unit, I found out that we only had flour and salt to live on. The 6th Department, which was located 14 kilometers (8.7 miles) from my unit, sent bread and, now and then, other things (groats and, rarely, frozen fish and, even more rarely, meat). The prisoners in the camp were starving, even though they were receiving their daily rations of bread.

The rules were as follows. Anyone who did not work the norm for a twenty-four-hour period, received 300 grams (about ten slices of bread) a day, those who fulfilled the work norm at 100 percent received 600 grams, and those who overfulfilled the norm received 800 grams. If a person fulfilled the norm by 150 percent, then he also received a bonus meat dish at lunch.

If there were no bonus meat available, he would receive bits of animal head, leg, or entrails. Those who were not fulfilling the norm did not get any bread, just a bit of soup. The civilians who worked on the tracks were also being fed badly. During that winter of 1940–1941, I nearly forgot what eggs, butter, milk products, and vegetables even looked like.

When winter set in, everyone began to come down with "tsingoi," especially the prisoners. In medical language, this is called scurvy, levels 1, 2, and 3. I myself came down with level 2 scurvy, which is when the body (especially the stomach) breaks out in small eruptions and the teeth loosen. With level 3 scurvy, the teeth fall out. In order to put the brakes on this disease, which is caused when a person does not get sufficient vitamins in his food, everyone, civilians and prisoners alike, had to drink a tincture made from pine branches.

But it was during this first winter at the camp that, by chance, I figured out a way to help feed everyone in my camp unit, not just the few civilians, but all the prisoners, as well. Here is how it happened.

As I already mentioned, I had brought my skis with me. Soon after getting to Permashor, one evening I went skiing in the moonlight in the area surrounding the camp. As I skied around, I spotted some fresh ski trails. These trails were strange in that they were without grooves in the middle, which meant that the skis were probably handmade. Of course I was very curious to find out who else would be out skiing near my prison camp, so I followed the ski trails in hopes of finding this person. The VOKhR armed guards never went on skis alone (and then, only on business), and the platoon commanding officer and the political instructor did not like skiing (although they had been given fabricated skis with grooves down the middle). And I knew that the closest Komi settlement was tens of kilometers away in deep snow.[15]

Soon, right in front of me, in the moonlight, I saw a figure on skis, someone unusually broad around the waist. It appeared to be a Komi, who must have lived in some settlement far from the camp. He evidently traveled to our area in a sleigh drawn by deer (as a rule, they used three to four deer on one sleigh). He had stopped close to the camp, strapped on his homemade skis, and placed snares in the bushes to catch birds. That year, there were many northern partridges around, and they seemed to congregate in bushes. These bushes, with their branches sticking out of the snow, grew all around the camp. They looked like islands in the snow.

The partridges would jump from branch to branch along the bushes and peck at the buds. Right in their path, the resourceful Komi had placed snares (loops of horsehair or small sticks), which he had tightened into lace between two branches along the holes in the snow. Once the partridge stuck his neck into a loop, he fell into the hole, hung himself, and froze to death. I watched as the Komi collected his "harvest" from the traps that he had set earlier, and set his traps up again. The partridges he collected hung on a string around his waist, which is why he had looked so unusually wide to me earlier.

I skied back to the camp and told the political instructor what I had seen. I had taken one of the Komi's snares off of a bush, and I showed this to him. Since we had several horses in our camp unit, I suggested that we cut some of their tails, and weave some nets (which I knew how to do since childhood, since I loved fishing). Then I proposed that we give the sick and weak prisoners a pass to leave the camp, and teach them how set traps for partridges around the zone. This idea produced results way better than I ever expected. That whole bleak winter, every person, including all of the prisoners, had partridge meat every day. We had had so many that we conserved some braised partridges in jars, as well.

Now that we had warm barracks and we had food in our camp unit, we could get down to the business of building our section of rail line.

Then, one day, out of the blue, a thunderstorm erupted over my head. Someone had found out what we had done to get the barracks built, and had reported us to the upper leadership of the camp. They accused us of "tufta" (giving phony numbers) and said that we had tricked the authorities. Nobody was interested in the fact that the monthly plan had been fulfilled. The emphasis was put on the first half of the month when we had "tricked" everyone. It was obvious that the leadership of the camp had decided to punish me and Volodia, so as to teach other camp bosses a lesson and keep them from doing something like this. And they would begin with me, since I was a candidate member of the party. (Volodia, as I already mentioned, was not a party member.)

Soon after I got wind of this trouble brewing, I got a message via the Selektor. It was a formal summons to a party meeting in the 6th Department. I went. The meeting took place in a pine log structure that had just been built. It smelled of soft pine and resin. The building was barely lit by primitive oil lamps. At the presidium sat the director of the 6th Department and the secretary of the Party Organization.[16] In the hall, there were several tens of Communists, basically from all the camp units near and far, and also from Department Headquarters. The majority of people at the meeting had worked in other parts of the Gulag before starting their jobs at Pechorlag.

Before he worked at a Gulag camp, the director of the 6th Department had been in the military. He had participated in the "liberation" of Western Belorussia[17] as a senior lieutenant, in the city of Belostok, where he had also found himself a wife. He had no training in construction work at all.

The secretary of the Party Organization ran the meeting. He started by angrily informing the group that there was a young specialist who not long ago had arrived from Moscow to this camp, who was also a candidate member of the CPSU. He said this young man had begun his working life at the camp with a deception, by undertaking a "tufta." Having named this disgraceful person, me, to all the Communists of the organization, he moved to exclude me from being a CPSU candidate member, and put the question to a vote. In the dark hall where all the people sat, you could see the breath being exhaled from their mouths. Then, a voice rang out, and someone suggested that they hear some words from the accused.

So they gave me the chance to speak. Seeing only the silhouettes of the audience, I nervously set forth my simple biography. I told them that although I had gotten the highest grades at my institute, I had elected to work somewhere to get some practical engineering experience on a construction site. Before I had even gotten a job, I was sent to work at the Gulag. I told the audience in detail what the Gulag officials from the Cadres Department, and the Communist Party officials from the CPSU Central Committee had told us before sending us to Pechorlag. I sketched out what I had been up against when I first arrived at my camp unit.

I described how Volodia and I had concluded that given the upcoming winter, we had to act quickly to save people's lives, since the prisoners were sentenced to work, not to simply die in camp. And I stressed that we had nobody to turn to for advice.

I explained to the crowd everything we did, from the earliest actions right up to the building of warm barracks. I honestly said that, yes, at the beginning of the month we consciously misled the authorities with "tufta," since we could see no other way out of this complex situation. I emphasized that by the end of the month, the monthly construction plan for railroad track building had been fulfilled and that the prisoners' lives had been saved. Now they were in the position to survive any kind of freezing winter. In the hall, I heard someone exclaim: "Great job!"

Several times the secretary of the Party Organization interrupted me and called for a vote to exclude me from party candidacy. But the crowd insisted that I be given the chance to finish speaking. Then from the hall, I heard another proposal spoken aloud: "He should remain a candidate of the party." When the secretary's proposal to "exclude me" came up, only the secretary himself and the department director voted yes. The entire crowd voted against the proposal, which was voted on first "in the order of presentation." When the second vote came "to leave me in," all hands in the hall, seemingly at once, were raised.

That is how their attempt to censure me in the party turned out. In the end, the 6th Department director issued an order (on the work front, that is, the NKVD side, not from the Communist Party) that strongly warned me and Volodia for our use of "tufta." Thus opened the first page of our personal affairs at the Gulag.

I returned from the party meeting with mixed feelings. On the one hand, I was bitter and bewildered because the leadership at Pechorlag refused to understand me. On the other hand, I felt confident that our actions had been the right ones and that the ordinary workers in the camp supported what we had done.

CHAPTER 7

THE UNIT BOSSES

As I already mentioned, aside from the security detail, there were only two jobs at the camp for civilians: the boss of the camp unit, and the foreman. The foreman was supposed to be a person who had some technical training. The boss position was reserved for people who had served in other subdivisions of the NKVD's GULAG, as a rule, and who did not have higher education. When I began my job at Pechorlag, I had been sent to work as a foreman. However, as I already related, when I arrived at the unit at Pernashor, where I was to work as a foreman, I found that I had to step into the boss job as well.

Then one day, I found out that I was being transferred to another camp unit at Pechorlag.[1] Once I made my parting remarks at Pernashor, where I was leaving my job as foreman and boss, I was warned that again there would be no camp unit boss at my new job. In fact, I was told, there would not be a boss at the new job for a while, so I would be expected to do both jobs. Again, that meant working as both camp unit boss and foreman.

After I had been working both jobs at my new camp unit for a few months, one day we heard that a unit boss had been named, and that he would soon arrive. I was looking forward to having him there with me. It would be a big help if he took over all the administrative and management matters, because this would allow me to concentrate more on technical matters. But as soon as he arrived at the camp, they took him away again. Actually, he was not sent to a new job, but straight into the zone, as a prisoner.

What happened was this. Before he arrived from his previous job (which was also at a forced labor prison camp), he had stopped over in Leningrad. While there it happened that someone stole his pistol off of him while he was riding on an overcrowded tram. Right away, he demanded that they stop the tram. They searched everyone on board, but did not find the pistol.

His case was under investigation for a long time, just dragging on and on.[2] By the time he arrived at Pechorlag, the inquiry had been concluded, and they had sentenced him to three years in prison. When his sentence was announced, they incarcerated him right then and there at the camp. With my own eyes I saw him being ordered up to roll call with the other prisoners, and I saw him return from the work site with them, too. He stood out from the other prisoners because he was wearing a sheepskin jacket ("from the outside," i.e., something purchased outside of the Gulag camp). I was surprised that the other prisoners didn't tear that jacket off of him, because he stuck out like a sore thumb among all their quilted padded jackets and lined shirts. Anyway, soon they transferred him elsewhere.

For me, this meant another long period of working two jobs at once. Finally, though, they sent us a new boss. I could never forget this man, even though we worked together only for a short while. (Not long after he arrived, they transferred me to yet another camp unit.)

I remember him because they appointed him unit boss after he had been in custody awaiting the death penalty[3] for eleven months. He had lost his mind from this experience, and then recovered. When the doctors decided that he was healthy again, they sent him to the Gulag to the most distant camp, to Pechorlag, to work as a unit boss. Upon arrival, he was assigned to the 6th Department's northern section, that is, to my unit. (Volodia's camp unit was actually more northern than mine, as I already noted, and his unit had a boss already.)

The new boss was a lean man, somewhere around thirty years old, with combed-back light hair and energetic facial features. He had a long, skinny nose with a protuberance, and his thin lips were usually pursed together tightly. His movements were sharp, and his judgments were categorical.

His dugout was right next to mine, so there was nowhere to go to get away from him. And as soon as he began to drink, he would come to me, sit for hours and recount the details of how he had been sentenced to the death penalty. It almost drove me mad, but there was no way to get out of it. All around us, there was only the dark night and the tundra.

I would be glad to forget his stories, but you can't order away memories. Here are some of things he told me.

To the question as to how he had gotten himself into such unusual work, he told me that when he had been demobilized from the army, he had been given a security job at Butyrka prison in Moscow.[4] One day, the prison's private vehicle arrived at the prison's courtyard with a contingent of arrested men. As it happened, the gates to the inner courtyard would not unlock, so they opened the doors of the vehicle in the outer courtyard and let the prisoners out. One of the prisoners noticed that the outer gates to the prison were still hanging open, and he took off running. As the security guard on duty, my unit boss at that moment had been standing next to the gates. When he saw what was happening, he did not hesitate. He drew out the sword that hung at his side and stabbed, right into the spine, the prisoner who was trying to escape.

The Butyrka guards who had carelessly left open the courtyard gates were punished. The security officer (our current unit boss) had prevented the prisoner's escape. For his decisive action, he was offered a transfer to a new job. At this new job, he would be carrying out "special commissions," that is, he would work as an executioner, shooting the enemies of Soviet power. He agreed to the transfer, and after some special training, he was sent with his new specialty to the ancient Russian city of Uglich.[5]

For days at a time, he said, from mission to mission, he sat around doing nothing. He rested. Then, when the prison had accumulated a large number of condemned prisoners, the authorities would set an execution date. A specially trusted group from the security department of Uglich's prison was then sent out to carefully select a place in the woods and dig a pit. The pit was guarded until the executions took place. Starting at night and working until the morning, the prison officials would transport the condemned prisoners in a closed truck to this pit. Besides the security men and the person who would ensure that the execution took place, he said, there was always a doctor on hand. It was his duty to certify the death and write up the necessary documents.

One at a time, they led a condemned prisoner from the truck to the edge of the pit, and forced him to get on his knees with his face toward the pit. The executioner then shot him in the back of the head, and the dead man fell in. From the blow to the head, the executioner told me, the body would turn over facing up, and straighten up on the bottom of the pit. The doctor then went down into the pit and certified that the body was dead. Then they went to retrieve the next condemned prisoner.

He told me that from time to time, there was a prisoner who would not do what he was told and go submissively to the edge of the pit. In these cases, the security guys had to help out, and the job for the executioner would be more complicated.

When the mission was finished and the pit was filled, they covered it with soil and tried to make it look as unobtrusive as possible. After every mission, he told me, he got drunk and tried not to think about what he had done until the next time they called. For a long time, though, he was convinced that his job was important and honorable, because he was destroying the enemies of Soviet power. He believed that not everyone could be as trusted as he was with such a job.

But then one day, he had to shoot a fourteen-year-old girl. The executioner was told right before he had to kill her that not only was she the daughter of an "enemy of the people," she was also a "German spy." Suddenly and involuntarily, questions sprang to his mind. He was to kill a fourteen-year-old girl in an ancient Russian small town far from the front, in a place that had no classified establishments? Where had this adolescent girl done her spying, and for whom?

When they brought her to the execution place, she held herself up firmly and was silent. But when they led her to the pit, she spoke up. She said that she did not understand why they were depriving her of her life. "Even Stalin said that children do not answer for their parents, so why me?" she asked. She was unaware, he added, that she was also accused of being a "German spy."

In the words of my unit boss, after this execution he drank himself into a stupor so profound that he felt nothing. Soon he was sent to a hospital for crazy people.

I was secretly happy when I received a new appointment and left this constant, unwanted interlocutor. When the Great Patriotic War began, the bosses of all the camp units were called into the army. All of their duties were handed over to the foremen, and as long as the camp was designated as vital to the military effort, the foremen were not generally sent to the army. Even if the foreman insisted he wanted to go to the front, he was not sent.

This particular camp unit boss I never met again, nor did I ever hear of him.

CHAPTER 8

A CHANGE IN LEADERSHIP
AT PECHORLAG

THE CIVILIAN EMPLOYEES AT THE CAMP UNITS HAD NO radios or daily newspapers. Instead, everything we knew about the rest of the country and about conditions in the other parts of the prison labor camp came from fragmentary conversations on the Selektor. Everyone, from the camp units and subunits, all the way up to the Camp Administration, relied on the Selektor. Any time you picked up the receiver and went to press the lever to make a call, the line was buzzing with talk. And it took a lot of work to connect to someone in particular. The things you could hear when you pressed the receiver to your ear! But this was how we received the latest news long before hearing anything officially.

I don't remember when it happened, whether it was in December 1940 or the beginning of 1941, but we heard that Moscow had taken drastic measures to change the entire leadership of Pechorlag, from the administration down to the departments.[1] I believe Moscow was changing the leadership because the news had reached the center of the huge number of prisoner deaths since the onset of the Arctic winter. They arrested Pechorlag's entire upper management, it was rumored, and shot them.[2]

I heard that they were also supposed to arrest the director of the 6th Department.[3] He tried to kill himself, but the bullet shot through his body right next to his heart. So when they rounded up the other department directors, he was in the hospital. Once he started to recover physically, he lost his mind. He remained in the hospital with this diagnosis for so long that he was forgotten. I heard that he eventually returned to normal life. There were other theories that he had survived being killed because he was such a skilled "operator." People said that he had faked his suicide very carefully, and then he had faked his craziness, plus he had managed to twist all the other "operators" around his little finger. And maybe they even helped him?

Moscow sent an entirely new leadership, from top to bottom, to Pechorlag. The prison newspaper, *The Rail Line for Stalin*, had high praise for those camp bosses who had not followed the criminal course of pursuing production results at any price. It also castigated the bosses who did not take care of the prisoners' needs, which had resulted in unnecessary deaths. The first thing the new leadership did when everyone was settled at Pechorlag, was to go after the materials imprisoned on those steamships and barges that were frozen in the Pechora and Usa Rivers. Those goods had been sent off to Abez in the fall of 1940, and we needed them.

With this in mind, a campwide directive went out to all the bosses, asking them to select some nonpolitical prisoners (that is, criminals) who were strong and healthy, to be sent to the 93rd Unit of the 6th Department. There, they would form a mobile traveling Gulag camp unit, which would lay foundation beams for an ice road on the Usa and Pechora rivers. Once this road existed, they could get to the steamships and barges that were stuck in the ice.

The Camp Administration could not risk using a large number of "political prisoners" from the camps for this work.[4] The politicals were not trustworthy, nor were they very healthy, as a rule. And they did not have the experience of surviving in the severe conditions of the north that many of the nonpoliticals had.

So, since the administration was not allowed to send political prisoners, they had to choose from among the hardened criminals when they formed the mobile camp units to build the ice roads. To head up these mobile units, they appointed former prisoners who had agreed to work in the camps as civilian employees. These men were very familiar with camp life from having served time, but now they had decided to turn their lives around, and work at the Gulag as civilians.[5] They were familiar with the lives and customs of the nonpolitical prisoners. Pechorlag's new leadership understood that it was important to get bosses for these mobile units who could actually have some authority among the hard-ened criminals. Especially given the conditions of life in the Gulag, not to mention the work out on a frozen river, where the bitterly cold north-ern winds constantly blew all around them.

That's how the Gulag administration managed so quickly to get an ice road laid down so the men could get to the freight stuck in the ice. Because, above all, we needed the food at Pechorlag.

CHAPTER 9

TRANSFERRED TO THE 93RD UNIT

Labor Force: Hardened Criminals

EVERYTHING THAT HAPPENED, I LEARNED LATER. THE CHANGES that directly affected me at Pechorlag began with talk I heard over the Selektor. I was told to go to the 6th Department for a new job. Once there, I found out that I was to become part of the local camp leadership. The 6th Department leaders praised me for taking urgent measures to save prisoners' lives at the beginning of the winter. They emphasized that I had conducted myself as a true Communist. And finally, they told me that they "had in mind" to entrust me with a new sector of work, which was at the 93rd camp unit. There, they said, I would encounter some very interesting engineering problems. The new camp unit was located just south of the 6th Department, not far from the Camp Administration offices.

The rest of the discussion revolved around what they called the "front of work" that I would face, meaning the engineering problems, and not a word was said about what kind of workforce I would find at the 93rd camp unit. Because of my own naïveté, I did not even think to ask them. However, when I did find out what kind of prisoners were there, it became clear to me that the workforce would be my main obstacle.

The thing was, at that time, the majority of Pechorlag's physically sound, nonpolitical zeks were hardened criminals, gangsters, and other kinds of felons. Many of them had been in prison previously. These men had totally acclimated to prison life, and they even had their own rules and customs. For them, the Gulag was a "second home."

Later, I came to understand that the most hard-boiled group of hard-ened criminals and gangsters in the camps obeyed only their own rule, which was: "We do not work." Following this rule, the only thing these prisoners were allowed to do was to work "for themselves." In other words, they could fix food, prepare wood, light the stove, and clean shoes, but nothing else. In preserving their own existence, the criminals had subordinated some of the inexperienced, simple, and healthy pris-oners, the "newbies," by using threats and intimidation. These new guys were forced to work "for two," that is, for themselves, and in order to defend themselves, for their "godfathers." The experienced bosses of the mobile units had not chosen these "godfathers" when they had picked out their workers. So when the selected prisoners left the 93rd camp unit for the ice roads, they left behind them the dregs of the criminal world.

The Camp Administration concealed all of this from me when they gave me my new assignment. I still believe that there was an ulterior motive behind this "new job." Most likely, the older camp cadres who had survived the recent purge had come up with this: "Akh, everyone bragged about how brave you had been in building those warm prisoner barracks earlier this winter. But now, you can show us that you are also talented enough to work with bands of hardened criminals and gangsters, the men that were even rejected by "their own." They were saying: "You think you are so smart and principled, so now we'll give you something nice and cozy to work with!"

When I met with the leadership of the 6th Department, they told me only that there would be around three hundred prisoners left once the mobile units had been formed. They also informed me that my new camp unit had no foreman and no boss, nor did it have any real admin-istrative structure in place. In other words, I would have to select an entire new staff on site, and then start to work. Oh, and at the moment, I was told, all of the prisoners in the 93rd camp unit had refused to go to work.

With that, the leadership introduced me to a young man who showed up dressed in zek clothing. He was around thirty years old, had a clean-shaven head, and an open, affable, ready smile. (As I came to know him better, I found that he had a great sense of humor and loved to joke around. He was always more than willing to make fun of himself. This was his way of philosophically coming to terms with the lives we were living.) It turned out that this young prisoner had been assigned to the 93rd camp unit as the labor assistant to the unit boss. The labor assistant was a category of worker in the camp for nonpolitical prisoners who were serving long sentences. These zeks were taught to work in the camps with the cadres, which meant that they worked assisting the bosses of the camp units, or the foremen. Their status allowed them to move about without armed guards within the boundaries of the department. They carried a special pass with their photograph on it.

In any case, we were told that we both needed to go to the assignments center immediately, without delay. The sleighs were already waiting. So, not understanding anything about what was what, and not having been shown even a blueprint of what we were expected to build, I was literally pushed into my new job.

We covered ourselves with hay in the sleigh. As we slid along the path, my new assistant told me about himself. Until he was sent to prison, he had been an NKVD employee, a security officer, in the city of Taganrog at a fish factory.[1] There he seduced the wife of his boss. The boss found out, and "slammed" his colleague off to the Gulag for ten years, supposedly for a barrel of rotten herring. (The official charge was "plundering socialist property.")

When I told him that I knew nothing about the type of prisoners that I was about to work with, he chided me for being gullible, and proceeded to tell me what sort of men I was facing. You can imagine how I felt when I finally understood what kind of a situation I had been caught in, all due to my naïveté and inexperience. My new colleague saw how hard I took this news. He tried to calm me down by persuading me that it was not that bad and that we would find a way to deal with it.

Later that evening we arrived at the 93rd camp unit. They sent us immediately to get some sleep. I was placed with the platoon security commander, and my colleague was dispatched to the camp unit's labor assistant.

Early the next morning, the labor assistant came to me and said, literally, the following words: "Well, Citizen Boss, permit me to report, that of the three hundred prisoners available, only ten people have lined up. And these ten have agreed only to stack wood, because there was no wood to heat the barracks."

I said I would be at the camp in a few minutes. The labor assistant and the platoon security commander both told me that going there would be useless. They said these were the type of prisoners who would not be talked into anything. All the same, I insisted, and we went.

In contrast to Pernashor, everything in this camp was depressing. There were no bushes, no spruce trees, and no paths. There were several large old barracks. The kitchen was outside the zone. We went into one of the barracks. Inside, there were no berths, only wooden planks from wall to wall, on two levels. The prisoners were lying on the planks. At the far end of the barracks sat a sturdily built middle-aged prisoner with a wedge-shaped beard, repairing shoes. As he soled a felt boot, he watched us carefully, paying attention to us as we talked.

What normally happened when the boss walked into a barracks was that the barracks orderly would give the command "Stand!" And then he would report how many men were at work, how many were resting after their shift, and how many were sick. When we showed up that day, though, nobody stirred, and nobody announced anything. They did not even look at us, as if we were an empty space. When I said, "Hello," the barracks answered with silence.

Then I asked an elderly prisoner who was lying on a wooden plank, "Why aren't you at work?" In answer, I heard, "I have been sitting for twenty-five years in the Gulag, and I have never worked for anyone. And you think I'm going to work for you, you little snot-nose. Fuck...your mother!" All at once, the whole barracks broke into guffaws.

I walked right up to the plank bed, and looked him in the face. Some watched me with curiosity, others with hatred. Several people simply turned away. I noticed a strong, obviously peasant chap with reddish cheeks and, out of the blue I thought: Nothing will get him, not even the North. I bet his family was "dekulakized." I asked him why he was not at work. That young man cast his eyes off to the side, making an effort to imitate the hardened criminal.

We left the barracks and the labor assistant said: "We won't get anywhere until we find the leader."

The commanding officer and I agreed with him. The labor assistant took on the painstaking work of finding their leader. I won't say how he managed that. But after several days it became clear that the leader was that prisoner with the wedge-shaped, professorial beard who had been repairing shoes that day we had come into the barracks.

I asked to see this leader, and we spoke for a long time. I asked him where he was from, if he was married, if he had children, where they were, what his profession "on the outside" had been, how long he had been here at Pechorlag, and how many times he had been in prison, and so on. At first he was prickly and answered my questions curtly, in monosyllables. But after a while, I managed to get him to warm up to talking to me. He told me that this was his second time in prison. This second term he had gotten because when he had only two more years to go until he could be released from his original term, he tried to escape. They caught him and gave him ten more years. He finished with these candid words: "Citizen Boss, don't even try. No matter what, we will not work."

Based on some advice I had received from the labor assistant, I told him the following: "Well, okay, but put yourself in my place. I am a young specialist, and I have no experience. But one thing I do know is that this prison camp, Pechorlag, has been given military status now. The war with Germany could break out at any minute. The first thing the Nazis will do is take the Donbas Coal Basin, so it will be out of service. Then all of our military factories will be forced to stop producing weapons and equipment to fight the war. The plan is for the Soviet government to get access to the coal in Vorkuta. I know that you prisoners have your own ways. But my task is to build a section of rail line to the coal at Vorkuta as quickly as possible."

I continued speaking: "If you refuse to get out there and help build these railway tracks, then I will have no choice but to send you personally and your friends to the Punishment Unit.[2] If you agree to work with me, then you may form your own brigade and organize it however you see fit; I will not interfere. I will have nothing to do with who is in it and who is not. I have made an agreement with the camp security men that your brigade will be brought back from the tracks to camp as soon as you fulfill your norm, even if the twelve-hour shift has not ended. Also, I will give your brigade the right to send your own representative to the kitchen to make sure that the cooks set aside any extra food that the brigade has earned for its cauldron. If your brigade fulfills the plan by 150 percent in any given twenty-four-hour period, then bonus meat dishes will be added to the dinner of each member of the brigade. And, if you think the brigade would like it, I could get your brigade all housed together in one barrack. I will help."

I told him that I would not wait very long for his answer. I told him to think about it and talk it over with the others. So, tomorrow, I told him, one of two things would happen. Either he would give me a list of men who would form a brigade, which would line up for work at 6:00 AM, or he and his men would be sent under reinforced convoy immediately to the Punishment Unit. I expressed the hope that he understood me correctly.

The labor assistant, the commanding officer, and I waited impatiently until the next morning. On that morning, we received a list of men for the brigade. Their brigade was made up of habitual recidivists, solidly built young men who had landed there during dekulakization, strong prisoners from Central Asia who spoke almost no Russian, and a number of other men whom the recidivists were clearly using as "dairy cows." In return, the recidivists protected the "dairy cows" from the pervasive mockery and brutality in the zone. It was always a mystery to me how the remaining recidivists who were not selected by their pals for the ice-road brigades were able to keep such strong, hardy prisoners (whom they exploited) for themselves.

By an agreement I had made with the security platoon, a separate security convoy accompanied this brigade to the work site. Their job was to dig into the frozen, clayish soil and widen the area that had already been dug out for the future railway line. They left for the tracks at 6:00 AM. At 7:00 AM, I walked past their work site. They all were sitting around a campfire. It was the same situation when I checked at 8:00 AM and at 9:00 AM. Then brigade leader then said to me: "Citizen Boss, let's have a smoke." I sat down and started a general conversation. He studied my face. I acted as if I had no doubts about what we had agreed on, and that the work would be done. I just sat with him smoking a cigar. Then I got up to go.

Suddenly the brigade leader stuck four fingers into his mouth, made a piercing whistle, and gave the command: "Well, gang, let's go!" Everyone, except a few men of the criminal elite[3] who remained sitting at the campfire, jumped up and began working at a good clip. At 2:00 in the afternoon, I heard a shout from down the tracks: "Foreman!" I went. The brigade leader said: "Check the work."

They had completed 150 percent of their norm. The men in the brigade put their pickaxes, crowbars, and shovels onto their shoulders and with a song full of curses, walked with their security guard past the other prisoner-workers, back to the zone. There, already waiting for them, was a substantial dinner. On this day, in addition to this very brigade, the remaining men also began to work. In a few days, the ringleader requested that his entire brigade be resettled into one barrack.

So about two weeks after my arrival at the 93rd camp unit, we started having normal workdays. It seemed that all was going well and I could be happy.

CHAPTER 10

ATTEMPTED PRISONER REVOLT
IN THE 93RD UNIT

WHEN THE ARCTIC NIGHTS ARRIVED, WE ONLY SAW THE SUN for a little bit every day. It was interesting to watch how the sky changed. Toward the south, because of the boundless snowy horizon, the sun would first appear as a small piece of a large red ball. You could easily stare at it with the naked eye, because its radiating light would not blind a person. But it sent extremely long shadows from everything standing above the snow, including things or people. Right there and then this part of the heavenly body disappeared, sending up to the sky what looked like farewell rays. Day after day, the sun grew bigger and bigger in the sky. Then, finally, it rose completely over the snow. This enormous, round, deep red mass looked as if it were sitting right on the edge of the horizon.

Gradually the days became longer, and the sun rose even higher and began to warm the snowy crust of the tundra during the day. At night, though, it got intensely cold again and refroze the upper layer of snow that had slightly thawed. The ice became thicker, and in a short time, it was so strong that you could walk on it without falling through. This was a dangerous time for the guards. Now, the prisoners could escape from the camp without getting bogged down in the snow. They would run, hoping to make it to the Ural Mountains and beyond, where capturing them would be very difficult.

On one of those evenings, I was eating dinner in my little hut not far from the zone when a frightened young security soldier came running to me. In a voice trembling with fear, he announced, "The Platoon Security

Commander sent me. There's a revolt going on in the camp!" I threw aside my dinner and hurried to the zone. Armed VokhR soldiers had cordoned off the camp, and they had installed machine guns on the watchtowers.

When I tried to go into the zone, the VOKhR soldiers refused to let me in. I insisted for so long and so loudly that they called the platoon commander. When he got there, he explained that the zeks had started a revolt, and were demanding to be let out of prison. It was not clear why this was happening, he told me, but it was too dangerous to let me go into the zone because I might be killed. I absolutely insisted that they let me go into the zone so I could talk to the leader of the revolt. The platoon commander finally relented, but he demanded that I write a memo stating that I had been warned of the dangers and that I took the responsibility for any possible consequences. After I had written the memo, they took everything out of my pockets. They said they would keep these little things in the security platoon, because if the zeks got ahold of anything, they could use them in any attack on me. I handed over my penknife, some money, and my documents. They let me keep a notebook and pencil, which I always carried in the zone with me.

I walked through the entrance into an almost empty courtyard. A few people were hanging around in the corners of the courtyard, but when they spotted me, they scattered to their barracks. I headed for the barracks where the elite of the criminal world lived. It was humming like a beehive. I walked over to it and went in. When I came inside, the place immediately went silent. I saw the agitated men sitting and laying on both tiers of the wooden bunks. The entryway was at one end of the barracks, and on the other end stood a big furnace made of stone and very poor local clay, crackling from the fire that burned steadily in it. The instigators of the revolt were sitting on benches at the large table just next to the stove. I saw that in order to get to the table, I would have to walk from the beginning to the end of the barracks, past the bunks that lined both walls.

I started walking. When I was less than halfway to the table, the leader who had been sitting facing the entrance saw me come in and suddenly jumped up, quickly went over to the furnace, and tore a large rock from its corner. He ran toward me, threatening me with the rock in both hands over his head, swearing like a sailor.

What to do? If I tried to run for the exit, he could throw the rock at my back, or someone could stab me with a knife. The thing I could do was to sit down again with the leader. Looking him right in the eye, I slowly walked toward him. He still held the rock above his head, but I could see that his arms were shaking slightly. I drew closer until only the table separated us. Very quietly, I asked him: "What's making you go crazy like this?"

With a groan, he dropped the rock behind his back, sat down at the table, and began pounding his fists on his head. He was so hysterical that it was difficult to understand what he was trying to say. I sat across from him, looking at him in silence. All the other prisoners surrounding us in the barracks also watched silently. Gradually, he calmed down, and I found out what had happened. It turned out that he was angry because the cooks in the kitchen were mistreating his brigade. Instead of giving them what they had honestly earned at dinner, the high-quality food I had promised them, the cooks had given them watery prison soup.

Right in front of me on the table sat a tub of this thin soup, with a scoop hanging on the side of the tub.

"Look at this!" said the leader, "This is what they brought us. This is an insult! You promised to feed us good food if we overfulfilled our plan. Is this what your promises mean? Yes, we are prisoners, so I guess that means that we are not people, and that you can cheat us and treat us 'any way you like'? And we believed in you." All the men surrounding us also began to get indignant and worked up, and started shouting out all around the room.

Experienced camp civilians already had warned me that the prisoners with long sentences, especially those who have already served a sentence previously, can snap easily. And sometimes something very small can make them lose it, and the explosion can be difficult to contain. So, they said, it was best to never let them get that angry. I knew that if I wanted this to pass without violence, I had to strongly control myself. I had been warned already not to curse, scream, or give orders, but to try to work out an agreeable solution that would clear the air.

With this advice in mind, I spoke loudly so that everyone could hear me. I reminded them that not only had I promised to feed them better for their successes at work, but that I had recommended to the brigade leader that someone from their brigade go every day to the kitchen to make sure that the cooks were adding the extras in the cauldron for the brigade. I then asked them if anyone had gone to the kitchen that day. The brigade leader turned to the surrounding men and asked them.

It turned out that, on this day, nobody had gone to the kitchen to make sure the cooks were adding the extras. Once that was established,

I then asked them to think about how they might approach the unit boss (me) in the future, and where they had gotten the idea that I was cheating them and treating them "any way I liked." Everyone fell silent for a few minutes. Then, they transferred their anger to the cook. They started saying that since the unit leader (me) had appointed the cook, then this meant that all the same was I was to blame. And so yes, they claimed, I was very being sneaky and trying to cheat all these men who were doing honest work.

I had to think of way to resolve this, so I suggested to the ringleader that the brigade itself appoint a cook. If they found a person to cook for them whom they could trust, I promised I would support their choice. They gave me the name of another prisoner who could cook.

But from this point on, everything got complicated. The prisoner that the ringleader and brigade wanted as their cook had worked "outside the zone" as a chef and cook at the best restaurant in Moscow in those days, at the restaurant of the Metropol Hotel. But when I told the commander of the security platoon that the prisoners wanted this man to cook for them, he categorically opposed it.

As I already mentioned, the kitchen at the 93rd camp unit was located outside the gates of the zone. The security platoon commander told me that this man, under no circumstances, would be let out of the zone. He was serving a twenty-five-year sentence for murder and for attempting a group escape. Moreover, he said, the escapees had brought a young, husky boy with them, promising him escape, too. But on the way to the Ural Mountains, they had killed him and eaten him.

So what to do? I gathered the entire criminal elite and asked them whether what the platoon security commander had told me was true. If it were true, I said, then how was I to understand their behavior and how could I from now on believe them?

In answer, I heard, "Let's ask the cook himself."

The men were all gathered on the benches around the table, and in front of them, on a separate stool, sat a tall, powerful, sinewy man who was around forty years old. There was something unpleasant in his appearance. It was his eyes, which were very close together, and they way he looked around in a piercing, prickly way. The leader told him that the unit boss had agreed to support him as their cook, as the brigade had requested, but that security had refused to allow him to go to the kitchen outside the zone, because they were afraid that he would escape. So this was the situation, he said.

The man answered: I have a twenty-five-year sentence, but I do not intend to be here that long. I absolutely will escape. I am a finished man, and have no hope. But if you (he looked over at the criminal elite) and Citizen Boss believe in me, then I swear (here he spewed out some criminal curses of the worst kind) that I will not let you down. I absolutely will escape sometime, but not now. I will go later. You may not believe me, but I will not let you down.

After this, I asked the cook to leave the room. All the prisoners in the room watched me carefully. I asked them: Do you believe what the cook said? They all answered that they believed him. And, they told me that if he lets us down after this, they swore they would search the world for him and finish him off for good. They added that the cook understood this, and that they had no doubts that he would keep his word.

In my gut, I believed in both the cook and the other prisoners. I got out my notebook right there, and wrote a note to security, asking that the cook be allowed to go outside the zone to the kitchen. I said in the note that I would be personally responsible for all possible consequences. Later, the security people tried to persuade me that I'd been hasty in writing this note, and they tried to talk me in to tearing it up. When I insisted on having it my way, though, they allowed the cook into the kitchen, but under heavy supervision. The troubles at the unit ended. Everyone went back to work.

The criminals continued to do their work as before. But the question of the cook and security was still not closed. Evidently, security had reported this situation to the Communist Party authorities. For something like two or three weeks, we ate the kind of delicious meals that we had never ever had before. Then came the order via the Selektor from "Sivaia Maska," that we were to send this cook to the 6th Department, which was several tens of kilometers away. Either the glory of his unique culinary skills had made it to them, or security had become alarmed. On top of that, we had just entered that period of the year when the snow forms its ice crust, which made it possible for a person to go anywhere he wished, undetected.

One way or another, however, we had to say goodbye to the cook. And when under strict security he got outside the boundaries of the territory that my unit answered for, that is, outside the bounds of which my camp unit had responsibility for him, he escaped.

There is one more thing that happened while I worked at the 93rd camp unit. It was something that in and of itself was inconsequential, but in my work life at the time, it made a big impression. As the foreman, every evening I called an operational meeting, where we went over the work indicators for the twenty-four-hour period, and for the night and day shifts. These indicators were important, because it was how we decided what sort of food would be given to every brigade and what kind of food every prisoner would receive the next day. The deputy foreman, the section foremen, brigade leaders, an economist, the labor assistant, the norms assigner, and the bookkeeper all attended this meeting. I always sat at a separate table with my back to the entryway. The participants of the meeting sat facing me. As always, someone was late, or someone was out doing errands.

When we three young specialists were training in Moscow before we left for the camp, we were given very nice penknives. These penknives had a link for fastening them with a metal chain onto our belt loops. And one evening, during one of these meetings, for some reason I stuck my hand into my right pants pocket and found that the chain was there, but the penknife was gone. But nobody had come close to me. Several people had walked past. Somehow I had not felt a thing, but right in front of everyone at the meeting, someone had come up from behind me and stolen it. Even though they had all seen this happen, they were all silent. They waited for my reaction. I pretended that nothing had happened, but inside I was very upset, since it would be impossible to get another penknife like this one. And in my life as a single man in the Gulag, a penknife like this was totally necessary.

One evening, after the attempted revolt had been averted and the unit was back to working like a well-oiled machine, I was holding one of our operational meetings. During the meeting, I slid open the drawer at the table, and there was my penknife. And I thought: This means that the criminal world at the camp unit has me in their sights.

Soon after arranging for the criminal elite to get their chosen cook, and his subsequent escape, I was transferred to the most southern unit of the 6th Department. It was next to the Camp Administration headquarters, in the village of Abez.

CHAPTER 11

BOSS AND FOREMAN AT THE 95TH UNIT

Labor Force: Political Prisoners

I WAS PERSUADED TO TAKE THIS ASSIGNMENT BECAUSE THEY told me that the new job would be more interesting to me as an engineer than the previous one had been. They told me that in addition to the usual work demands, we needed to build a dam and a large railroad station. Perhaps this was the reason. But I had the distinct impression that the main reason for transferring me out of my previous camp unit was because I had enjoyed too good of a relationship with the elites of the criminal world.

While instructing me on my new duties, the departmental leadership told me that unexpectedly, the 95th camp unit was without a boss or a foreman. The existing administration of the camp unit consisted of prisoners.

The problem with the unit being run entirely by prisoners was that the department could not send food and essential building materials to a prisoner-run camp unit. The other problem was that this camp unit still had not provided the department with its accounts for 1940, the previous year. The department needed a list of what materials they had used, and for what purpose. According to the Camp Administration, this camp unit had missed all the deadlines for filing these accounts, and actually, until the administration received the proper paperwork, they would not authorize anything for this unit. Even if a civilian boss requested the food or goods, they would get nothing.

From what the department could tell, the unit had already prepared its accounts, but since there was no civilian boss or foreman to sign off on the papers, they were not valid. So my first job was to go to the camp unit, check over the accounts and certify that they were correct. These accounts needed to include a list of what materials were used and on which projects they had been used. Then I needed to send the accounts to the department.

They gave me three days to get things in order and send my signed account. In the worst-case scenario, the camp unit would stop getting any food. All responsibility now rested on me.

I had to get myself to the new job as soon as possible. The department gave me a racing sled, the same type I had taken to my last job.

Because of the experience at my last camp unit, before I left the Camp Administration, I decided to ask the leadership about the kind of prisoners I would find at the 95th camp unit. They told me that this was a strict-regime unit made up of prisoners who had committed serious political crimes.[1] All of them had been given long prison sentences. They warned me to be very careful with them, since many of them were very smart people, including professors, scientists, and other well-known figures in science and culture. All of them were embittered toward Soviet power, and at any moment they could initiate a provocation.

As in the other places I had worked, my sole support at the new work place was the security garrison (the VoKhR guards), especially if there were any Communists or Komsomol members among them. There were no other civilians at this camp unit. Upon my arrival, I met the security people, and emphasized that I wanted us to have a good, honest working relationship. The security men briefed me about both the people in the unit, and how they were doing on fulfilling their work plan on their sector of the railway building.

Then I went into the zone. This camp unit had a large population, mostly of older people. These prisoners were very dignified. There was no cursing, and they acted politely and with restraint. Their barracks were very orderly. There were places for sleeping in two tiers, with two berths below and two above. The workday was the same as in other units, in twelve-hour shifts.

I gathered together the prisoners who were working as administrators of the camp unit. They were all highly educated, and a trained specialist worked in every administrative area. The deputy foreman and section foremen were both rather old, but experienced engineers. The economist was an economist by training. The same could be said about the bookkeeper, the accounts clerks, and the medical personnel. By the way, this camp unit also had a small field hospital, since many of the prisoners became sick not only from colds, but from illnesses due to their advanced ages (that is, problems with heart, kidneys, liver, stones, and others).

After I became acquainted with the life and activities of the unit, I looked into the accounting situation for 1940.

When I asked, they put on the table a volume of work with appendixes, and certified that everything in it was correct, and that all the data had been checked and rechecked. But the account was never sent because there was nobody to sign it. The previous civilian boss did not have specialized training and was afraid to sign it, and dragged his feet until the Camp Administration dismissed him. Everyone tried to convince me to believe the account, sign it without checking carefully, and send if off quickly.

All the same, I decided that since I was given this job, I would check it out. I still had two days left to investigate matters. But the main complication was that the section of track this camp unit was building was about 20 kilometers (about 7.5 miles) long, and it was almost totally covered with a thick layer of snow, more than a meter deep (3.3 feet). Snow depth was measured only at the places where work was being done. With this much snow cover, it would be impossible to find out exactly how many sleepers, rails, brackets, and linings had been put in, how many hammered spikes there were, whether or not had they dug the ditches all the way, and so on.

This camp unit, luckily, had several horses. The deputy foreman (who was a prisoner) and I saddled a pair of them and, with great trouble because of the snowdrifts, we went to several sites along all the tracks. He tried to explain things as we went along. It became clear that the total picture of what the unit had done on building the rail line in 1940 would emerge only when the snow disappeared, that is, at the end of May or the beginning of June. It was only March (of 1941) at this time, and there still were frequent snowstorms and blizzards. However, a little bit of sun was already pleasing those of us who had missed it so much.

Again the question arose: What to do? Right now, there was no way to check the accuracy of all that was included in the account. But people had to eat, they could not be put off. There was only one thing to do.

I had to take the word of the elderly, serious man who had prepared the account, and sign it. When I got back to the camp unit, that is what I did. The account was sent. This was how I began my job at the new camp unit.

Prisoners in the zone could usually be divided into two groups. The first group was made up of the intelligentsia, who were basically Russians, Ukrainians, Belorussians, and also sometimes those who came from other republics, who were in prison under Article 58 for anti-Soviet activities (nationalist displays, anti-Soviet propaganda, etc.).[2] The second group was made of those people who had little education, and who had come out against Soviet power with weapons in their hands. Among these were many Basmachi[3] who often barely understood Russian. There were also those people who had taken part in anti-Soviet demonstrations in other regions of the USSR, and a large number of the so-called dekulakized peasants.

All these were grouped around one of their own, a person with a certain authority. I paid special attention to these men. Often, they were strong-willed people, who were able to hide their thoughts and accommodate themselves to any situation. They were often extraordinary characters.

The prisoners who came from the Central Asian republics had the worst time in the camps. They usually spoke Russian poorly, or did not understand anything that was said to them. Mostly, they were the Basmachi. Most of them were young or middle-aged, and they were all physically very tough. Every brigade in the camp unit tried to get them to join their brigade, because a Basmachi prisoner could be exploited and coerced into doing the work of two men. In this way, the Basmachi would increase the average level of output of each brigade, and at the same time, the average level of each member. It was almost the same situation for the "dekulakized" peasants. These were mostly physically strong people from the provinces, and they were usually both semiliterate and frightened by the situation they found themselves in. The intelligentsia was especially skillful at using these people for its own interests.

Once I had familiarized myself with this camp unit, I asked for a private meeting with one of the Basmachi's leaders. Unlike the other tall and well-built Basmachis, he was a short, skinny fellow with a narrow, intelligent face and a thin, little mustache on his upper lip. He was about fifty years old. He spoke Russian well.

This is basically how our conversation went:

I asked, "How are your fellow countrymen doing here at this camp unit?"

He answered, "And what, Citizen Boss himself cannot see for himself? Why does Citizen Boss ask this question?"

I then went on to propose that we move all his fellow countrymen into one barracks, and create independent brigades from just these men. Just as I had done so successfully with the hardened criminals in my previous unit, I promised to stay out of everything and let them form the brigade themselves. I said I would not pay a bit of attention to who was in them and how much their members worked. I told him that if their twenty-four-hour norm output reached 150 percent, then we would reward the brigades with some bonus meat dishes in addition to their regular meal. I proposed that we find someone in their barracks who could cook for them. With the brigades' earnings, he could get special foods, and prepare some of their native dishes. And finally I said that I would get security to agree that when the brigades' output reached 150 percent for the day, the brigades would not have to stay out on the tracks in the freezing cold until the end of the shift, but would be brought back to the zone earlier, to rest.

The results tell the story. The brigades that the Basmachis formed regularly produced at 150 percent, and they often tried to get up to the level of 200 percent. In their barracks, the men created a genuine cult around the leader. They covered his bed with eastern fabrics, making me wonder where they had gotten them out here in this boundless tundra. The leader himself did not work. He sat on his bed as if on a throne, with his legs crossed so that the knees stuck out. His head was covered by a turban. When his fellow countrymen approached him, they would put the palms of their hands to their faces and bow very low, whispering some sort of words in their language.

After that, I repeated the same experiment with the "dekulakized." They also were all moved in together. I put them all on one side of the barrack and fenced it off from the others. There, they all worked, including the brigade leader, and their output also reached 150 percent.

I had a harder time with the intellectuals. They had not been taught to work when they had been children, and they were not used to heavy physical labor. But once they understood that they could no longer exploit the strong but semiliterate inhabitants of the unit, they saw that in order to survive, they had to adjust to the new reality. I tried to help them out by putting them on the sections of the track where they could rely on their native smarts to grasp what they needed to do. I did what I could to make it possible for them to produce no less than 100 percent of their norm.

As a result, in the Socialist Competition[4] for the May 1, 1941, holiday (then we were still having these competitions) the 95th camp unit took first place!

CHAPTER 12

THREAT OF ARREST

THE MONTH OF MAY ARRIVED. IN CENTRAL RUSSIA, THIS WAS the happiest time of the year. The cold winter fades away, and in comes warm weather. Nature wakes up, and everything all around becomes green. Gardens flower and birds sing. In contrast, at the Arctic Circle, the first half of May still meant whistling snowstorms, blowing winds, and hard freezes at night. But nevertheless, the days began to be longer and by the end of May, the snow goes away, grass appears, the trees turn green.

Unfortunately, though, this is the beginning of the most unpleasant period of the year. This is when you can see dark clouds of midges[1] everywhere over the boundless tundra, and there is no way to get away from their bites. They even get under your clothes. They bite and sting anything that is alive. It's especially hard to look after the horses when you are riding them. Their entire bodies get covered with layers of midges, which are smaller than gnats, and even the horses' very long tails cannot chase these pests away. If the rider places his hand on the horse's neck for a second, instantly the horse's blood oozes out from millions of crushed and satiated insects.

So, midges or no midges, May arrived and we were finally able to clear my unit's rail tracks of snow. We barely managed to get the snow moved around when the Selektor watchman brought me a short Selektogram. The gist of it was the following. In the yearly account of my new camp unit for 1940, it said that a railroad branch of about one kilometer had been built at Abez station. Upon inspection of the place, the authorities had found no such branch line. They demanded to know where a whole list of things that had been requested for the nonexistent branch line had gone. The list included rails, sleepers, brackets, liners, spikes, nuts, bolts, and so on. The Selektogram stated that if we could not produce these things, they were ready to set in motion a criminal case against the boss of the camp unit (me), the person who had signed this account. They said they would bring the matter to court, with all the unavoidable consequences. These consequences were very clear to me: a minimum of ten years in the Gulag for "plundering socialist property."

I thought back on the conditions under which I had signed this ill-fated account. At the time, I had absolutely no other recourse than to sign it. I had to make sure the prisoners got fed, and plus, it had been impossible to check for every little bolt under the thick layer of snow. But what now, and to whom could I prove this?

I began by getting two horses ready and grabbing the deputy foreman from the prisoners. Then we rode on horseback to Abez station.

Once we arrived at the station, I had the deputy foreman show me where the branch line began. The switches for the track that they had laid on the branch line were there, but further, there was only an embankment that had been prepared. On the embankment, there were no signs that sleepers and other things had ever been put down. The deputy foreman said that he clearly remembered that right before the onset of winter, the unit at Abez station had received the rails, the sleepers and all the necessary pieces for building the branch line from the supplier.

Near the switches, the deputy foreman found these materials that had been stacked on wooden beams right before winter arrived. These beams, like everything else, had been pressed into the earth. Once the freezing cold came and the blizzards began, the supplies moved from their storage place. I had trusted the brigade leader and section foreman who were responsible for the building of the branch line, and I had approved their weekly accounts. The deputy foreman now admitted that it was his fault, and asked in every way possible for my forgiveness. But it wasn't going to be easy for me to get out of this.

I sent him back to the camp unit, and went to see the head of the State Security Department[2] at the Camp Administration. This man was around fifty years old, was totally bald, and had smooth, reddish cheeks. He seemed like an intelligent fellow with a sense of humor, sharp yet laconic.

He listened attentively to me, and expressed his sympathy, but he said that if I didn't find the missing property, then State Security[3] would have no alternative but to prosecute me.

"But don't despair yet," he tried to console me. "Rails, sleepers and the other missing materials are not like chocolate," he said. "In a place like Pechorlag, a person cannot just drag them around and sell them on the side." He went on to say that in the fall there would be an inventory of the camp's entire construction site. He advised me to go see the head of the Department of Technical Supplies, tell him my situation, and get him to assign to my unit any extra building materials they find while doing the inventory. He promised to call him today, and also call his colleagues in security and tell them to hold off on my criminal investigation and case until the inventory took place.

Well, this was something, at least. But since I already had worked as a unit foreman, I had walked along the railroad tracks of the site in all times of the year, and more than once I had seen what the zeks did when filling in an embankment. If they found a pile of rails or other equipment that had been dropped off earlier, they did not move them from the road, but instead they would use them as fill in the embankment. It made their work go faster, and also they did not have to lug any heavy things off to the side to the tracks.

During the winter, we brought in all of the property via sled tracks that went along the line of the future railroad. A couple of times I had had to force the zeks who were doing this work to dig out partially covered materials and store them next to the tracks. Knowing this, the head of State Security's kind offer had not removed the stone in my soul. Although he had lowered the probability that I might be charged with this crime, the threat still hung over my head.

That evening, I went to see the head of the Department of Technical Supplies, whom I already knew, at his apartment. He treated me very well. First he served me some liquor to calm my soul, and then he told me honestly that he did not believe that the inventory would turn up the missing materials. I then asked him who in the world would have the idea to steal this stuff, since materials like these could not be eaten, nor could they be sold in the camp.

The department head told me to put myself in the shoes of those supply workers (who were also prisoners), who were sent to get materials at the construction site's base at headquarters. Maybe they would go and order the materials from the supply section, take the time to put them in the guarded warehouse, go and get the sleigh and load them, and then immediately go back to their camp unit. Or maybe, he proposed, they would go to the supply section, and on the way, they might see some materials just sitting outside of the guarded warehouse. And then, instead of doing all that moving of materials and loading, they would have a few days off just to hang out and live a little freely. Then they would grab the unguarded load, take it back to the unit. That, probably, is what happened. Of course, over the course of the long winter, it would be impossible to track down who might have done this, and when it might have happened.

Nevertheless, he insisted, there will be a solution to this problem. He said that when he had arrived at Pechorlag to take this job as head of the Department of Technical Supplies, he had noticed that someone, sometime before Pechorlag even existed, had built a railroad branch from the port on the river Usa to the village of Abez. It turned out that he had never entered this branch line into the books. He had kept it as a reserve, thinking he might need it someday. "You see," he explained, "I am the supplier. And if, as a result of the inventory-taking your materials do not 'show up,' I can write off this section of rail to you. So, don't be depressed."

After that, my friend and I got drunk "to the devils," and I begged God that my friend not be transferred before autumn, because that happened so often in the camps.

In the end, by autumn, everything had turned out all right. However, all summer I worried terribly, tormented myself and put all my hopes on the sole thing left to me, on luck. Out of the blue, I thought of what my mother used to say. She once asked me if I knew the significance of my name "Fyodor" in the holy scriptures. I, naturally, answered that I did not. Then she told me that it meant "God's gift," and she told me to never forget this in everything I do, and to treat others with heartfelt warmth, even when they did not deserve it. I somehow return to her words when I consider how indulgently I have been treated at times.

When the prisoners from the camp unit administration found out what kind of threat was hanging over me from having convinced me to sign their account at the beginning of the year, the atmosphere between us changed. On the one hand, they felt moral responsibility. On the other hand, and what may have been more important, they did not really know me and could not know that I would never "rat them out" and blame them to save myself. Even if I were brought to trial, I would never do that. Maybe they thought that as a preventive measure I would immediately tell the Chekists to look for guilty parties among them. Then for all of the guilty ones, all this would do would be to add even more time onto their already long years of imprisonment.

In the zone, the prisoners' attitude toward me greatly improved as it became clear that I was not trying to deceive anyone, and that I was exploring all my possibilities and using all my connections to solve this problem. After the troubles had been resolved, our relationship got even better. I guess that earlier, these prisoners were wary of me. What could really be expected from a twenty-two-year old inexperienced youth, who, although trained as an engineer, for many of the zeks was old enough to be their son? But nevertheless, after we solved the camp unit's problems with the Camp Administration, I began to detect warm feelings in my conversations with these prisoners. I got the feeling that they wanted to help me now, and to keep me from making mistakes from not understanding things properly. My work became easier. My closest circle of zeks no longer doubted my sincerity, and we all moved on to a more trusting relationship.

Mochulsky (right) and
Nikolai Gradov graduated
from the Moscow Institute
of Railroad Transport
Engineering in spring 1940.

Mochulsky (right)
with fellow student
and civilian
worker Nikolai
Gradov on board
The Vologda steam-
ship that they took
up the White Sea
and the Barents
Sea on their way
to Pechorlag,
October 1940.
The next several
pictures depict
their journey.

Mochulsky and his friend Volodia Kravtsov (in dark hats, far left) on a steamship on the Usa River in Komi, with other Gulag NKVD employees, in October 1940. The prisoners who were being transported to the same Gulag camp are held below.

An early snowstorm caused the boat Mochulsky was taking to Pechorlag to get frozen in the Usa River. On October 20, the passengers disembarked and made their way across in smaller boats, preparing to walk the rest of the way to the labor camp.

A contingent of civilian Gulag employees and prisoners crosses the Usa River on the way to Pechorlag.

When the steamship transporting workers and prisoners to Pechorlag froze in the Usa River, each Gulag employee was made responsible for getting two horses to the camp, which meant a harrowing eighteen-day walk over muddy, marshy land.

The author (right) stands at a temporary encampment in a Komi village, as the three young Gulag employees and six horses make their way to Pechorlag.

After eighteen days of walking, Mochulsky and his friends arrived at Pechorlag's main Gulag administration facility in the village of Abez, in time to take part in the camp's celebration of Revolution Day. A banner hails the twenty-third anniversary of the Great October Socialist Revolution.

On November 7, 1940, their first full day at Pechorlag, Mochulsky (right) and his friend Volodia Kravtsov attend the camp's Revolution Day celebration.

Local residents of Komi province came to the Revolution Day celebration at the Gulag camp. Mochulsky (far right) stands with his friends Nikolai Gradov and Volodia Kravtsov near the reindeer.

Mochulsky's friend and fellow Gulag employee Volodia Kravtsov outside Pechorlag's main administration building. He is wearing the sheepskin coat and
padded pants that distinguished the staff from the poorly dressed prisoners at
the camp.

Gulag prisoners build a rail embankment at Pechorlag in summer 1941.

Convicts clear the rail tracks after a snowstorm. On the left with a spade in his hand is First Regional Chief of Pechorlag Aleksandr Davidovich Tsfas.

Mochulsky stands in front of the mud hut the prisoners built for him. He wears the badges he had earned earlier for mountain climbing and parachuting, which were the pride of young people in those days.

The winter of 1941-42 saw the arrival of the first trainload of coal to come from Vorkuta on the rails Mochulsky's camp built.

A grenade-throwing competition for Gulag staff members at Pechora Station at Pechorlag, in the summer of 1943.

CHAPTER 13

THE WAR

THE NEWS OF FASCIST GERMANY'S ATTACK ON THE SOVIET Union came when I was out on the tracks.[1] The labor assistant told me this. He had just come from Abez after escorting some prisoners from a neighboring camp unit. He himself had heard the broadcast from Moscow on a local radio station in the camp headquarters. He did not have any more details. Anxiously, I took off on my horse, which was the fastest way to get back to my camp unit. Neither the 6th Department nor the Camp Administration had sent any news to us. With difficulty, I managed to reach my director at the 6th Department on the Selektor. He confirmed that the war had started, and then he gave me the order to speed up our work on constructing the railroad.

That same day, I also spoke to Nikolai and Volodia on the Selektor. Now that the war had begun, we three agreed that we should go to the Military Commissariat and demand to be sent immediately to the front. Nikolai and I both had been awarded "Voroshilov Stars," that is, we were qualified to be snipers. Nikolai was an expert mountain climber and an excellent skier, and had many times won prizes for the institute in these categories. I was a qualified instructor in mountain climbing, parachuting, glide piloting, and also skiing. Volodia was not at all sporty, but he knew three foreign languages. In fact, he spoke German perfectly. (This was later confirmed when at the end of the war the government recruited him to work as an interpreter in counterintelligence, and the imprisoned Germans could not distinguish him from their own men who were accused of betraying the "fatherland,"[2] that is, their country.)

Anyway, we left our work sections and went to the Military Registration and Recruitment Office in Abez. There were lots of other men just like us there. Since we were engineers, the Military Commissar himself saw us. But once he met us, he did not even give us the chance to make our impassioned speeches. He reminded us that the Gulag camp was integral to the war industry, and in sharp tones he lectured us about leaving our jobs at such a dangerous and crucial time. He told us to get back to work right away. He did promise, though, that if we were needed, they would call us.

The news that the war had started spread to the prisoners in a flash, although there had been no instructions about informing them.[3] In my camp unit, the reaction to this news was restrained. On the surface, nothing seemed at all different, except that now the prisoners wanted to hear the latest news. I could tell that all the prisoners were deeply worried about what was going on, especially when it became clear that our army was suffering defeat after defeat, and that the Red Army was retreating deep into the USSR. Although the politicals were housed at this camp unit, I never heard any mean comments, heckling, or any remarks at all from them. The security officers who worked at the camp unit said that some of the nationalist prisoners from the intelligentsia, especially those from the Western Ukraine, were happy that the Fascists were succeeding.[4] But they hid their personal feelings from other zeks, probably fearing physical violence or being reported to the authorities.

In those first days of the war, the insistent propaganda from the prewar days was still being broadcast all across the Soviet Union. It was saying, essentially, that "we are not after foreign land, but if war is thrust on us, then we will wage war on enemy territory until we beat the enemy." Likewise, there were films (*If Tomorrow There Is War*, and others), songs ("To a Far-Off Region the Comrade Flies," and others), impressive military parades, publicity about military maneuvers, and so on, all in this same vein, all the same propaganda campaign. So in the first days of the war, naturally, all the civilians and prisoners expected an early Soviet victory.[5]

But in just five short days, the Fascists had occupied Minsk, the capital of Belorussia, and they quickly captured the villages and cities of the Ukraine. Suddenly, the loss of the Donbas coal basin and other vitally important centers of the country hung over us, and everyone's disappointment and disbelief gave way to alarm for the fate of our motherland. For those of us at Pechorlag, it meant that the leadership stepped up its demands. No matter what, we were told, we had to finish building those railroad branch lines to the coal fields of Vorkuta by the end of 1941.

Winter, with its ferocious snowstorms, plagued our region, which stretched from the Pechora River to Vorkuta, for almost nine months of the year. And then, in the summertime, the railroad embankments that we had built using local tundra soil would shift, so we knew that we had to get better sand and soil from quarries that unfortunately, were not nearby. The best possible thing would have been to lay down some spur tracks and bring huge amounts of sand and soil back by rail, but because of the wartime emergency, we did not have the time to build them. And the Arctic winter was already approaching us at Pechorlag.

To extend our railway to Vorkuta during the coming winter, the camp leadership decided to build temporary track on those sections of the planned rail line that had not yet been built. During the winter, they told us, instead of building bridges across the many rivers and streams that the tracks crossed, we were to lay sleepers and rails right on the ice. And by the spring of 1942, that is, May 1942, then, by hook or by crook, we had to build all the bridges on all these places and all the approaches to these bridges along the wide swampy floodlands. And we had to construct them correctly, with the proper soil and sand, which all had to be trucked in to us.

This was the task that they gave us and, in the interest of defending the country, we absolutely had to do it. Everything had to be done 100 percent correctly, because any section of badly joined track in any place could disrupt coal deliveries, which would then hold up production at the military factories in the European part of the country.

Moreover, shortly after the Great Patriotic War[6] began, the Americans and the English promised the USSR deliveries of war materials and other necessary materials that were needed at the front through the Lend-Lease Program.[7] These goods would come through the unfrozen port of Murmansk. The USSR told the Allies not to weigh down their ships with their own fuel for the return trip, but to fill their ships to total capacity with our coal. In other words, we promised to supply their ships with coal for the return trip. When the agreement was announced, the coal could only come from Vorkuta. That is to say, we did not even have a rail line that went all the way there, but the coal was already promised.

Shortly after this, a huge assortment of commissions and departmental representatives of the leadership from the 6th Department

Headquarters, the Camp Administration, and also Pechorlag's Communist Party Committee took to dropping by our camp unit and the other subsectors of the camp. The bosses were checking to make sure that we were doing everything we could to speed up the construction and to get our workers (that is, the zeks) to work, because they were demanding absolute fulfillment and overfulfillment of the plans. Sometimes these visitors appeared in the deepest night, like at 3:00 or 4:00 AM, when people were getting some sleep. By 6:00 AM, the night shift was returning from its twelve-hour shift at their work places under the open sky, and we were forming up the day shift brigades, giving them their assignments and making substitutions. As the foreman and boss of the unit, normally, I managed to get two or three hours of sleep before this. (This was exactly what all the other civilian bosses at other camp units were doing.)

But, as I said, this was just the time of the night when the visitors loved to show up, so they could later report to the authorities various instances of "disclosures of disgraceful behavior," or "a criminally negligent attitude toward fulfilling their service obligations" of the camp unit bosses. Out on the track where the zeks worked, these same visitors were abusive, and sometimes they would threaten us by saying that if this "disgraceful behavior" were repeated, we ourselves would be sent to the zone as prisoners. They often sent their own inspectors who would go with the foremen out to the portions of the track we were working on, sometimes covering our entire stretch of track (remember, our unit's section was about 20 kilometers, or 12.4 miles long). These inspectors were checking the progress of our work, watching to see how much work was done during the night, as well as during periods of hard frosts, snowstorms, and frequent blizzards. There were even times when commissions came in from Moscow.

One of these most serious allegations against a foreman and boss at a camp unit would be to have "refusers" in their unit, that is, prisoners who refused to go out and work. At mine, the 95th camp unit, where the politicals were kept, that sort of thing never happened, either before or after the war.

But the camp units that housed the hardened criminals (thieves, bandits, and so on) had lots of prisoners who regularly refused to go to work. These hardened criminals loved to make fun of the camp leadership. There was one story that sounded like it had been made up, but the criminal prisoners told all the time. It went like this:

A very important member of the leadership, a Big Boss, once came to a camp unit. He went into the barracks, where he saw a healthy fellow lying down on a berth with some sick prisoners. The Big Boss asked why the healthy man was not at work. In answer, he heard: "Citizen Boss, look at me. You see how big and strong I am. But they gave me a small wheelbarrow for moving earth. I beg you to make me a special big wheelbarrow. I will set records."

The Big Boss gave the order to make a large wheelbarrow. The prisoner requested that it be painted red, since it would be the one to break records. And while the wheelbarrow's paint was drying, they had to feed the emaciated future record-setter. The corresponding commands were given. But by the time they took the wheelbarrow out to the tracks, the Big Boss had already gone away, and the zek announced that he had changed his mind. Let the Big Boss push such a heavy wheelbarrow, he said. And he thanked the Boss for feeding him so well for all those days.

Some camp security officers told me another of these stories. They claimed to have actually witnessed this. Some high-ranking bosses from Moscow paid a visit to a women's camp. In the female prisoners' barracks, they saw various prisoners who were sick or who were simply resting after the night shift. In the middle of them, lying on a bunk, they spotted a very pretty young woman wearing a light dress, with her legs crossed so that her legs were bared above the knees. The person showing the bosses around pointed her out to the most senior boss and said, "she is a constant refuser."

The boss asked why she refused to work. She said, "Citizen Boss, I have been asking the unit boss for a long time to let me do what I'm trained to do, but he won't." The boss turned in anger to the unit boss, and said, "What? I had to come all the way from Moscow to solve such a simple problem? Tomorrow, she does what she's trained to do." Then the woman spoke up again. "Citizen Boss, you never even asked what my specialty is." The boss said, "Yes, you are right. What is your specialty?" And she answered, "I am a prostitute."

At that, everyone in the barrack dissolved into laughter, and the high-ranking Moscow bosses and all the people accompanying him, quickly turned and left the barracks.

Once the war began, though, the problem of "refusers" began to fade away, because the refusers, for the most part, were the criminal prisoners. And starting in the early part of the war, they began sending these nonpolitical prisoners to the front in penal battalions.

Before the war, I had supervised the work going on along the tracks mainly during the day. And what work had been done by the night shift workers, I then checked in the mornings. In those days, I hardly ever went out to the tracks at night. But beginning in the summer of 1941, this changed. Along with my normal daily supervision, I began to regularly visit the other construction divisions at night. I had to even get another saddle horse, since one could not hold up. I slept about two or three hours a night, and sometimes even that got broken up. I learned how to doze in the saddle. After a few weeks of constantly sleeping too little, one day I got a fever and the whites of my eyes turned red. But now, at least, the prisoners understood that their work could at any moment be checked, and labor discipline on the night shift improved.

As I mentioned earlier, the prisoners' food portions depended on how much work they did every day. Those who did not fulfill the norm by 100 percent were given, for one twenty-four-hour period, in all 300 grams (10 ounces) of bread and a bowl of watery soup. So, in order not to die of hunger, everyone tried to fulfill the plan, and actually, they often did fulfill it. Also, there were those record-setters who fulfilled 150 percent of the plan and more, and they got an increase in their food. But sometimes, we had bad weather days. We had hard frosts with winds, snowy blizzards, and very thick snowfalls in the winter, and in the summer, we had protracted, cold rain and hurricane-force winds.

When the weather did not cooperate, it was almost impossible to work up to the norm. And sometimes, the nasty weather would last for days. If we kept strictly to the existing regulations and fed the prisoners just 300 grams of bread while they sat doing nothing, they lost their last bit of physical strength and became emaciated. I have to say that before the war, we solved this problem by filing a special climate report[8] that allowed us to keep the prisoners inside, but after the war began, this possibility had been eliminated. How could this be?

So Volodia and I came up with this tactic. Every month the department held a meeting with the foremen (including Volodia and me) where we drew up a projected plan of work for the next month. In our plans, Volodia and I added in the kind of jobs that would be impossible to check: the clearing of ditches, the taking away of the top layer of earth in the sand pits (Go on, check it out! Just how high was this layer?) and others. On the days when the weather was too nasty for working outside, we simply added these unverifiable jobs to the brigades' "fulfillment," which brought their output up to 100 percent. This was how we made sure that every member of the brigade would receive the normal food ration the next day. The prisoners knew about this even at the camp unit's highest level of administration. Nobody ever spilled the beans, even though our country had entered a period when everyone was denouncing everyone else for something.

It is possible that nobody ever blabbed because they feared reprisals from one of "their own." Sometimes these reprisals ended in death. Moreover, figuring out who did what among the prisoners was impossible. In the camp units that housed the hardened criminals, the prisoners played a card game called "Put it in the kitty." In this game, instead of playing for money or chits, they would play for a person, sometimes even a civilian, whom they hated.

One of their methods of punishment for the person they hated was as follows. First, they prepared their weapon: They took a thick board, about 1.5 to 2 meters (4.9 to 6.6 feet) long, and drove a very big, long nail into the end of it. Then, they would manage somehow to clear the barracks of its inhabitants for a short while. Once the place was empty, the prisoner who was to carry out the sentence, waited for the doomed person near the barracks' doorway, holding the board by its other end. As the doomed man approached the barracks, someone gave a signal. Then, as soon as he opened the door and stepped inside, he was hit on the head with a very strong blow of the board. The nail would break right through the skull and cause immediate death. And no matter how hard or how long the Chekists (the security detail) investigated this crime, they could never find out who had committed this murder.

This sort of retribution did not exist among the intelligentsia, the educated political prisoners. They tended toward refined "intellectual" methods. Here is what they would do. Somehow, a rumor would start to circulate about an intended victim, that had him involved in preparing a "political plot" or "plans for escape" at the work unit. This "information" was then brought to the Chekist who served the unit, frequently a young, inexperienced fellow, a recent graduate of a special school.[9] All this was collaborated by "witnesses" and sometimes, "documents." It often happened that the Chekist who investigated the rumor would impose a severe punishment on the person.

The intellectual zeks could create (and sometimes did create) a big deal out of nothing about civilians they did not like. For instance, they might spread the rumor that a person is speculating (buying and selling) with the prisoners, or supplying the zone with forbidden products, or extorting (in other words, buying for money or food) watches or gold pieces or other things that some lucky zeks had managed to hide.

Just try to prove that something had not happened if several specially prepared "witnesses" are insisting, in one voice, to the unit's Chekist, that "it was a fact," and not just something they had heard, or that it was something they had accidentally seen and they would give written "testimony." The case would be undertaken, the judicial powers would be set in motion, and "washing it away" would not be easy. Sometimes, it was impossible.

Of course, nobody really trusted the politicals, especially when just one person would make the accusation. But when lots of different people showed up and repeated the same thing, and described all of "the details"? Then, any honest judicial employee would have to think it over, and in the best-case scenario, the accused would be dragged through an interrogation. And in the worst-case scenario? At the very least, there would always be that feeling afterward about the "accused" that, well, "something was not right," as they say, or "either he stole a coat, or a coat was stolen from him, but something happened."

Anyway, getting back to our nearly impossible task at hand out on the tracks in the fall of 1941, we had most of the bases for laying the sleepers and rails on our unit's section of the rail line. But we had not built anything yet in the places where streams and rivers crossed the track. We knew that we would have to build many bridges, or at least install large pipes under the track to remove the water. The problem was that we knew in the spring, when all those river spurs coming down the Ural Mountains started melting, huge amounts of water would run down and those rivers and streams would turn into powerful flows of water. They would easily wash away the barriers that stood on the tracks, which were the very parts of the rail line that we worked so hard to build. But in that climate, bridges with their high ditches leading up to them could only be built in the spring (that is, only in 1942). But now we were at war, and time would not wait, as they said. So on those places we quickly built bypasses, with the goal of laying sleepers and rails on the ice of the rivers and streams when the ice hardened enough to hold the weight.

It was about 10 kilometers (6.2 miles), not counting the water barriers, from the Camp Administration in the village of Abez to my camp unit. On this segment of the rail line, we lay the sleepers and attached rails to them, right onto the unsteady permafrost. We had steam locomotives pushing open goods cars of sand as close as they could get to us, and we then moved it ourselves. The sand flowed under the sleepers and in this way gradually an embankment appeared, upon which a heavy steam locomotive could travel. Just like this, step by step, we all built a rail line heading north to Vorkuta.

Toward the end of the summer, the rail line went past our camp unit to the first water barrier. In order not to lose time, we built the further sections of the rail line without machinery, that is, by hand. We prepared the base so that, with the oncoming winter weather and the arrival of locomotives and their open goods cars that were loaded with everything necessary, we could quickly finish laying the rails.

The steam locomotives that brought things on open goods cars were called whirligigs, and we began to use them to transport brigades of workers. But then another large obligation surfaced for my unit, which was not of course included in the construction plans. We had to gather wood. The thing was that our camp unit's section of rail line had thick forests from the spurs of the Ural Mountains right next to the tracks. Pechorlag's administration began to send us whirligigs to pick up wood for administration headquarters. And the headquarters was very large. All of the inhabitants needed to stay warm in their houses and have wood for preparing food. War may be war, but we all still have to go about our daily lives.

The administration of Pechorlag was the highest power around, so when they wanted something, we had to obey. The plan for constructing the rail line was a sacred matter, and it was forbidden to violate it. So we not only had to build the rail line in a hurry, we also had to gather wood for them, all with no increase in the number of workers. The feeling was: You can do it all. Just work each and every prisoner as hard as you can. So, after a twelve-hour workday, you can sleep a few hours, and then go on to cutting and hauling wood for the Big Bosses. As they say, "You can complain . . ."

CHAPTER 14

ILLNESS

I SETTLED INTO A PUNISHING WORK SCHEDULE, AND BECAME totally worn out. I got so little sleep in those days that I lived in a fog until November, when the hard frost and snowstorms began. My sleep debt grew so great that one day my body protested. I woke up, very early as usual, but I felt awful. I went out for the changing of the brigades, sent the night shift off to sleep and the day shift off to work, and instead of going out to the tracks as I normally did, I went back home. There, I took my temperature. I had a fever of 40 degrees Centigrade (104 degrees Fahrenheit).

I called in the deputy foreman, and told him to take over my work for the day. I notified the commander of the security platoon. I made some tea, and drank the entire teapot, thinking that I could sweat out the fever. I was afraid to eat anything, since I didn't know what was wrong with me. So I wrapped myself up warmly and fell asleep for a long time. When I woke up, I felt that I had managed to sweat it out. I changed the bedding, and again took my temperature. It was the same, still at 40 degrees. And it went like this for four days. Nothing hurt, but I was very weak. And I had a high temperature.

I didn't report anything to my boss, the director of the 6th Department. At first, I drank only tea, because I was never hungry. The weakness in my entire body got worse. I slept for hours and hours. On the fifth day, when I saw that my temperature was again at 40 degrees, I decided to catch the Camp Administration's whirlygig when it left with its next load of wood, and get myself to the central hospital in the village of Abez. I spoke to the leadership of the 6th Department by Selektor, dressed warmly, and hit the road. When the whirlygig arrived, I told the driver that I was sick and needed to go to the hospital. He lay me down in the tender (where they kept the coal for the locomotive) on a bench and we started off for the capital of the camp.

When we were all settled in the train, the engine driver began to steer the train whose cars were loaded with wood, straight toward the branch line at the Usa River. The branch line dipped steeply down into a tunnel of unbroken snow about 1.5–2 meters (4.9–6.6 feet) high. Suddenly, the driver saw that there was another train at the end of the branch line. He started braking furiously, but the descent was very steep. We were going to crash into the other train. He yelled at me to jump out immediately, into the snow, and he jumped out after me. We ended up on our heads in the snow, but we still heard the crash, and the grinding of the toppled cars.

We pulled ourselves out of the snow. The driver went to the train and I walked to the hospital, which was about two kilometers (1.2 miles) away. I walked up to the building, climbed the porch, rang the bell, and fainted dead away. When I woke up, I was sitting in a warm bath. A doctor and nurse were there next to me, and they began anxiously asking me how I felt, and where and what hurt. I answered that nothing hurt, only that I had this general feeling of weakness. They transferred me to a bed, and took my temperature, which was still at 40 degrees.

I stayed in the hospital for around two months. At that time (the end of 1941), there were lots of civilian specialists at Pechorlag. Luckily, there were a lot of very knowledgeable medical personnel among them, mainly from the blockade of Leningrad.[1] Several of them had come to work at the hospital in Abez.

After two weeks in the hospital, my temperature dropped a bit, although it was still fairly high. After X rays, analysis, and other checks, the doctors called me in for a consultation. The head doctor told me: "Since you are a grown man, we are going to tell you the truth. You have quickly advancing pulmonary tuberculosis, in both lungs. If you like, we can treat you here. Or, the camp leadership has authorized sending you to the Gulag hospital in Altai Krai.[2] There, at least, the mountain air will benefit you. And we will send a nurse along with you, to help get you set up."

When I was a child, my father talked often about his older brother. When this brother was fourteen years old, he wanted to become stronger, and so he drenched himself with cold water on the porch of the house. He kept doing this, even during the winter. But then he came down with quickly advancing tuberculosis, and in the spring, he died. This illness strikes young people, I was told. They cannot survive it, and they die, as a rule, in the spring. Therefore, my father warned me not to "go too far" with hardening oneself, because I, too, probably had a weakness for this disease.

When the doctors gave me their verdict, I was twenty-three years old. That is, it seemed to me that their diagnosis and prognosis could be correct. But since childhood, I had loved sports, and had done mountain climbing, skiing, parachuting, and gliding. I always spent my days outside, in the fresh air. I refused to believe that I really had quickly advancing consumption.

In November 1941, Hitler's troops stood on the outskirts of Moscow. The country was mustering its entire strength to stop the enemy. And when I heard what the doctors were proposing, I thought: "The last thing anyone needs is to worry about me." And at the same time, I thought about how difficult it was just to get from Abez to Kotlas, the first station stop where the rail line to Vorkuta began. (Trains carrying coal on the temporary tracks had begun to make their way into the heart of Russia, but with great difficulty and with frequent crashes.) The doctors promised that I would be taken in a heated goods car, along with the nurse, on the two-week trip. (At that time, neither passenger trains nor even passenger cars went to Abez.)

Many questions surfaced in my mind. Where would we eat, and where would the coal come from for the "little heater" in the heated goods car? And further, who would couple my goods car to the right train? And when? And the further we traveled from Kotlas into Siberia, there would be echelons of wounded men from the front being transported; and there I would appear in my heated goods car.

I thought it over in this way, and then I turned down the trip to Altai. I told them: "I'm staying here."

While I was recovering in the hospital, I became friends with the nurses. They felt sorry for me, since they knew that I would not live until to see the spring. They treated me with compassion. One day, when my temperature had dropped to 37–37.5 degrees C (98.6–99.5 F), I asked them to bring a sheepskin coat, clothes, leather boots, felt boots, and a fur coat to the hospital ward. The nurses hid all of these things from the doctors in the cupboard. In the evenings, when the doctors went home, I dressed warmly and went out walking. I visited a club where they showed movies, and on their "dance nights," I danced with pleasure. I even saw some old acquaintances whom I'd befriended when I had arrived at the camp. With their hands over their eyes, the nurses watched my travels, and kept them secret from the doctors.

I did not fall into despair over the doctors' sentence. I thought about it a lot, but I never really believed what they had told me. I never told anyone anything about my illness or the doctors' diagnosis, not my parents, brother, sister, or friends in Moscow or at the front. My thinking was that if, despite my optimism, the illness and its quick sad finale suddenly came to pass, then all the same, nobody could help me. So why upset them beforehand? Just the opposite—I sent them bright, cheerful letters.

During this period, something happened to me that I always felt made my recovery possible. One day, the nurses came in and told me that someone wanted to see me. This person had come earlier when I was out, saying that he would return later. So in he came, a tall, pleasant, plump, middle-aged man. He was smiling happily as he greeted me. He told me that by sheer chance, he had heard I was sick, and he was happy to have the opportunity to help me. I stared at him, desperately trying to remember who he was and where our paths had crossed.

As if reading my mind, he said, "No doubt, you don't recognize me. That's no surprise. When we last saw one another, I was a walking skeleton." And then he mentioned the 93rd Unit, my old camp unit. This was the unit that housed mostly hardened criminals, but it also had some working folks with nonpolitical status. Then I remembered him and his story.

While I was working at the 93rd Unit, one day the labor assistant had come to me and said that a prisoner wanted to talk to me face to face. I agreed. In walked an old, drooping, thin man. He told me that he was from the Ukraine, where his wife and children still lived. He also told me how much he loved his family. He went on to tell me that before his arrest, he had been the director of a large store, and they had lived well. Suddenly, one of those government commissions that often showed up and checked stores, came in to look over his store. After a while, the members of this commission approached him to say that they had found problems and violations in his work.

He was sentenced to five years in prison, sent to Pechorlag, where he found himself subject to "job work."[3] Because he was a healthy, strong man, the criminal prisoners started using him as "a dairy cow," that is, he had two norms to fulfill on his shift, one for himself, and another for them. He could not refuse to do their work, or complain to the leadership, because the criminals had threatened to punish him violently if he did. In exchange, the criminals protected him from the other prisoners. Since he was a "newbie" at the camp, he would otherwise be picked on and mocked.

It was March, 1941, when he had come to see me in the camp. In that meeting, he had told me that when his term ended in May, he would be going home. He said: "My wife and children cannot wait. But look at me, can I really show up at home looking like this, as a skinny, emaciated man? All of my relatives will be horrified."

I asked him what he wanted from me. He answered that the laundry room boss was leaving the Gulag, and that he wanted to nominate the man standing in front of me to take his place in the laundry. The camp unit's laundry room was outside of the camp zone on the edge of the forest near a small stream, in the "free zone." For me, it would mean, if I agreed, that I would need to get permission from the security platoon to release him from escort. The man went on to press his case, telling me that he had worked, without complaining, for five years doing double work. If there were a possibility for him at the laundry room, then he would be free of the criminals' demands. Even though he would no longer be doing their heavy physical labor for them, this way, they could not torment him in his last months before freedom.

His status was nonpolitical and the question of him going outside the zone without a guard was not especially difficult. The man looked at me with hope, and in my mind, I saw myself in his shoes. His skinny, worn-out body especially depressed me. So I consented. His eyes lit up—he was suddenly giddy with happiness. Right in front of me, he seemed to totally transform. He straightened himself up and vowed that he would never forget what I had done for him.

Right after that I was sent to work at the 95th camp unit, and I hardly had time to think of this again.

And now, here we sat again, this time in a hospital lobby, next to each other. He told me that after he was let out of prison, he started working on getting himself back to the Ukraine. One day, the Camp Administration's Gulag Economy Department invited him to come and see them. They offered him a unique job as a civilian in the village of Abez, and they said that if he took the job, they would bring his family to Abez. They promised to set the whole family up in an apartment in a nice building reserved for the camp leadership. So he decided to stay on as a civilian employee in Abez.

And it was a unique job. It turned out that the Camp Administration had a small store with all the necessities, just for the higher leadership of the camp. A large assortment of fresh foods arrived every day from Moscow. Considering his experience in managing a store, they proposed that he become the director of the Camp Adminstration's store. He took them up on the offer, and they brought his family from the Ukraine. The family managed to get out just before the war started, and now they lived happily in Abez. By the time we met each other at the hospital, their hometown in the Ukraine had already been occupied by the Fascists.

"I heard from my boss that you were sick," he said. "In gratitude for all that you did for me back at the 93rd camp Unit, I feel that it is my duty to do anything I can do to help you get better."

As if to confirm what he had said, he opened the large bag he had carried in with him. He had brought many things that I had long stopped thinking about here in the North: fresh fruits, grapes, raisins, dried apricots, eggs, which I loved, but had already forgotten how they smelled, expensive red fish that melts in your mouth, sour cream, butter, and chocolate.

I did not know how to thank him. I offered to pay him, but he categorically refused. Then he promised to come again. He visited me regularly right up until the day I was released from the hospital and left Abez, and every time, he delighted me with an incredible diversity of foods. There was nobody else in the ward with me, obviously, because they were afraid that I might infect others around me, so the nurses brought in two bedside tables especially for the gifts. I shared all of my gifts with the nurses, and they in turn, did not tell anyone the secret of why I needed the tables.

CHAPTER 15

RECOVERY AND RETURN
TO WORK IN THE SOUTHERN
PART OF THE CAMP

I HARDLY NOTICED THAT TWO MONTHS HAD GONE BY IN THE hospital. At the end of December 1941, after careful observation, analyses and X-rays, the doctors again called me in for a consult. This time, there were more than five of them at the meeting. They were all elderly, eminent men, with intelligent, businesslike manners. By that time, my temperature had stopped increasing even at night, which would be typical for tuberculosis patients. Also, my night sweats had passed, and my appetite had returned. And now, our local gods of medicine informed me that there had been a medical miracle. The quick-developing tuberculosis of both lungs had disappeared, and I was left only with a small dark spot at the top of my left lung.

They proclaimed me practically healthy, and said I could go back to work. But I needed to be careful, they warned, and I had to go in for periodic check-ups with a doctor. They said that they had recommended that the Camp Administration transfer me to the village of Pechora, at the very southern part of the camp. This village sat on the right bank of a very large northern river, also called Pechora. The doctors felt that this transfer made sense because there was a pine forest along the Pechora River. Beyond that lay only the endless tundra, all the way to the Arctic Ocean. And that boundless tundra was nothing but bogs and their summertime clouds of midges, which would oppress anyone, even a healthy person.

To finish the story of my illness, I was under the care of doctors for the whole rest of the time I worked at Pechorlag. Every month I had to pass a medical exam, and I accumulated a big pile of their assessments on the state of my health. In 1944, the Gulag sent me to another camp whose headquarters were at Orel.[1] On my way to Orel, I stopped in Moscow to see my father, and while there, I became sick again. My father looked through the pile of papers documenting my illness. He became very upset, and went into action. It turned out that one of his friends was the director of the Scientific-Research Institute on Tuberculosis in Moscow. My father called him, and soon the director himself welcomed me to his institute. After he had looked through all of my medical papers from the Gulag doctors, he himself examined me carefully.

Then he told me, "Young man, you may burn all those medical reports and conclusions. You did not have consumption, nor did you have tuberculosis. You are absolutely healthy. You had lobar pneumonia in both lungs, which had never been treated.[2] This is often mistaken for tuberculosis, since a mass of bubbles can appear on the lungs. No doubt the X-ray machine your doctors had was very old and not very powerful."

There was no end to my happiness! Suddenly it occurred to me that if the camp doctors had not made this mistake, then I would not have been transferred from the northern part of the camp to the south. I would have been surrounded by other people, and my life could have turned out differently. As the believers always say: "Everything is in God's hands."

At the Camp Administration, where I was newly assigned, they congratulated me on my recovery. They told me that for the time being, the doctors recommended that I be put on a job with a somewhat easier schedule so that I would not overdo it and get sick again. I was now going to work in the 1st Department of the 1st Region of the Gulag camp,[3] as an engineer/inspector in the Department of Technical Control. The headquarters of the 1st Region, 1st Department were in the village of Pechora on the right bank of the Pechora. They told me to go there immediately.

Freight trains carrying coal traveled regularly now from Vorkuta. Because the rail line in many places was not finished, and the rails and sleepers had been put down on frozen tundra and iced-over rivers, track-building was continuing. Accidents were frequent. Sometimes these accidents resulted in death for the people who worked on the train, or the occasional passengers who, for some or another reason, decided to risk taking the coal train to the southern sections of the camp instead of the sleigh. The only advantage the train had was that it was fast, that is, if it actually arrived at the destination.

I never considered taking the train. I decided to travel by sleigh, so I collected my bags, preparing for my departure. Because they would not drive a sleigh with only one passenger, I had to wait until another fellow-traveler showed up. The other passenger turned out to be a very unconventional person who had been let out of prison early. He had been a well-known cameraman and documentary maker in the second half of the 1930s, famous for his film footage of the Spanish Civil War. Once he had been freed from prison, he had taken off with the active-duty army to one of the fronts of the Great Fatherland War. This had earned him respect.

But, on the other hand, he had been sent to Pechorlag for conceivable and inconceivable sexual perversions, which were punishable by law. (These perversions included things like rape, corruption of minors, and others.)

It turned out that I was together with him in one sled (just like "in one boat") and then in the one barracks for civilians in the village of Pechora, until a passenger train heading south showed up. All in all, we spent about a month together. This was during the most horrendous period of the war, when the whole country was focused on stopping the Fascist attack and on trying to turn the tide toward our side out on the fronts. The war and the great Soviet push to win notwithstanding, all he talked about during the trip, and on those long, drawn-out evenings when we were together in Pechora, was the difficulties of male-female relations. Of course, he meant sexual relations. Unlike me, he had had extensive experience. At the time I was keeping a diary, writing down many things that he said. (There is more on this interesting person in chapter 25.)

In any case, sometime during the first week of January 1942, we covered ourselves with straw in a sled, and set off for the southern part of Pechorlag. We traveled from camp unit to camp unit. After each stop, we switched sleds, drivers, and horses. Sometimes we had to wait a few days, because all the available sleds were out driving the expanse of the camp units. But this just made me happy. Now I had the opportunity to become better acquainted with the people I met on the road, to get to know the situation at this or the other camp units, and feel the happiness and pride of work from the foremen and bosses of the units I was so close to and familiar with. At the same time, I could see with my own eyes what kind of state the railway tracks were in, which at the end of 1941 were facilitating deliveries of coal from Vorkuta.

The difficulties that plagued every camp unit were similar to the ones I'd had at "my" unit. The state of the track was also familiar. Work was continuing on all of the main projected sections, especially on those sections that included bridges and approaches to the bridges. The temporary bypass tracks were causing much worry, effort, and anxiety, because they were built from local swamp earth or lay directly onto frozen tundra in violation of all permissible norms of construction. For instance, the minimal turning radius for a railroad was supposed to be 600 meters (656 yards), but some of the bypasses of the future bridges that sloped down toward the river had a crooked radius of 300 meters (328 yards). And the actual descent was several times shorter than permitted for normal operation.

The consequence of this was that the heavy trains loaded with coal sometimes went off the rails. Every accident delayed a delivery of coal and was viewed as the most serious crime, for which someone absolutely had to answer. The guilty ones were always from among the "little mice," either the foreman or the railroad master, or the station guard, and so on. If the person were a civilian, then they sentenced him and threw him into the zone as a prisoner, and if it were a prisoner, they lengthened his term. In my head, I thanked God that I had stopped being a foreman just when the rail line went into service.

When I finally arrived in Pechora village, I found out what the job of engineer/inspector at the 1st Department entailed, and I met some of the people there with whom I would work. To me, my new duties seemed like a paradise when compared to what I had experienced while I worked elsewhere at Pechorlag. Here, there were no white nights, no responsibilities for equipment, and almost no contact with prisoners, that is, I did not have to be their boss, or even work with them. It was such a great pleasure to have this chance to live in the village with other civilians. After work I could hang out with other young people, of which there were many. They were there as engineers, technicians, doctors, nurses, and so on. In the evenings, I might meet young ladies and women. There were very few of them at the time, but still, there were possibilities. We were young, and we all had the same craving for personal contact. In the camp unit, there had been no time to think of such things.

Nevertheless, daily existence was difficult. Upon arriving at Pechora, I was given a berth in the dormitory for civilian men. It was a large barrack with three levels of berths containing several tens of beds. In the center of the barrack were two stoves, and next to them stood two bare (without tablecloths) long wooden tables with benches of the same length. Dim lamps hung over the tables. All around the stoves, people had put things out to dry: felt boots, foot wrappings, socks, underwear, and clothes, which gave off their corresponding odors. People who lived in the dormitory stored their personal things, like books, in boxes or suitcases under the beds. As soon as you left the dormitory, other people rooted around in your personal belongings, sometimes appropriating for themselves things that attracted them (except toothbrushes). The toilet was in the courtyard. We washed with water in pots from the porch of the barrack.

Many former prisoners who had stayed to work in the Gulag system as civilians also lived in this barrack. They "set the tone" of life and daily existence in the barrack. For instance, if I was lying on my bunk resting after work they would pull me by the leg and call me to the table to play cards, usually, "ochko." If I refused, they tormented and nagged me. It was better to agree, just to keep them from dragging me from my rest.

I came up with a method for playing cards with this bunch. I emptied out both pants' pockets, then put 300 rubles (10 notes worth 30 rubles) into one of them. If I lost, I left the card game, and nobody minded. They left me alone. If I lucked out and won, and sometimes I took the whole bank, then I put the 300 rubles back into my pocket, where they had been when the game began. I kept the rest of the money from my win in my other pocket. And then, I risked everything on this money that I had just won. Sometimes I won, wildly. Most often I played out of the pocket with my winnings. Then I would stand up and leave, as if the "good" card would not come to me (for instance, an ace). And I still had the money I'd taken at the beginning of the game. I kept the statistics. It turned out that in a month "I kept what I'd brought" even considering the frequent ups and downs of my fortunes that month.

Now and then, the one club in town showed old films. Since the beginning of the war, the dance nights had ended (unlike in Abez). There were no libraries in town. We read the literary magazines that others brought with them to Pechora, and we traded books with each other. If we wanted to read in the evenings, we sometimes went to an office and read there, sitting at a table. Or sometimes we would hang out there with friends, talking late into the night, if nobody was working there that night and the building guard hadn't locked the doors.

After a while, I made some friends and found comrades in the town. Since we usually worked twelve to fifteen hours a day, we hardly ever got together during the week. But on Fridays, we looked for someone who had a private room or apartment to hang out in. We would talk and play cards (like "proferanc" or poker) deep into the night. (Normally, the private rooms were given only to families for a certain time or as a reward for good results at work.)

As for my new job as an engineer/inspector for the Department of Technical Control, I worked out on the rail line they were building in the 1st Department. Just like in the entire camp, people were working like crazy to get this rail line up to speed. So it was my job to make sure that the construction work met technical norms, that there were no deviations from the approved plans, and that the prisoners were doing quality work.

For example, the plan called for one portion of the rail line to go along a hillside. Sometimes when track is laid along a hillside we cut into the hill, and then the foundation is stable. But there are times when we have to fill in an embankment on a hillside. If you put earth directly on the slope of a hill, the embankment can wash away in any rain, be it a downpour or the springtime melting of snow. If this happens, then any train traveling on this track will absolutely wreck. So to make sure that the fill in these places is stable and won't wash away, we grade the hillside and elevate the embankment. On the mountainside, we put in ditches so that the water flowing from the mountains will be led away from the embankment.

If these kinds of places along the track are not inspected during construction, then later it is impossible to know whether or not the prisoners graded the embankment or whether they filled it in by putting the earth directly on the hillside. The prisoners working on the track, however, had only one concern. They wanted to do the least amount of work possible so their section foreman, who was also a prisoner, would note down a high level of output for them. And sometimes, the daytime civilian foreman on this section of track might, for some reason, be absent. (He could be on vacation, or sick, or resting, and so forth.) Therefore, this "double checking" was totally necessary. If the foreman was not there to see what was going on, then the engineer/inspector was obligated to carefully ensure that they had done the work within the technical norms of construction.

After my experience of being a daily foreman, this job as inspector was easy for me and did not take much work. What I did was to systematically go out to the track and inspect what the camp unit was doing at work. I quickly found a common language with the foremen at this camp unit. They knew almost immediately that they could not trick me or "pull the wool over my eyes." We developed very good working relationships.

Unfortunately, this "heavenly life" did not last long, actually, only a few months. Then I was thrown back into real work.

CHAPTER 16

BOSS OF A MILITARIZED SECTION

Labor Force: Captured German Prisoners of War

AT THE BEGINNING OF 1942, MOSCOW SENT A NEW MAN IN as the chief of the 1st Region of Pechorlag. We three young engineers who had graduated from the Moscow Institute of Railroad Transport Engineering (MIIT) knew him already. Before we left for our jobs at the labor camp, back in 1940, we had seen him in the Gulag Department of Cadres, where he had worked at the time as the deputy head. Soon after he had arrived in Pechora to take up his new duties as chief of the region, he called me. He told me that he remembered our meeting in Moscow, and that he was interested in finding out where I and my two comrades were and how the work was going for us.

At our meeting, I described my work in great detail, starting from the first day on the job at the camp up to the present. He then informed me that the job I'd been doing as engineer/inspector, was really for old fellows, and not suitable for such an energetic young man like me. He added that he was sorry about the illness I'd gone through, and that he understood that I had needed this period for getting back up to speed at work. But he finished our talk by promising to assign me to a new job that would be more in line with my skills, in a few months.

Somewhere around the end of February 1942, he called me in again for a more serious discussion. Here's the thing, he told me, when we had sat down, the entire 500-kilometer (310 miles) length of track on the territory of Pechorlag will finish, if you look at the rail line from north to south, with an exit to the railroad bridge across the Pechora River. That bridge will have to be big and quite tall, since large steamships will have to travel under it, even when the water level is high, like during the springtime floods or after long rains. The construction work on this bridge was going full speed ahead, he said, and by the time the ice breaks and begins to float on the river in May, it should be ready. But on the northern side (our side) of the river, the bank is low, so the rail line's lead-out at the upper point of the bridge has to be built high. At the same time, it will have to have a very wide base at the embankment, and it has to be quite long, because the ascent up to the bridge must be gradual, that is, no more than 12 meters (13.1 yards) per one kilometer of track (as provided for in the technical norms.)

Since the Pechora is such a large river, he continued, the water pressure on the embankments during the flood periods will be very powerful. So, we need to take into consideration two things: first, the actual embankment has to be very stable, not made from any old soil, but from high-quality earth; second, it is crucial that the embankment be built up to the uppermost point on the plan, so that even during the highest flood, no water can cross over the embankment. Otherwise, the whole embankment could be washed away, and we will have done all that work for nothing. It is imperative, of course, that we do not, in any way, shape or form, have any disruptions in the flow of coal from Vorkuta.

He said that Pechorlag's highest bosses and some officials from Moscow had just been here, looking at the place where the huge embankment needs to be built. They saw for themselves that the work on building this approach to the bridge is at its earliest stage. Their main conclusion was this: If we leave it all as it is, and the embankment does not get built this year, this means that the entire rail line heading north from the Pechora River will be cut off. There are practically two months until May. Therefore, Pechorlag's bosses have decided that we must quickly mobilize all the camp's resources toward this, and by May, have the approach to the bridge built and finished.

They have designated the construction of the bridge and its approach as an emergency, and the project has been give military priority. The boss of this project will have a lot of power. On my recommendation, he continued, they have nominated you as the boss of this preferential military site. I will tell you this honestly: If you pull this off, you will get an award;

if you don't, we will shoot you. It's wartime, it's bleak, and we cannot tolerate any disruptions in the deliveries of Vorkuta's coal.[1]

The boss of the 1st Region continued: We have already given all the orders for transferring truck drivers and other necessary technical workers to the construction site, as well as the workers and technicians that you will need. So right now, you need to get yourself to this newly designated military site, familiarize yourself with the situation and give us your recommendations immediately. Right now, workers are building you a temporary house with a telephone, and you will also have service personnel, a horse, a car and chauffeur. We don't want you to think of anything except the construction of this bridge.

From now on out, he went on, Pechorlag's bosses will show up at the construction site every day to monitor the pace of work. Here is what must happen: The volume of earth moved every twenty-four hours must increase tenfold, otherwise the tasks will not be completed and flooding will wash everything away. The previous region chief was too lax, and things did not get built as they should have in this area. He was dismissed from his job and will be punished as befits wartime conditions.

I had no choice but to obey the orders. I went immediately to the construction area. Actually, I saw no signs of any sort that approximated the grand scale of construction that the chief had mentioned. I saw brigades of prisoners transporting gravel from the nearest sand pit in wheelbarrows, on planks they had laid down. For the gigantic future embankment that the bosses envisioned, this was a mere drop in the ocean. It was clear to me that first, we had to find some very large quarries of excellent sand. And second, we also would have to immediately build temporary roads and railroad spurs leading to the quarries, so we could bring in the sand by both rail and truck.

For three days, I and my closest two assistants, civilian engineers who had been selected on an emergency basis from Department Headquarters, rode horses along the right bank of the Pechora River looking for the necessary quarries. When we found them, we drew up plans for building roads from the quarries to the base of the embankment. Whenever possible, we lay these roads out on the frozen Pechora River. Then we calculated how many freight trains, railway platforms, drivers, and so on, we would need so that work could progress around the clock.

After that, I went to back to the region chief to tell him what we needed. He blew up on me, saying that for the last three days, the indica-

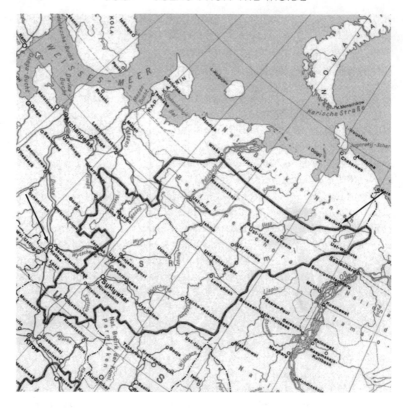

In this detail from a captured Nazi map dated March 1941, there is no evidence of a railroad being built. Nevertheless, the first load of coal was shipped on the Vorkuta-Kotlas Rail Line in the winter of 1941–1942. This 310-mile rail line ran from Vorkuta (Workuta on this map) in the northeast to Kotlas. Princeton University Library.

tors for work done on the embankment had not increased. The camp leadership from Abez was circling around him and was "working his ass off," as they say. I depended on you, he told me, and then you go and disappear somewhere and everything is back to where it was.

But a little while later, he agreed with my plans on how to organize the work, and he promised his total support. He said that he would take care of everything in his control. He also requested that we speed up the construction as much as possible.

Another four days went by as we searched for sand pits and then built access roads for both truck and rail transport. The camp leadership came completely unglued, and on the eighth day, all of the bosses appeared unexpectedly at our construction site. And exactly on that day, we had increased our dirt-moving capacity by tenfold. However, we still were not at peak capacity, because not all of the quarries we had discovered were operational yet.

That is how the work got done: with stretched nerves, cursing, and sleepless nights.

One new thing for me was that I had German prisoners of war working in the biggest quarry. Regular Soviet prisoners were working on the other sections. Our country was a participant of the Geneva Accords on Prisoners of War, which stipulated that captured officers could not be put to work.[2] With my own eyes, I saw German prisoner soldiers loading sand into the trucks at the bottom of the quarry, while the officer sat at the top and did nothing but smoked. This was in striking contrast to how the Hitlerites treated our prisoners of war.

In the beginning, the camp leaders were upset that the prisoners were not making their daily norm. This of course affected their daily food ration and, in turn, their energy level. One day, on the way to the large quarry, I noticed that my driver, a German soldier prisoner, understood a little Russian. I had studied German as a child, so we started to talk. I asked him why the German soldiers who worked in the large quarry were not working up to the norm. I told him that fulfilling the norm by 150 percent would bring them an increase in food.

The German gave an interesting answer. "The only thing you Soviets do," he told me, "is use propaganda and persuasion on us. But we are not used to this. What we need are commands, orders, and directions. Figure out yourself how many trucks of sand should leave the quarry every shift so that we will be better fed, and give us the command. Then you will get your result."

So, that's exactly what I did. Was I ever surprised to find that the exact number of truckloads that were needed to fulfill the plan by 150 percent left the quarry that day. (Let's say I told them that three hundred truckloads of sand needed to go out on their shift. At the end of their shift, we could count exactly three hundred truckloads. No more, no less.) In working like this, the soldiers cheered up, and the embankment was filled in more quickly. Soon, representatives from the camp unit that housed the Germans started coming to me at the militarized section, "to study this outstanding experience."

One thing about my job as the boss of the militarized section was that I only dealt with the prisoners as a labor force. I did not have anything to do with their maintenance or daily lives in the way I had been involved in my previous jobs as camp unit foreman and boss.

On May 1, 1942, about two weeks before the large floating, melting ice blocks would appear in the river, we finished the embankment to the bridge. Again, the Big Bosses showed up unexpectedly. This time, the group included high-ranking Camp Administration bosses, some big shots from Moscow, and the secretary of the Komi Regional Communist Party Committee. (The rail line was on the territory of the Komi ASSR.) All of them were wearing leather coats with fur, white felt cloaks, and fluffy beaver caps with earflaps. They arrived, looked around, and saw for themselves that the approach to the bridge and the actual bridge were ready. They stayed to witness the first train with Vorkuta coal crossing the bridge to Pechora (and not on the ice of the river, as had been before). After they congratulated the local leadership and the builders, they left.

Later, the regional chief asked me: "What would you like as your reward?" I answered: "Give me a room to live in. I've had it with living in the barracks with 30 men in one room." He said, "When you get back to the town, there will be a place."

In June 1942, I returned to the town of Pechora, and there really was a room for me.

Somewhat later, the regional chief called me to his office again. When I got there, the secretary of the Komi Regional Party Organization was there, as well. The regional chief said, "We would like to congratulate you. The leadership of the camp, along with the Komi Regional Committee of the CPSU, have come up with a list of people to recommend for a governmental award. We have recommended you for the "Red Flag Order of Labor." I thanked them.

However, I was only on the "awarded" list for a short while. When the list of awardees arrived in a directive from Moscow to the camp, my name was not on it. As they later explained to me, I had been recommended to receive "too high of an award." In all of Pechorlag, only a few people were awarded the "Red Flag Order of Labor." I was told that they were using the opportunity to give them out to some people who worked in Moscow at GULAG NKVD (although none of them had ever even been at a prison labor camp). "Don't worry," they said to console me, "you are young and still working. You will get your Order another time." Other, more seasoned builders told me that, actually, if they had awarded me a medal like, "For Labor Excellence," then I would have received it. They told me that I would just have to wait until the next time.[3]

CHAPTER 17

BOSS OF A RAILWAY DIVISION

Labor Force: Professional Railwaymen

EVEN THOUGH THE FLOODING DANGER HAD PASSED ON THE Pechora River, and the enormous embankment to the bridge had withstood the pressure of the spring waters, this section of the track retained its military status since it was necessary to continue with reinforcement work. But the emergency situation had passed, and the authorities gave me permission, as the boss of the section with military importance, to go and live in the village of Pechora. From the village, every day I went to work in the floodlands of the river. In July this work finished and again, the regional chief called me to his office.

He congratulated me on my success in completing my embankment job, and then went on to tell me the next plan. It does not make sense for you to return to the job of engineer/inspector, he told me. This, as I told you earlier, is a job for old fellows. Physically, you held up very well while doing heavy labor on the militarized section of track. So, I feel comfortable trusting you with this next very crucial job, which will demand a huge amount from you physically, as well as good engineering training.

Until recently, continued the regional chief, the camp's chief job was to lay down railroad track from Pechora to Vorkuta as quickly as possible. We had to do this because, as you know, of the serious situation on the fronts and the loss of the Donbas and its seams of coal. The access to Vorkuta's coal literally saved the country. Now the track has been laid, the coal is moving from Vorkuta, and most importantly for the camp, the railroads have begun to operate. But since we built it quickly, in record time, it turns out that in many sections we used substandard materials or low quality dirt for the embankments, and we allowed deviations from the projected plan.

In some places, he continued, we are still using track that was built for temporary usage. And heavy freight trains hauling coal are driving on them, one after another. But we need to build up the road and do some maintenance, which will be very difficult because of the railroad's normal operating conditions. The work has to be done in the intervals between trains passing by.

The current railway division boss on our section of the track, he said, is an old but very experienced railroad engineer from the prerevolutionary days. He loves his work and is very devoted to it. He is willing to work day and night. But, he is physically weak and often ill for a long time, and now the doctors have forbidden him to go out on the track. However, he never pays them any attention, and as soon as he feels better, he goes to work. As a result, then he is bedridden again, for a long time. At this point, he has been at home in bed for two weeks already, without any real prospect of getting back on his feet anytime soon.

Therefore, said the regional chief, I am proposing to make you senior engineer of the railway division, a job you will do while in fact fulfilling the duties of boss of the railway division. Once the current boss gets a little better and comes back to work, we are going to send him to Moscow to recover there. But as long as he is still here, try your best to learn from him, ask his advice often. Be open with him. He will value it. And when he goes, you will become the boss of the railway division. So prepare yourself. Go out to the track often. Learn from the people who are working there on the track, especially the unescorted prisoners who are railway engineers by training, both here and in the regional headquarters. Let me know what you think.

What could I do? I accepted the job. And then I made a request. Since the only communication out on the track was the Selektor, which was overloaded with a million work matters, I asked the regional chief for one fixed hour a day on the Selektor's lines, to be reserved only for the railway engineers. I wanted to do it that way so that others knew, and they would not bother with the railway engineers. The regional chief said that this was an intelligent suggestion, and promised to issue the corresponding order to make this happen.

So every day (excluding days off and holidays), at a specified time, all the workers of the railway division along the entire track settled down at a Selektor. In this way, they told me what was going on at their section of the track, and then I gave them their instructions. When I went out on the tracks, no matter where they were, at the appointed time they all gathered together at the Selektor. Discipline among the workers at my new job immediately improved, because everyone knew that the work was being scrutinized daily.

I found out later that the regional chief had listened in on my entire first "brief conference" on the Selektor along with the railway engineers on the track. He told me later that before I had come along, nobody had thought of this and the leaders of the other services had started demanding that they get "their hour" on the Selektor, as well. He did not give them their hour. He told them that this was done exclusively for the railway engineers, since guaranteeing a reliable operating rail line was right now the main task.

The next thing I had to do was go get myself out on the tracks and acquaint myself with the people. I also needed to visit and inspect those places where, from the point of view of operations, the rail line was most vulnerable. This was just what I did on those first days of my new job.

I also started visiting the ailing boss regularly at his house, telling him the things I had done in his absence at the railway division. We shared our plans and doubts. He knew the people who worked out on the tracks very well, their strong and weak points, and his advice and observations really helped me. But his advice was also useful in solving concrete engineering problems. His knowledge and practical experience, to my mind, were unique.

Despite the great difference in ages, gradually we formed a warm, close, and trusting relationship. He told me a lot about himself, his childhood, and the first years he worked as an engineer. I described how, immediately after graduating from my institute, I had declined to become a graduate student and had asked to be sent, like all graduates, out to do some practical work. He was very glad to hear this, he said. He approved of my decision.

However, our heartfelt talks ended after about six months when they sent him back to Moscow to recover. Since he was an interesting man and had a lot of experience on Russian and Soviet rails, I have included some of his recollections in chapter 21.

To continue, after the old boss of the railway division left for Moscow, I became the de jure boss. This turned out to be very troublesome and dangerous personally. It was accepted practice in railroad transport to have the track inspectors go out to the tracks every day with mallets, to carefully look over the state of the rails. They had to ensure that there were not any bent rails, standing water after a rain, split sleepers which the rails were fastened to with stakes, stakes that had come out of their places from the heavy train traffic, and intentional damage (such as loosened nuts that connect the rails, stakes pulled out, and so on).

Besides this, the road foremen regularly checked the accuracy of the gauge with a specialized trolley, because after the trains passed by, especially on the crooked parts of the rail line, the rails can separate a little. Even a little spreading of the tracks can cause an accident. These trolleys recorded (on tape) the actual railway gauge. So if an accident occurred, this tape was the proof that this railwayman was not at fault when they went looking for someone to blame. Even if the accident were caused by some other reason, not evident on the tape, a railway worker would be blamed and sent to prison.

Prisoners who were allowed to move around without an armed escort worked as the permanent railwaymen and road foremen. These prisoners were ill-fed and lived in difficult circumstances; many of them were emaciated and worn out from long imprisonment. Plus many of them were depressed. With their situations in mind, I knew that there was no way to totally trust them to be vigilant, watchful, and careful when they checked on the state of the tracks. And we cannot forget the special characteristics of the polar climate (ferocious snowfalls, freezes, winds, endless rains, the darkness both day and night), which had to influence how well they looked over the tracks every day.

The brigades that repaired the rail lines and maintained them in normal operating condition were also made up of prisoners, so all those things I just mentioned also hindered their work.

Of course, these prisoner-railwaymen of the Gulag knew what kinds of punishment awaited them if there were an accident and they were blamed for carelessly checking the track, or repairing it superficially, or being negligent in guaranteeing the safety of the trains. Despite everything, they still preferred to "hang on" to this work, since it was familiar to them and it provided them the possibility of resting a little from the cruel camp regime. Therefore, as a rule, these men tried to do their best. And they trusted in their fate.

And as to my job as boss of the railway division, I was responsible for the entire state of the railroad in this section. If an accident occurred because of carelessness in track maintenance, then I was responsible. Once or twice they (the upper management) might content themselves with prosecuting somebody who was absolutely guilty from among the men "at the bottom" (the track inspectors, the brigade leaders, the road foremen) if the accident was minor. But if there were many accidents in one railway division or there were a major accident due to some discernable reason, they would put the railway division boss on trial alongside the lower-level workers.

During the time that I worked as railway division boss on this portion of track, there were three accidents. Each time, an authoritative committee, made up of representatives of the three main services (railwaymen, moving stock and operations, plus workers of the security forces) arrived immediately at the place where the accident had taken place. They stayed there until they figured out why the wreck occurred, the section of track was restored, and train service on this track could resume. It goes without saying that each of the representatives of the three services tried to uncover facts that would lay the blame on someone who was not from their service, but from one of the others. Sometimes the reasons were obvious, but there were times when they had to really work to "get to the bottom" of what had taken place.

Happily, the reasons for the accidents on my section of track were not the fault of the railwaymen. In two of the cases, the trains drove onto a section of track that had a train already on it, and in the third, freight car that was carrying a load of coal broke its wheel axel.

My job as the railway division boss was very stressful. I was always nervous, and I got physically worn out, since I had to be out on the track so much of the time. But I got used to the job. I became better acquainted with the people who worked at the railway division, and I developed a good working relationship and a mutual feeling of trust with them.

Then, after about six months or so, the leadership decided to move me to another job.

CHAPTER 18

THE "LIBERATED" SECRETARY
OF THE COMMUNIST
YOUTH ORGANIZATION

THE DEAL WAS THIS. NOT LONG BEFORE THE EVENTS I
wrote about earlier, the brother of a Ukrainian writer who was very famous
at that time, by the name of Korneichuk, was appointed head of the Political
Department of Pechorlag. His brother was well known for writing the novel
Front, which caused a huge sensation when it came out.[1] In this novel, he
ridiculed the civil war commanders and went on to promote younger, very
talented commanders who were showing their military skills on the fronts
of the Great Patriotic War.[2] That's why there was such interest in the brother
of the writer when he arrived at the camp. He was a tall, compact, pleasant
man, and had the rank of commander. Now and then we saw him from afar.
I never thought that I would meet him face to face, or even more, that
because of him, my life would do a complete turnabout.

One day, at the end of February 1943, the special passenger car
belonging to the Political Department head arrived at Pechora Station.
The regional chief was on vacation. Korneichuk, as the head of the
Political Department, was hosting a number of people at his place. I was
aware of this, vaguely, but I was busy with my railroad concerns. I had
no idea that this visit had anything to do with me. Then, out of the blue,
the secretary of the Regional Party Committee told me that Korneichuk
wanted to see me. When I asked "Why?" he replied, "You will see."

I thought back over all the work I had done on the railroad division, and still could not figure out why he needed to see me. So, perplexed to the bottom of my soul, I appeared in front of the high-ranking leadership.

We greeted one another, and he asked me to take a seat. Korneichuk studied me a bit, and began what seemed to me a strange discussion. After a short digression into my biography, and a few questions about my parents, he suddenly started to ask what I had read and was reading, how well I knew Tolstoy, and Ostrovskii, what the difference was between Gogol and Hegel, Babel and Bebel, and so on. Then he turned to questions about the situation on the fronts, and the state of affairs in the international arena. I followed all of this, answering precisely, but thought to myself: "Why is this necessary, and where is he going with this?"

Soon everything became clear. Korneichuk then began talking about the regional Komsomol[3] organization. It seemed that Komsomol members were scattered along the more than 100 kilometers of the Gulag's railroad tracks of the camp. However, nobody was in charge of them, nobody was doing any kind of Komsomol work with them, not even collecting dues. The organization did have a secretary, he said, but his real job was with the security platoon. Plus, he had only an elementary education, which was a problem. In this region, there were many Komsomol members who were engineers, technical workers, doctors, and nurses. They had nothing in common with this current secretary, and he himself avoided them for the most part.

He went on to tell me that there were several hundred Komsomol members here at the camp, and only some of them came from the security organization. It had been decided that this lack of any work among the young people in the region could no longer be tolerated. So the Political Department had decided, and Moscow had agreed, to bring someone into the 1st Region to work as the secretary for Komsomol Affairs. This person would work directly for the Communist Party Committee, and in order to do this job, the person would be "liberated" from his other job at the camp. This way, the new secretary could focus totally on the problems connected with educating young Communists. We in the Political Department, he added, have in mind to propose you as our candidate for the job as secretary of the Komsomol Organization.

I pleaded with him, saying that this did not make sense. The government had spent a lot of money on me to train me as a railway engineer.

Now I had some experience, and I liked the work. I did not want to switch to political work. I'm not the type to be a political worker, I told him, I am terrible at public speaking. I get extremely nervous if I have to speak even a few words at a meeting. So if I take this job, I think the Komsomol will suffer, and so will the section of railroad at the camp where I am boss. I swore to the regional chief that I would do whatever they needed me to do. But now that I had earned the trust of the workers out on the track, why change everything?

Korneichuk answered that he too, like me, had been trained as an engineer. He had graduated from a military-transportation academy in Leningrad. However, he emphasized, the party had needed him for political work, and that's how he had found myself here, at this camp, as head of the Political Department. He said, "I will be honest with you. I need an energetic, young take-charge deputy to the head of the Political Department for Komsomol Affairs. The last guy was over thirty-five years old, and had no feeling for the job. I have been watching you already for several months. You suit me, and I think we could work together."

He continued: "As for you not yet having any experience in Komsomol work, you will get six months as the 'liberated' secretary, then I will make you an instructor in the Political Department for this work. After a few months, I will name you as my deputy for Komsomol Affairs. So do not argue, do not object, it's already been decided. Tomorrow, you will go to the regional Komsomol meeting at the club."

I had nobody to talk to about this. The regional chief was still not back, and there was nobody else to whom I could turn to plead my case. The next day I went to the meeting at the club. It was full of young people. I sat in the very last row, hoping that nobody would notice me.

At that time, I did not know any of the "intrigues" that surrounded the election of the Komsomol Committee and its secretary. I sat in that hall and watched. First, the secretary delivered a very weak report, after which others made presentations, and then they began to suggest some possible candidates for forming a new Komsomol Committee. Almost none of the names they proposed were familiar. When they had reached the end of their slate of candidates, Korneichuk went up to the microphone. He said that considering the large size of the organization and how its membership was dispersed along the tracks for more than 100 kilometers (62 miles), the Political Department would like to propose another young party member as a candidate of the Komsomol Committee. He went on to say that this young party member knows the kind of people who are living out along the track, he has a lot of energy, and he possesses a broad, all-around background. Then he uttered my name.

The committee finished its election procedures. And after that authoritative recommendation, I was elected to the committee. Immediately following the election meeting, Korneichuk led the first session of the new committee. At this meeting, he nominated me as secretary. I was confirmed unanimously.

When the members of the committee had gone home, Korneichuk stayed to meet with the secretary of the Regional Party Committee, who also had been present at the Komsomol gathering. Korneichuk told him to help me out and support me in the coming days. Then, turning to me, he suggested that I hand my production work over to the senior engineer of the railway division tomorrow. He wanted me to begin my job as the secretary of the Komsomol Committee immediately.

When it was my turn, I told him that I could not abandon my post as the boss of the railway division without the agreement of the regional chief, and I asked that he allow me to continue working as boss of the railway division until the chief returned to the camp. Korneichuk did not object. Not long after that, though, he left the region, without even waiting for my boss to get back.

Upon his return, the regional chief was enraged at the willfulness of the party workers,[4] and he demanded that I continue to do my job on the tracks. For a few days, the regional chief and the Political Department head argued, but in the end, I had to leave my work as an engineer, as it later turned out, forever.[5]

They moved me to the big office of the secretary of the Regional Komsomol Committee of the region, where I had to switch gears and start working with young people. I really did not have the heart for this job. But I did it, once the regional chief called me and said, "There is nothing to be done." (He meant that I could not keep my old job.) "I guess you have to get involved with Komsomol work."

Today, it's just a thing that happened long ago. But at the time, I could not get rid of the feeling that all around me, people were doing real things. And here I was, forced to switch to something uninteresting, something that did not require any specialization or long years of training, and something that any normal person could do. And this was during the most terrible times of the war, when the situation at the Soviet fronts was very serious. But every time I went and requested that I be allowed to go and fight at the front or with the partisans (recruiting of volunteers was then going on, and I had registered), they turned me down. The answer was that Pechorlag was considered a "militarized zone," that the factories needed the coal even more since the Fascists had attacked the Donbas, and that without Vorkuta coal these factories would cease production. They insisted that I, as an engineer, was more vital to the camp than to the army.

I understood their reasoning, but in my heart, I did not agree. My brain simply refused to understand the necessity or the rationale of taking me from responsible, productive work on the tracks and not letting me go and fight at the front. Instead, here I was getting involved in educating civilian youth on the southern flank of Pechorlag.

However, I did not have a choice. And since I had never done anything halfway, I moved into the office of the secretary of the Regional Komsomol Committee and dove into my work, "up to my neck," as they say.

I began by visiting the entire length of the track of the 1st Region. I acquainted myself with the Komosomol members at each place, identified the local Komsomol organizations, helped them to elect sensible and intelligent young people as members and secretaries in their local organizations, and assisted them in putting together a work plan. The most important part of these new work plans turned out to be making these young people understand, to the extent possible, how to help get work done out on the track, and how to help the families who had relatives at the fronts. At Pechorlag, this last thing was extremely important, since now several hundred families had received the telegrams that cancelled the man's reserve status and told them to report to active duty. The families, particularly the ones that had small children, were left without food, and there was practically nowhere to turn to for help.

The tundra surrounded us completely. A person could not get to any town, nor could he turn to the leadership. There were no stores and nothing to buy, only allotments to the workers.[6] There was no kind of public transport at all. And wood for burning in your place and for cooking food? And clothing for your kids? Where to get felt boots and schoolbooks for their school-age children? These and a huge number of other practical problems faced the families whose fathers or husbands were sent to the front. These problems literally knocked on the door, and they had to be solved, not put off. To start, we had to make clear just how many of these people were in every village, and what they needed, so we could help them. We also made a work plan for organizing sports and cultural activities.

When I got back to Pechora, I met with the local secretaries of the Komsomol organizations and its members. With spring drawing near, we knew that the snow would be melting and that the rivers would begin to break into big ice pieces. We got the leadership's permission to let Komsomol members be on daily patrol along the entire section of railroad and the outlying regions, especially in the places that were most in danger of being flooded. As I mentioned earlier, normally unescorted prisoners who were on the staff of the railway division did this job. But we had an important job to do, and things to consider. We had to keep the rail lines open and accident free, we had to deal with the North's unpredictable climate, and we had to use possibly unreliable prison labor. So this extra assistance from the Komsomol members in this crucial period would help immensely.

As it turned out, this Komsomol initiative had tangible results. The Komsomol prevented several accidents that would have happened because of unexpected thunderous snow meltings. For alerting others on time and participating in the prevention of the accident, the Komsomol members were awarded a prize. In my work diary, in the section titled "Reports on Incentives and Awards," I have an entry that I am proud of to this day. I wrote: "For exemplary fulfillment of the task of keeping back the spring waters, I was presented with a pair of calf leather boots and two pair of socks as my reward. Order No. 220, May 31, 1943." The boots I long ago wore out, and the socks, too, but the memory remains.

The Komsomol members searched out the families with children whose men were at the fronts, found out what they needed, and asked the regional leaders for help. They told me that they took firewood to them, and distributed clothing and food for the families, especially for the children. The Komsomol members themselves had to figure out how to get the wood chopped and cut, and also come up with ways to pay the person who did the work. The Komsomol members took it upon themselves to make sure that the families who had a family member at the front had enough wood to keep their houses warm. To pay for the needed clothing and food, the Komsomol's Committee of Special Funds for Essential Needs began to hold auctions from time to time. The leadership met them halfway, that is, they gave them the rest of what they needed.

The Camp Administration's civilian employees who participated in the auctions understood why they were there and how the things were collected. In addition, they knew that even though their salaries were high, there was nothing to buy at Pechorlag. Therefore, some things sold "by auction" for huge sums of money, for instance, a scarf that cost a few kopecks was sold for 700 rubles. The very fact that everyone knew one another helped to raise the level of competition between participants. Nobody wanted to stop bidding in front of his or her coworkers. At the same time, when a woman whose husband was at the front would shyly bid on an item, hoping to get something for the children like clothing or food, the Komsomol committee members who ran the bidding quickly stepped in to give the thing up for sale literally for kopecks, and the others waited for "their time" to be included in the bidding.

Aside from the auctions that the Committee of Special Funds for Essential Needs held, the regional Komosomol Club organized talent shows. They charged admission to the shows, and advertised where these pricey tickets could be purchased. The population of the village responded enthusiastically to this kind of event, all the more so because every family expected that their breadwinner would soon be called to the front, as well.

In this way, the young people (and not just them) were excited to participate in the talent shows.

At the Arctic Circle, the snow stays on the ground until the middle or end of May. But starting in February, every day there is more sun and the days get a little longer. We used these days to organize skiing competitions that became like holidays for all the civilians at the camp We started with the leadership. We talked our highly respected bosses into getting involved by reminding them of the days when they were young. We told them that if they skied with us, then their deputies would have to compete, and then, after them, all the coworkers, and not just the young ones. We leaned on them to get the wives and children of the Camp Administration's workers to attend the competitions, too. They could come out, we said, if for no other reason than to skate and have fun with the others, and to enjoy watching the successes of the participants.

We posted amateur brass bands at the starting and finish lines, we hung bright flags and banners, we put together a table of food, and we talked the leadership into giving prizes to all the folks who had the best time on the tracks, by age group. We found a photography buff, who again, with help from the leadership, got hold of some film and paper, and conscientiously printed photos of the entire run of the relay race. The photographs showing this were hung later in the club.

When the short northern summer began, just like we did with the skiing competitions, we held sports competitions in which, considering the military time, we tossed grenades and did the leopard crawl.

In the club, accompanied by an amateur string orchestra and an accordianist, we began to have regular evening dances and competitions for the best dancers, which included photographs of the winners. After a while our collective's amateur nights became famous outside of the region, and we started inviting the neighboring villages.

Since the war was going on, we got the security services to help us and lend us their weapons, to set up a shooting range where young people could be taught to shoot guns. (The participants were not only men, but also women, who did not shy away from this.)

In time the civilian employees became accustomed to seeing the photo stands that regularly displayed the life of the Komsomol organization. These pictures hung in the Camp Administration buildings, in the club and in the dining hall. All of this increased the Komsomol's respectability.

When I first settled into the big office of the secretary of the Regional Komsomol Committee, my telephone was stubbornly quiet, and for days there were no visitors. Soon everything fundamentally changed, but by that time, catching me in the office was not easy. My main job took me out along the railroad tracks, this time, though, for my work with young people.

As if to top off all these activities, I had the pleasure of getting the news that I was to be given a special commendation from the CPSU CC, on our national holiday of November 7, 1943. By then, however, I had been transferred again and was no longer at Pechorlag. Korneichuk, the head of the Political Department, had kept his word, and in August, 1943, I was assigned to work as an instructor, in the Political Department, on Komsomol affairs.

Before I left Pechora for my new job, they asked me to write out an account of my work there. I had never compiled any kind of record, so I did not know how to do it. First, I described the conditions that the young people were living in when I was chosen as secretary. Then I briefly described how the Komsomol Committee had tackled the problems of young people. I illustrated my account in detail with some of the photographs we had taken. It never once occurred to me that this report would have a decisive influence on my future.

The thing was, soon after my transfer to the village of Abez to work in the Political Department, Korneichuk, the director of this department, was sent from Pechorlag to the center for a new assignment. Another fellow who took over entirely as deputy director of the Political Department for Komsomol Affairs arrived to take his place. And I "got stuck" as an instructor. I hoped that maybe now they would let me go to the front. But my fate was to be otherwise.

When Pechorlag's Political Department sent its record of my work to Moscow, they included my own account to illustrate the situation on the ground. In Moscow they looked my version over and someone told me later that they concluded that this was the kind of Komsomol secretary who should be a working as a full deputy director of the Political Department at the camp. Since the corresponding suggestion did not come from Abez, but from the center, the Political Department of the Gulag itself then took the initiative and decided to appoint me as deputy director for Komsomol Affairs in another of its camps.[7] This is how it happened.

Since my new title would be deputy director of the Political Department for Komsomol Affairs, which appeared in the NKVD's list of positions, they recalled my personal file from Pechorlag to Moscow.[8] That's how I broke free of the tenacious embrace of the Gulag in the North, but still remained in the system.

CHAPTER 19

FASCIST MILITARY LANDING FORCE

SYKTYVKAR, THE CAPITAL OF KOMI ASSR, WAS LOCATED
very far to the east of the Pechora-Vorkuta rail line. Before the Great
Patriotic War began, we almost never saw airplanes fly over the area of
Pechorlag. Probably in the past, Soviet flights from Vorkuta had made connections to other flights in Syktyvkar. Soon after the war began, though, we
heard and saw the first Fascist airplanes making individual reconnaissance
flights over the areas where we were constructing the rail lines. However,
these flights were few and far between. Those airplanes with their crosses
painted on the wings flew high and never took a shot. And the Soviet side
never fired at these planes, neither from land nor air.

As I mentioned earlier, next to our Gulag camp, there was a forest
tract about 10 kilometers (6.2 miles) wide, stretching from the Pechora
River to Vorkuta. Further out lay the endless tundra, which went all the
way up to the Arctic Ocean. In the winter, the only way to travel across
this terrain was by using relay teams of reindeer. In the short summers,
the riverbeds of shallow rivers and creeks were the only transport arter-
ies. Along the banks of these rivers and creeks, there were small hamlets
of the citizens of Komi, all spread out far from one another.

Even before the war began, the civilian staff of Pechorlag felt that if
Hitler's Germany attacked the Soviet Union, the Fascists might try to
land paratroopers and weapons near the prison camps that were building the railroads. Their goal would be to set free and arm the prisoners.
Then the prisoners could be used to fight under the command of the
Fascist officers inside our country, and also in the western regions where
the USSR borders Finland, which, at that time, was an ally of Germany.

After war broke out, the party and the Komsomol formed military detachments in every city or town near Pechorlag. Working alongside the subunits of the security platoons (VOKhR) and the Chekists, these party/Komsomol detachments were put in charge of patrolling the prison camp around the clock. In the event that the Fascists landed near the camp, these detachments were to encircle and destroy them before they could come into contact with the prisoners. (There were no army sections at the railroad construction sites.) They appointed me as the head of one of these detachments, which included mostly engineers and technicians.

If you looked at our prison labor camp through the eyes of the Fascists, then of course, the idea of landing troops near it might look very tempting. It would be possible to think that they could easily take by force and arm an enormous embittered group of prisoners, and move them from the North to Moscow.

This was in theory only. But in reality? Where would these paratroopers land? And at what time of the year could they land? The only forests were near the Pechora River. In the tundra, the winters meant deep snow, and in the summers, impassible swamp. Near the railroad tracks, there were no good-sized towns to speak of. To get anywhere, they would have to go by rail, and since the rail line was not completely built yet, they would have to go on foot or on horse. And along the entire 500-kilometer (310-mile) stretch of projected track, there were only a few hundred horses available.

Clearly, the Fascists' attempts to provoke an uprising of prisoners in Pechorlag by landing troops there never came to anything during the war. However, the Germans did attempt to land a few times, near Pechora village, which was surrounded by forests.

It was early in 1942, when the residents of Pechora village first heard the unfamiliar rumble of a low-flying large airplane, circling slowly overhead. We clearly saw the swastikas of Hitler's Germany on the fuselage. The airplane flew over our village from the west to the east, and then, descending still further, disappeared over the expanse of the nearby pine forest.

Soon after that, the Camp Administration called in the heads of the party/Komsomol military detachments, and a representative of the Chekists told us that the Fascists had landed some paratroopers several kilometers from the village. They commanded us to mobilize our military detachments quickly, arm the members, and go out and liquidate the Germans.

Everything worked out well that time. We all got ready, and then we encircled the region where the paratroopers had landed. The Germans themselves came out voluntarily and surrendered to us as prisoners. Of course, not all of the them, because a large group of them, immediately after landing, neutralized the commanding officer and several of the zealous Fascists. After the leaders were turned over to our Chekists as prisoners, the paratroopers (who were themselves Soviet citizens) told us that the Fascists had taken them prisoner at an earlier date. And then, they explained, in order to get back home somehow, they had gone to special intelligence schools. All of them, after interrogation, were sent under escort to Moscow.

Clearly, the Germans learned something from this, because after that they began to carry out their landings in secret, without crossing the railroad tracks and without flying low over the villages. I think that on their first "visit" they did not fire at the village from the plane, since they could not tell by looking where the civilian employees lived and where the prisoners were being held.

Another time, something very strange happened. A smart-looking NKVD major came into the barracks of the camp security platoon. Upon seeing such a high rank, the watchman jumped up, and commanded the platoon: "Stand! Attention!" He was about to report to the major about who had just entered, but the man interrupted him and demanded that he call the security platoon's commander. The watchman-soldier shot off like a bullet to carry out the major's order. At the same time, the guest walked over to the stand of weapons along one wall of the barracks, and began to pick up the rifles that stood among them, one after the other, clicking open the breech-blocks and checking how well the guns were lubricated.

The frightened platoon commander came in, and after standing at attention, put his palm to the peak of his military cap and began to speak: "Comrade Major…" His guest interrupted him and said, "I am not a major." Then the platoon commander, shocked at these words, began to yell, "Security, get your guns!"

Then the "major" told him, "Stop screaming. Get a soldier and come with me. I could take you prisoner for not going out to the German paratroopers that landed not far from you in the nearby woods. The ones who didn't want to become prisoners, we either tied up or killed."

But there weren't always such happy outcomes. It seems that the Germans learned quickly. One of their landings took place far from

Pechora village, and they managed to capture a brigade of prisoners who were working on the tracks. They armed the prisoners, shooting those who refused to go along with them. Then they headed for the prison camp to free the zeks who were being held there, and then move them eastward to the Soviet-Finnish border. As the entire group approached the camp, we managed to encircle them and as a result, we destroyed much of their battalion. According to a nurse I liked who took part in this operation, many men were killed and wounded.

Since all the operations to liquidate paratroopers that landed were undertaken in secret from those who did not take part in them, it is impossible for me to tell the whole story of the battles with the German troops that landed near the tracks of Pechorlag. But what was clear was that for the ingenious Fascists, as I have already said, nothing useful ever came of these. They never managed to affect the regular movement of loads of coal from Vorkuta to the inner part of the USSR.

It surprised me that the Fascists, whose airplanes flew unimpeded over the tracks of Pechora camp, did not bomb the railroad bridge across the Pechora River and the approach leading up to it, especially in the flood season. If they had done that, they could have stopped coal deliveries to the military factories in the inside of the country for a long time. They could also have severed the supply of coal that was headed for English and American ships in Murmansk, which would have impeded us from getting the goods through Lend-Lease that we badly needed.

Aside from landing paratroopers near Pechorlag, the Fascists also tried to recruit Soviet civilian employees to work for the German secret service. This was very difficult to do in the Komi ASSR where Pechorlag was located, since the Gulag's civilian employees were not Komi ASSR locals, but were assigned from Moscow. Nevertheless, they tried.

When I was working as the "liberated" secretary of the Komsomol organization of the 1st Region of the camp during the summer of 1943, a young Komi man came to me and asked to be registered as a Komsomol member. Like all Komi, he spoke little. But in answering my questions, he told me that he had been at the front, and had been seriously injured. After getting out of the hospital, he had been released from military service because of poor health, and he returned to his native area in the Komi ASSR. Since he knew how to drive, he decided to apply to work as a chauffeur in Pechora village. The Regional Cadres Department had checked his documents and had hired him as a chauffeur. Everything seemed to be in order.

But when I started to look over his Komsomol records, I noticed that the Komsomol dues that he had paid were not in line with any kind of wages we had at the time, no matter where he had worked in the Soviet Union. I did not say anything about this, I wished him success, and we parted. However, the security people also had noticed this. Later, they told me that this young man really was a Komi by nationality, and he really had been wounded, but that he had not spent any time recovering in our hospitals. The papers on this part of his life had been forged. The Nazis had captured him, taken him as prisoner, and sent him to study at an intelligence school. After that, he was sent to Pechorlag to try to form a secret service at the camp, and do what the German Command ordered him to do. By working as a chauffeur, they felt that he could be extremely useful to the Fascists.

CHAPTER 20

Deputy Boss in the Political Department for Komsomol Work at the NKVD's Road-Building Camp No. 3

At the end of March 1944, I arrived at camp headquarters in the town of Orel[1] for my new job, as deputy director for Komsomol Affairs in the Political Department at Camp No. 3.[2] My new Gulag camp was working on the restoration of the highway from Moscow to Kharkov that had been destroyed by the war.[3] In the Briansk Woods off to the side of this highway, there was a special camp unit of prisoners preparing timber for the construction job. The camp stretched across Tula, Orel, Kursk, and Belgorod, and in these towns, and in other towns in between them, there were several supporting camp bases, each with its own headquarters, bosses, mechanized units, and zones of prisoners.

At this camp, lots of young people from the rural areas and towns along the highway worked right alongside the prisoners. Most of these young people were between fourteen and sixteen years old (in 1944, you had to be seventeen to go into the army), including girls too, who were around that age and older. After they had worked for eight to ten hours a day in a place, generally, not far from where they lived, they were being taught to drive, by the "quick and simple" method. This way they could drive the trucks and other road-building machinery, such as bulldozers, earth-moving machines, rollers, small excavators, and others. Because there were so many of these young people at the camp, compared to Pechorlag, Komsomol leadership over them was even more important.

Orel and Belgorod had been liberated in August 1943, so when I arrived in Orel, the reconstruction work had just begun. The Komsomol organizations had not yet been organized, and there were only incomplete records of Komsomol work done among the young people there. First, we needed to improve the way these young people were living. The towns along the road had been almost totally destroyed. These boys and girls were living with their relatives (if they had survived the two onslaughts of war that came down this road), and in the best cases, in partially destroyed buildings or in dugouts nearby.

They heated their places with "little stoves" of tin plate that they had made themselves. These little stoves not only kept them warm, but they were also used for cooking food. They dressed mainly in "second-hand clothing." They wore old adult clothes they had found, or abandoned remnants of military uniforms that they bartered for at the "second-hand markets" that had spontaneously popped up all over the place.

Working at the Gulag camp gave them a minimum of food and a bit of money. There were a lot of these young people around, so there was no problem getting enough workers to do the jobs.

Besides the local young men and girls, the center had sent engineers, technicians, administrative and medical workers, soldiers, and VOKhR officers to this camp. There were also demobilized Soviet Army soldiers, who had been wounded or who had become ill and who had then been sent to work in the various subdepartments of the camp.

Using my experience from working with the Komsomol organization at Pechorlag, I began by traveling along the road. I made an inventory of the youth who were working at the camp. Then I created "local" Komsomol organizations, and helped them elect a secretary and put together a work plan.

After this, I prepared and led a meeting in Orel for the secretaries of the Komsomol organizations and the young activists. I even invited the deputy head for Komsomol Affairs of the Political Department of the Gulag. (He did not show up, but he sent an employee of the organization.)

I convinced the boss of Camp No. 3 Main Administration of Highways NKVD to speak about the construction tasks, the director of Camp No. 3's Political Department to speak on the political situation in the country and overseas, the commander of military operations about the situation on the fronts, and the secretary of Orel's regional party committee for Komsomol Affairs to speak about the role of young people in partisan activities in the oblast (county) during the occupation, and about the tasks ahead of us after liberation. I also spoke, telling them what kinds of things we needed to address to get these young people taken care of at the camp.

In this way, everyone at the camp and in the local organizations knew the Komsomol. This was very useful for those many times when the Komsomol went to them with various requests for schoolbooks, a site for a pioneer camp, and for sports equipment.

I will not repeat myself in recounting how I got things going for the young people working on that road. I tried my best to direct them as much as I could to help the reconstruction work on the road. All in all, I spent one year and nine months at Camp No. 3.

After I had moved to Orel, I continued to go to the leadership from time to time and request that I be sent to the front. After some time had passed, one day I heard that there had been an order issued by the minister of the NKVD. Among other things in this order, my name was on a list of people who were to be given the title of lieutenant. After that, my boss told me to stop bombarding them with requests to go to the front, and to just relax and do the work I had been assigned to do at the camp. I found out later that of the nearly sixty camps in the Gulag system that had deputy directors of Political Department for Komsomol Affairs, only five of them were given the title of lieutenant.

In my opinion, this was intentional. During our meeting in Moscow at the CPSU CC, the head of the Political Department of the Gulag had told me outright that they had plans to send me to do Komsomol work at the biggest Gulag construction site. This was the camp that was building a rail line from Komsomolskaia to Sovetskaia Gavan.[4] And I was told that on down the line, I would be transferred to party work. That kind of future did not really suit me; I wanted to return to the institute and study science. But during the war, all personal plans were pushed aside, and I had no choice but to go on their predetermined path toward management.

In any case, the road-building site at Orel needed freight trucks. After we had smashed the Fascist army in the Baltics, the Soviet government had allotted around one hundred trucks to us. But we were told that we had to go to Vilnius for the trucks,[5] and drive them back to Orel on our own. The camp bosses met to discuss candidates for this job. They all agreed that there was no better candidate than the deputy director for Komsomol Affairs in the Political Department (me), and the drivers who would go along with him to bring back the trucks would be those quickly trained fifteen- and sixteen-year-olds. They formalized this by signing my name on all the papers, then gave me the money they thought would be necessary for all of us, plus some assorted foodstuffs. In addition, they included a couple of officers who had been injured on the front and, after recovering in the hospital, had been assigned to our camp. So off I went with my gang of half-starving teenagers who were not easy to manage, and a supply of gasoline.

Somehow we economized on our food supplies, the young guys managed, the officers won their favor, and our supplies lasted until we got to Vilnius. Even though it was absolutely forbidden, we picked up passengers for money all along the way. Then we bought food at the local markets with the money we got from these illegal passengers. This is how we managed to get enough food for everyone. Also, when we would pass a field with ripening potatoes and vegetables, there was absolutely no controlling the young folk. The column would stop and they would run all over the field, returning only after they had gathered enough for a little reserve.

On the way back from Vilnius, these inexperienced drivers who had just completed their driving course were to go in pairs in each truck. We put one driver in the front vehicle, and one behind that, in the truck that we had hooked onto the first truck. (We attached the wheels of the second truck to the body of the first truck, and the back wheels followed the front wheels.)[6] The road was long, and much of it had been destroyed by the war. It was autumn, and it rained frequently. At night, we slept in the fields. (We did this on purpose to keep the young men from being tempted to run from house to house looking for food if we stopped in a town or a city.) As surprising as it sounds, we made the entire trip to Vilnius and back without anything major going wrong. The inexperienced young drivers did very well on the return trip, and all of the trucks were delivered to the camp.

One day I was called to Moscow, to attend a conference for the Political Department's deputy directors for Komsomol Affairs, for the entire Gulag. All of these deputies were working at camps under the jurisdiction of the Main Administration of Highways NKVD. While there, the colonel general,[7] an elderly, gray-haired man who was the chief of the

Main Administration of Highways NKVD, held a meeting with us. We were seated around a long table. The colonel general asked us to speak about the kinds of difficulties we were encountering in our work with young people, and if we had any requests for him, the chief of the Main Administration of Highways NKVD. He requested that we speak out to everyone, in a "roundtable" format. Several people spoke briefly. I was surprised that my colleagues from other camps only talked about their successes at work. (Maybe they did not want to upset an old man, or maybe they hoped to be remembered as successful workers.)

I was seated close to the colonel general. When it was my turn to speak, I told the truth about how hard life was for the young people at my site, and how they were all from a region that had only recently been liberated from Hitler's army. I emphasized that for the youth to work successfully, we needed to not only think about the quality of the work done, but about the timeframe we had for this restoration work. For the young people with whom I worked, I asked in particular for a sleeping car and bedding, winter and summer clothing, and some shoes. And as rewards for the very best twenty workers, I requested some good wool fabric for suits, which none of these young people had. And further, I said, if this request were to be granted, then Camp No. 3's assistant boss for Economic Affairs should not be allowed to do as he pleased with these things when the goods arrived. To ensure this, I continued, it would be best to send them with a special stamp that said "Attention: Deputy Director of the Komsomol."

The chief of the Main Administration of Highways NKVD looked shocked. In sharp tones, he said that I was trying to delude him and the other participants. To corroborate, he called his deputy for Economic Affairs and demanded that he report how many consumer goods had been sent to Camp No. 3 in the last quarter. When he brought in the numbers, they looked very impressive. Now all eyes were on me.

I then asked them to separate these numbers into those things sent from the center for the civilian employees and members of their families, and to think about what was left for the young men and women from the liberated areas. These youth had no normal housing and nothing to wear, nowhere to sleep, and at night, they had no protection. I added that I myself often walked along the road, and that I saw it all. It would be wrong to conceal this situation, I said, or not to notice it in the general statistics on relative provisions. The colonel general was persuaded, and in the presence of all the participants of the meeting, he commanded his deputy to send to Orel a sleeping car with the goods I had requested with the obligatory attachment of a stamp that said "Attention: Deputy Director for Komsomol" on them.

All the other people the meeting immediately began to recall that their camps needed the same kind of help. But the chief of the Main Administration of Highways NKVD reminded them that they had said nothing of the sort in their presentations, and he turned them all down. He told them that the next time, they needed to be smarter about what they said.

Since I had recently been given the title of lieutenant, the colonel general ordered that along with the car of goods I'd requested for the young people at the site, I was to receive some fabric for a greatcoat, and an officer's uniform made from the same material that was used for generals.

Upon returning to Orel, I told Camp No. 3's boss, who in his youth had been a deputy director in the Political Department for the Amur Flotilla, about the convention in Moscow and the instructions of the chief of the Main Administration of Highways NKVD. I requested that if the sleeping car did arrive, that we not allow his assistant for Economic Affairs (his name was Bliumkin) to twist either me or him around his little finger. It was good that I warned him, because when the sleeping car arrived, Bliumkin tried to claim to the boss of Camp No. 3 that he, Bliumkin, had requested the car be sent. He also claimed that he had requested the fabric for an officer's greatcoat, and an officer's uniform made from material used for generals, especially for the boss. In order to convince him, Bliumkin even showed him the fabric for the greatcoat and the uniform. Was he ever surprised when the boss asked to see the documents and said that he knew the history of the car already.

Although the assistant boss for Economic Affairs tried to do some sneaky maneuvering, in the end, not one meter of fabric nor one thing was lost. We distributed the things we received by collective decision. Linens and bedding went to everyone. The clothing we gave out for good labor results, plus gifts for some newlyweds. Because as always, life continued on its way, and people still got married.

Soon after this something happened that could have ended my Komsomol activities and changed the whole course of my life.

The boss of Camp No. 3, as I already mentioned, had himself been a Komsomol worker, so obviously he was very sympathetic to me. At the end of August 1944, he called me in and told me that in connection with an inquiry from Moscow, he had decided to send me to the NKVD's Higher School. They were running a closed recruitment for employees with higher education. The term of study was two years. At the end of it, I would be sent immediately to a higher-ranking job, from department boss of a regional NKVD Administration to deputy chief of the Main Administration.

At the time, I did not realize that this recruitment had been announced after one of the periodic purges of the organization, when many of its leaders had been simply executed by shooting. And now they needed new victims, for the Stalinist-Beria[8] regime still had ten years left to rule, and there would be many more purges in the NKVD system. They were looking for people who, above all, would be submissive and would carry out commands from above without thinking much. Since the thinking was that "there's an opening so we must fill it," they had to prepare new cadres for the spots that had opened up.

At the time, though, I thought that this proposal was a sign of special trust in me. On the other hand, if I went to the NKVD's Higher School, I would always be connected to that system. Most of all, I loved the idea of going off to study, but not in an NKVD school. I wanted to be a graduate student in science instead. But at the time, it was uncomfortable to turn it down, and everyone around me, as they said, "would not hear of it." So I dragged my feet in the hopes of getting out of it somehow.

And it happened. On October 10, the boss of Camp No. 3 received a telegram from the deputy minister with this order: You are to post the candidate, F. V. Mochulsky, who has been selected to attend the NKVD's Higher School, to the ministry. He must be there no later than October 12." Two days later, the boss of Camp No. 3 sent this reply: "The Political Department objects to sending Mochulsky, whom you have chosen as a candidate to the NKVD's Higher School, since we do not have anyone to replace him in his job. I wait for your orders." On October 18, the deputy minister finished with this note: "Mochulsky is to remain in political work. As soon as possible, please send."[9]

In the end, I never had to get myself established in the NKVD after all. Needless to say, a future in the NKVD had never appealed to me.

Back at work, we started getting alarming reports about the Briansk Woods camp unit prisoners who were supposed to be cutting and sending wood out to us. The wood was not being delivered. It was impossible for us in Orel to understand what was happening because of poor communications. But the main thing was that valuable time was being lost, and we needed to straighten things out very quickly. And also there had been heavy snowstorms, so snow blanketed all the roads to the unit. Nobody could drive or walk there now.

The boss of Camp No. 3 called a meeting to try to think this through together, and figure out what was really happening at that camp unit. They decided that they needed to give someone from the camp leadership "emergency powers" and send them out to the unit. If necessary, we had to be ready to remove the unit boss and the foreman from the job. We would have to get the approval of the local NKVD and the regional party committee, and then assign someone else to the job, maybe from among the local activists, former partisans, or demobilized soldiers. In any case, this person from the camp leadership would have to stay there until the problem was solved and the prisoners were again back to cutting and sending wood out to us on schedule.

During the meeting, someone remembered that I had brought my skis with me from Moscow. They started talking about how it would be impossible to get to the Briansk Woods camp unit without skis. A sled could only get to the edge of the forest. And how would anyone get any further?

In a unanimous vote, they confirmed me as the candidate, and Moscow sent its agreement, as well. They gave me the documents with the emergency powers to carry in hand, then they called the head of the NKVD of Briansk Region and the secretary of the Regional Party Committee, to make sure that if I needed their help, they would be available. Finally, they wished me a good trip.

I took my skis, compass, flashlight, map, revolver, and a supply of cartridges, and I set off. During the German occupation, the Briansk Woods had been taken over totally by partisans.[10] Then, after we had defeated and expelled the Germans, the woods became a haven for those who hadn't managed to get out with the collaborators[11] and other Fascist underlings, who hid out there to avoid being punished for their crimes. As I already mentioned, in the last several days, there had been several snowfalls, and snow had completely whitened the roads. While skiing on those roads was not easy, the thought of bumping into some bandits in the woods weighed on me even more.

I realized that there was no way out of this situation. Painstakingly, I followed the road to the woods that held the camp unit, and once there, I asked around in Briansk to find someone who knew how to get to the unit. I decided that it was better to travel through the woods at night, when there would be fewer chances of encountering an enemy ambush. It had stopped snowing as I climbed out of the sleigh on the edge of the road that led down to the woods. The moon lit up the sky, delighting the eyes with our classically beautiful Russian nature. As a child in Belorussia, I had adored the woods, and I often went into them on skis. I would ski on the sleigh paths that were covered with snow, with a feeling of harmony in my soul, which helped to soothe any internal disharmony or feelings of fear.

Around 4:00 AM, covered with snow, I skied into a village that had been nearly burned to the ground by the Fascist death squads. It sat just a few kilometers from the camp unit. I had been told of this village beforehand, so I even knew how to find the house of the village leader. I had heard that during the war, he had been a partisan, and that I could trust him completely. The village leader was extremely surprised to see me. Still, he fixed me a nice breakfast, and while we ate, he told me what he knew about the camp unit and what was going on there. And he knew a lot, because the boss of the camp unit had a lover in the village. It seems he came to see her often, using a trotter and small sleigh. In fact, last night he had come to the village. "If you like," he said, "I could introduce you to him right now."

I declined his offer, and asked him not to tell anyone that I was here. I explained that I wanted to see with my own eyes what was going on at the camp unit, to find out why plan fulfillment for cutting and processing the lumber had fallen so dramatically. I told him that I wanted to get to the camp unit in time for the morning shift (at 6:00 AM), so the village leader offered to take me there by horse.

We stopped at the little building that housed the commander of the security platoon at the camp unit. The village leader introduced me to the person in charge, and after that, he invited me to drop back over to his place for a long chat when I got back. Then, he left. I explained to the security platoon commander why I had come and asked him to help me. Together, we watched the camp as it woke up. The prisoners ate breakfast, then formed lines, and left for their job sites. I looked over the camp units accounts. Everything was familiar to me from my work at Pechorlag.

Finally, somewhere around 10:00 AM, the camp unit boss tooled in on his trotter. He was a middle-aged man who seemed cheeky and dull-witted. When he saw how young I was, he assumed I had no idea about working with prisoners, so at first he was defiant and clearly wanted to "pull the wool over my eyes." Later, when he had more or less figured things out, he stopped being defiant. He promised to make things right and get plan fulfillment "back on track." He and his foreman were, as they say, "in it together." They got drunk and went out carousing with each other, figuring that the leadership was so far from them that they'd never find out anything.

I met with the camp unit's other civilian employees, the commander of the security platoon, and the political instructors, who monitored daily life at the camp, the secretary of the Regional Party organization (who was the former commander of the partisan detachment in these regions) and the head of the NKVD's Regional Department. We all agreed that the camp unit boss and the foreman needed to be dismissed from their jobs immediately. They all recommended that we replace them with two local people, a teacher and an engineer. Both of them had been partisans in the Briansk Woods, and they each had the necessary authority for the job.

Using the emergency powers that had been given me, I changed the leadership at the camp unit. Since I was very familiar with running a camp unit, I stayed several days to help them set up and get going on the job. I showed them how to come up with a new work plan, and how to best run successful meetings with the camp administrators (who were mostly prisoners) and of course, with the camp's civilian employees. I went out to the prisoners' work sites with them.

The new camp unit leaders and I went to see the commander of the tank regiment that was stationed on the outskirts of the Briansk Woods, to ask him for help. We had the idea that they could drive their tanks down the road leading from the Unit to the railroad station, mash down the snowdrifts, and make truck traffic possible.

Then I went to see the village leader at his house, where I had left my skis on the day I had arrived. He told me everything he knew about the people who were working at the camp unit. He also spoke to me in great detail about the partisan struggles in the Briansk Woods. We took a sleigh and visited the battle sites and the places where there had been ambushes. We also went to see the partisans' camp, which had only recently been abandoned.

After two weeks, the camp unit was back on schedule with its job of getting the wood and dispatching it on time. It was time for me to abandon this legendary but remote corner.

On the way back, I stopped in Briansk to meet with the chief of the NKVD's Regional Administration and the secretary of the Regional Party organization. I told them what had taken place at the camp unit, and we discussed my other job of rebuilding the highway between Moscow and Kharkov.

Once I returned to Orel, I once again got back into my Komsomol work. We all were so happy with the news from the fronts. Our work on repairing the highway was going very well. The Komsomol members of the camp were beginning to make a real contribution to the restoration work. And then, the long-awaited Victory Day came.[12] Finally, we no longer had to mobilize all of our country's energies toward winning the war.

Once the war ended, they dissolved the Political Departments in many areas of the Gulag, which meant a job change for the employees of Camp No. 3 of the Main Administration of Highways NKVD. In my work booklet for January 1, 1946, I wrote these words: "Released for reassignment by the Political Department of GULAG NKVD."

PART III

INTERESTING ASIDES

SOME RAILROAD RECOLLECTIONS

As I mentioned in chapter 17, I worked for a time with an older, very experienced railroad engineer from the prerevolutionary days. He told me a number of interesting things about railroads and railroad building in old Russia.

Before the revolution, both the Petersburg and Moscow Institutes of Railroad Transport Engineering were very privileged educational institutions. These places were so elite that they did not even accept all of the noblemen's children who applied. And from the poor families, these schools only accepted the most talented students. The railroad engineer I worked with ended up at the Petersburg Institute in that latter category. In those days, once a person graduated from one of these institutes, he was set for life. The graduates had large apartments, summer homes, and transport (a horse cab, a horse, and a driver). They could teach their children foreign languages and music (for which they would have a piano in the home), hire the highest quality teachers, travel with their families to the South, and so on.

In those days, most engineers worked only for money, and in order to make more of it, they resorted to various tricks. They took advantage of the fact that the clients who were building the rail lines normally did not understand engineering. For instance, my rail expert friend told me that in the planning out and the laying of track for the rail line from the town of Vitebsk heading west, the engineers projected and built high embankments with large turnarounds on flat ground, even though both of these were totally unnecessary. All they really needed to do was to lay straight track and build small embankments so that when it rained the rail line would not get water on it.

Why did they do this? Because they were paid much more if they built turnarounds than if they lay straight track, and the same thing was true for high embankments. By the way, when I was still a student at the railroad transport engineering institute before I was sent to work at the Gulag, I once visited Vitebsk for practical training. I had seen this crazy thing with my own eyes. At the time, though, none of us had any idea why it had been done that way.

My friend had been a working railway engineer his whole life. For many years he had worked in Belorussia, in the Ukraine, and in Siberia. During the years of Soviet power, though, he also spent some time in the Gulag. He was arrested for something someone else did, but he could never prove his innocence. He served his ten years, but his health had been damaged. He never wanted to tell me about those years that he spent in prison, and I did not pester him about them.

But he did tell me some stories that are especially tantalizing for a Russian railroad buff. Once when we were talking, I mentioned that even though I had graduated from a Moscow railroad institute, I still never understood why the railroads in every other country in the world used a track gauge of 1440 millimeters (except tiny Japan, where it is 1000 millimeters) but the track gauge in Russia was 1524 millimeters. It always seemed to me that this would not be so odd if the gauge were, say, 1500 or even 1520, but why did we have those extra four millimeters?

He told me that when he had been a student all those years ago, he had puzzled over the same question. Then one old professor had offered an answer. When Russia first started building its railroads, people all around the world already used the meter as a unit of measurement, but Russia still used the "sazhen."[1]

But the old professor had heard an even more interesting version. This one had to do not only with track gauge, but with the section of the railroad between Petersburg and Moscow. It seems that when they made the plans for building this line, high officials went for instructions to Emperor Nikolai I.[2] In his office, they spread out a map of Russia on the table. The emperor then took a ruler and placed it between Petersburg and Moscow and drew a straight line with a pencil. But, right where the emperor's finger held the ruler, the pencil slid off the ruler and drew around the finger. So that was how they built the rail line, straight as an arrow, except for where the emperor's finger had been. And in fact, the railroad track today between Moscow and Leningrad still curves off in a semicircle, "around the emperor's finger."

As for the railroad gauge, these high officials told Nikolai I that all over the world, the gauge normally used was 1440 millimeters. And they asked him: "Should we do the same, or make ours bigger?" And the answer they got was: "By the cock...bigger." When the officials left the emperor, they thought it over. How were they to understand the words of His Highness? If he were speaking metaphorically, then these words would mean "why bigger?" and then they should make the gauge at 1440 millimeters. But what if he really had in mind exactly what he'd said? None of the high officials would risk returning to the emperor's office to ask him what he had meant.

They decided to enlist help from Nikolai I's personal physician. They asked him to tell them how big the body part was that the emperor had mentioned. The doctor told them 84 millimeters, which they then they added to the 1440 and came up with 1524 millimeters.[3] So from that time on, the gauge of our railroads has been 1524 millimeters. And nowhere else in the whole world will you find this gauge.

As a result, when our trains have to go outside of our borders to foreign countries, we have to transfer all of the railcars and locomotives to wheeled trolleys. In the same way, when Russia is at war with neighbors, in order for us to attack outside our country, the railway troops have to alter the gauge. For a retreat of our troops, the enemy has to do the same thing on our railroads, which delays their advance into Russia. Such is how we live.

CHAPTER 22

PESCHANKA, A VILLAGE OF DEKULAKIZED PEOPLE ON THE RIVER PECHORA

WHEN WE WERE BUILDING THE APPROACH TO THE railroad bridge across the Pechora River in 1942, and I was out searching for good sand quarries, I heard about a nearby Russian village from the locals. Peschanka village sat in a forest on the high, sandy slope of the Pechora River's left bank. Russian peasants who had been dekulakized and forcibly moved to the North had built this village.[1] I found that the sand there was excellent, but it was too far away for us. Later, when we visited this place where the resettled people had made themselves at home, and we found that these folks were willing to barter with us for things we needed. We brought them clothing, and they gave us agricultural products, which all of us—the civilian railroad builders at the camp—greatly needed. At that time, in the spring of 1942, I did not have much time to focus on food very much, but the civilians' rations were very limited.

With fall approaching and the long Arctic winter looming, my comrades from the Camp Administration's 1st Region and I decided to ask the camp leadership for permission to go to that village. The leadership gave its blessing, and even promised to help with transportation. We went there twice. In the summer, we traveled by boat, and in the winter, we skied on the iced-over river. This village, especially compared to the small towns that the Komi lived in, made a big impression on us. In consisted of one long street along the river. All the houses were built on high foundations on deeply buried piles, since the local sand could not hold moisture. The homes themselves were made of high-quality pine logs, and they had large windows with shutters. The windows, doors, and porches on many of them were decorated with various jambs and lintels. Inside, the rooms were spacious, and every house had a large Russian stove. Each courtyard included various other buildings that they had built, as well.

When we arrived from Pechorlag, the people were noticeably distrustful and suspicious of us. It took a long conversation where we talked about ourselves and our views on life before the owner whose home we came to "softened" a little toward us. We very carefully asked them about their lives and their children, but they held their tongues and told us little. They also refused to accept the small bottle of liquor that we had brought along for them. Instead, when we settled up, they took it as partial payment along with the clothing we offered, for the food they were giving us.

Since the summer at the Arctic Circle was short, the "gifts of nature" which grew there in the sandy soil were limited. There were no tomatoes, and cucumbers were grown under glass, in forcing beds. But these peasants managed to get potatoes, turnips, onions, carrots and several other quick-growing vegetables, and so these were the things we got from them in our exchange.

The men in the village sported beards, and the women wore their hair in braids. These folks had a very vague understanding about what was going on in the world. They did not even know very much about the Soviet war with Germany. They listened to this part of our conversation with great interest.

The owner of the house I visited had a boat. The men in the family managed to catch fish at the fishing hole not only in the summer, but in the winter as well. So they gave us both fresh and dried smoked fish, too, as part of our exchange. In the fall, the entire family went out mushroom gathering, since there were lots of mushrooms in the surrounding woods.

I felt that they had a big grudge against the government, which had torn them from their native land. (They never did tell us where they had come from.) They had put down roots in the new place, and even if they got the permission to go back, they were not inclined to do so. "Now our home is here," said the wife, and the husband nodded his head in confirmation.

On our second visit to them, they were more polite. They thanked us for the presents we had brought for their children. They invited us to come back. But when we spoke with them, it was otherwise; again they were very reserved and cautious. My comrades and I came to the opinion that this caution and reserve was something that had resulted from the suffering they had lived through in being uprooted and resettled. We felt that this was a characteristic that they would have for the rest of their lives.[2]

As I sat with some of the residents of this village, I recalled what we had been taught in grammar school and at our institutes: The kulaks were class enemies of the Soviet people. But faced with a concrete example, like the peasants in the village of Peschanka, I started to believe otherwise. (I had had these sorts of thoughts earlier, too.) Now I understood that these people, in reality, were the hardest-working people we had in our countryside. They loved the land, and they learned how to work it well. And from an early age, they taught their children the skills for this difficult rural labor, which did not even allow free or normal "days off." For every day, from sunup to sundown, they devoted themselves to what they loved.

The earth, in turn, rewarded these workers, and they prospered. And for that very thing, the Stalinist regime unfurled its persecution on them. Millions of these peasants were physically destroyed, and others were condemned to hard labor camps or to exile in the depths of remote areas where the climate was difficult.

But a real toiler never disappears. The villagers who lived in Peschanka were an example of this, right before my very eyes. I left this village with a heavy heart and much turmoil in my soul. Why had the Communist Party, the government and the Soviet leadership done this?

CHAPTER 23

THE COUNTRYSIDE OF KOMI
ON THE RIVER USA

IN AUGUST OF 1943, I AGAIN RETURNED TO THE
headquarters of Pechorlag in the village of Abez. At this time, I was working as an instructor in the Political Department for Komsomol Affairs.
I spent a lot of time making trips throughout the entire camp, from
Vorkuta to Pechora, working with the Komsomol members.

While in Abez, I managed to find out what had become of my acquaintance who had been the director of the secret store for the leadership.
He was the person who had helped me so much by bringing me those
"deficit foods"[1] at the end of 1941, when I was recovering in the hospital.
It turned out that he had been transferred to another Gulag camp that
was located in a warmer area.

One day while I was living in Abez, a new comrade from the camp's
Political Department asked me if I wanted to go with him to the countryside, where the Komi people lived. They were settled very far away from
Abez, on the Usa River. He said that it was possible to trade a half-liter of
liquor for a deer carcass, and by doing this, we would have enough meat
for ourselves to last the whole winter. At that time, each civilian employee
received a ration card for one half-liter of liquor every month. I wasn't
that interested in drinking, although I was not against "knocking back a
few" now and again with good friends. The comrade himself got the permission from the leadership for the trip and for a low, wide sled with a
prisoner as our driver to go along with us. So he got it all together, and
the next Sunday we set off.

We left at dawn. A young female employee of the Camp Administration came along, as well. She was hoping to barter with the locals in the village. She brought along some ladies' clothing that she wanted to exchange for a little bit of butter.

Other people we knew who had already been in this Komi village had warned us that there was a certain way we needed to act to deal with the Komi. What our friends had told us, boiled down to this. We had to keep in mind that the Komi had lived century after century in a severe climate where for several months of the year there is hardly any sun, no electricity, and no radios. The distances are far between villages, and some villages consisted of just a few families. So, their communications with others is very limited. They live off of reindeer meat. These families exist on their own, with their herds of reindeer, for many months, wandering around the endless tundra, where you hardly see even a bush. These friends also told us that the Komi were strong, stern, phlegmatic, and intolerant of lying and cheating, but that they also very much valued real friendship, honesty and compassion toward others.

Knowing these few things helped us. Our friends told us that when you go into a Komi home, you should greet them, and without waiting for an answer, sit down on the bench near the exit. After you sit, then you tell them why you came. Let the woman take a look at you, study you, and think you over. After that, they will answer your questions, but they will take their time. If you do not follow this advice, our friends told us, you may end up getting nothing at all.

Once we got to the village, we saw ourselves how things were. The female friend who came along broke off from us and went off on her own to look for butter. My comrade and I chose two nearby houses and each of us went into "our own" houses. When I stepped over the threshold of that house, here is what I saw. Right in front of me, on the other side of the large room near the window sat the husband, making a harness. On the right side, the wife was bustling around a large stove. There were also several children in the room. When they saw an unfamiliar person come into their house, they ran up the nearby staircase that led to a landing just below the ceiling (where it's always warmer) covered in reindeer pelts. The children threw themselves down on these skins, but after a little while, I started to see their curious dark brown eyes looking at me.

I said, "Hello." The man and the woman continued to go about their business, as if nobody had come into their house and nobody had spoken. According to the advice I had received previously, I sat down on the

bench near the exit and asked the question: "Do you have any meat?"
Silence. After several minutes, the man asked, "Do you have any liquor?"
I answered, "Yes." For several more minutes he continued working on the
harness, then he lay down his awl and waxed thread, stood up, and went
into the unheated part of the house.

As recommended to me the day before, I stood up and followed him.
We went into a large unheated room with dirt floors. On poles that went
from wall to wall, hung the processed carcasses of reindeer (without their
skins and innards). The man pointed at them and said: "Pick one." Then
he held his hand out for the bottle of liquor. I gave it to him. He cleaned
the sealing wax from the cork, opened the bottle, and walked over to a
wooden block with an axe stuck in it, near a window. He put a couple of
drops of the liquor onto the block. Then he took some matches out of his
pocket, lit one and held it close to one of the drops of liquor. That scared
me: What if it does not catch fire? In fact, I had not tested it. But the
liquor lit up. The man smiled, and then led me, with my reindeer carcass
out of the unheated room to the front door.

That's how I came to have enough meat for the winter.

As I approached our sled with my reindeer carcass, the girl who had
come along with us showed up and said, in an agitated voice, "I am never
coming back here! Never in my life! I want to go home now!" I asked,
"But where's your butter?" And she replied, "What butter! It's impossible
to talk to them. These people are so rude!"

As it turned out, it was not rudeness at all. Because of the subtleties of
the Komi language, they had misunderstood each other. This girl had
waited a long time before deciding which house to go into. Finally she
picked one, went in and asked the man who lived there, "Do you have
any butter?" He answered her, "No meat, no butter." But he had spoken
to her in Komi. And this sounded like: "Yai abu, vyui abu." He had spoken the words very quickly. And in her mind, she separated each "ya" and
the two next words pronounced together became "vyuiabu."[2] Since the
man was totally drunk and alone in his house, she did not wait around to
see what would happen next, and shot like a bullet out of the house and
into the street, and all the way to the sled. I calmed her down. I explained
that in Komi, "abu" means "no" and "vyui" means "butter."

I went with along with her to another house where she managed to
exchange her things for some butter. Soon the third member of our
group came along with his carcass of reindeer, and we, feeling satisfied,
set off back to the camp.

The special features of life in Komi and the climate of the region influenced the architecture of the houses we saw in the village. There were two parts to their houses, a warm section and an unheated section. Since it is cold for most of the year, the ceilings in these houses are low and the windows are very small. If they have settled in an area that is not near a forest, the Komi live in big tents made from reindeer hides. The people also wear reindeer hide as their clothing. Their shoes are sewn from skin taken from the legs for the reindeer. They look very comfortable, warm, and beautiful.

That's how the Komi lived in the rural areas. In the cities, such as Syktyvkar and Vorkuta, the architecture of houses and the life of the population are the same as in other cities in other regions of Russia.[3]

CHAPTER 24

WOMEN AT PECHORLAG

I WANTED TO SHARE WHAT I KNOW OF THE FATE OF WOMEN who were sent to do time in prison and served their sentences in this northern subsection of the Gulag. Before starting, I should say that the units that I worked in housed only male prisoners. But once, in the middle of my time working at the 93rd Unit,[1] they sent a brigade of women to us. We were told to house them outside of the main camp, and in no circumstances were they to have anything to do with the male prisoners.

This was understandable. The prisoners, both men and women, who had been given long sentences and had been deprived of their rights to have relations with the opposite sex, sort of "went nuts" concerning the question of sex. They were willing to use any kind of contrivance or perversion to "taste the forbidden fruit."

On the other hand, if a female prisoner managed, despite the rules, to get pregnant, then all the same, she could lighten her heavy load. (She would see a decrease in the amount of physical labor, an increase in food, however meager, for the time she was breastfeeding, and so on.) Sometimes, if she had been sentenced as a criminal, not as a political, and she had served most of her time, then the pregnancy would mean that they could send her out to the settlement surrounding the camp, or even just set her free. And if she managed to prove that she had become pregnant from a civilian, or even better, an employee of the camp, she would have even more reason to hope for indulgence and for them to look more kindly on her future.

Therefore, the leadership of the camp kept close watch over both the female and male prisoners, to keep from having any contact with anyone of the opposite sex. They especially wanted to keep the prisoners from the civilian employees. Prisoners, by fair means or foul, tried to make connections with the opposite sex. If they could not hook up with someone, many of them went in for all kinds of perversions to somehow satisfy their sexual needs.

One of the most scandalous cruelties of our judicial system, I am convinced, was handing a prison term in the camps to a young girl, for some, small, insignificant crime. In the camp, no matter what her strengths and wishes were when she came in, the very circumstances could corrupt her "completely" and turn her into a prostitute.

For example, one time a young girl arrived at the unit for female prisoners. During a frank discussion I had with her at that time, she told me how before the Gulag, she had worked as a cashier in a store. Once, at the end of a workday, an object that she had needed for a long time turned up for sale in the manufactured goods section of the store. This happened on the evening before payday, and she did not have the 100 rubles she needed to pay for it. Since the next day she would be getting her pay packet, she decided to take this small sum from the cash register, thinking that the next day when she got paid she would return the money to the cash register.

So she bought the thing she needed, but before closing the store, a government commission descended on her. This commission discovered the shortfall of 100 rubles in her cash register, so they wrote her up and sent the matter to the court. She explained herself over and over again and tried to persuade or plead with them to let her give back the money, but they did nothing but commiserate with her. A hearing was held, and she was sentenced to three years in the Gulag. Normally, with such a short sentence, they did not send the person to a remote camp, but they sent her far away. Clearly, someone was displeased with her, or maybe things just turned out that way.

And then they put her in the "Black Raven,"[2] a closed truck for transporting prisoners to drive her from the prison to the courts. On the way, they stopped and pushed in another prisoner, a healthy man who also was being taken to court. As soon as the door of the truck was closed from behind and bolted, he threw himself on her and raped her. That's how she became a woman. And there was nobody to complain to about this.

After she was arrested and sent to the women's cell, that night, several recidivists fell on her. They brought out a little bag they had made and filled tightly with buckwheat groats in the shape of a male member. The recidivists held her hands and feet down, and violated her with it. When she resisted, they beat her unmercifully. The other women nearby were afraid to get involved and did not react to what was going on. The recidivists threatened her, saying that if she complained to the security guards, they would maim or kill her. So she kept silent.

Then when she arrived at Pechorlag she found out about lesbianism. Since she was so young, the barracks leader, the "Atamansha"[3] forced herself onto her, and she had no choice but to put up with her "fondling."

How could I help her? In the context of the camp, other than feeling bad for her, I could do nothing.

Another time, again at the 93rd camp unit, a group of about thirty women arrived, under armed guard. Since I had been told of this beforehand via the Selektor, I had managed to prepare a place for them, away from the main camp, in a nearby forest where there was a little flowing creek. On the banks of this creek sat a large building that had a fairly roomy bath with a steam room, a delousing chamber, and a place for drying, ironing, and storing the laundry. There were already women living in the back rooms, and we quickly built a shed nearby for storing the laundry and sewing. The women washed and ironed linens, and repaired the prisoners' clothes and sheets.

The day after we settled the new brigade into the building we had allotted for them, the labor assistant came to me and said that the brigade leader of the original group of women in the camp would like to see me. And until I agreed to see her, she told the labor assistant, not one woman would go to work. I told him to bring the brigade leader in to see me.

And into my office walked a very pretty young woman. She had a sort of a Gypsy look about her, with a strong, slender figure, long legs, and large dark eyes. Her long wavy dark hair was tied back with a red ribbon. She was very sure of herself. She greeted me and sat across from me at the table where I was sitting. She purposely moved her chair away from the table so that I could see her entire seductive figure. She pulled her skirt above her knees, crossed her legs, moved them close to me so that, as they say, "I had something to look at." Then she started a playful conversation.

However, before she had even arrived in my office, I had already asked the labor assistant to find out what she was about, and why the other women obeyed her without complaining. I also asked the labor assistant to think about whether or not she should be the brigade leader.

After looking into it, the labor assistant recounted an unbelievable story. It turns out that this young woman had developed physically very early and being very pretty, started seducing officers (the most financially secure sector of society). After dinner in a restaurant, she would then invite them to go with her to a secluded place just out of town, at the edge of a forest, where there were no other people. And then, just when the officer had gotten on top of her, she would kill him in cold blood with a knife to the heart. Then she stole his money and documents and disappeared. And she went on to look for the next victim. In the end, the authorities caught up with her, and arrested and sentenced her. The sentence for crimes like these is usually death, but since she was underage, they gave her ten years. All of the other women in the brigade were panic-stricken and feared her. And even though she was only seventeen years old, they obeyed her unconditionally.

Of course, before asking to meet me, she already had gotten her own reports on the leadership. She had found out that I was around twenty years old, that I was a bachelor, and that I did not have a girlfriend. So she decided to play on this. But I immediately put her on notice that we were not going to have any kind of close relationship. I wanted her to be perfectly clear about that.

Then she told me that she had a "camp husband" who worked at one of the nearby camp units as the labor assistant. Once a month he went to the headquarters of the 6th Department, which was near our unit, with his unit boss, their foreman, and an economist, to examine and approve their unit's plan for the next month.

"Let's do this," she said. "When they come to department headquarters, you arrange for them to stay over night in our unit. And since they travel without any guards, you can let him come and stay the night with me. If you do this, in exchange, I promise you that all the women in my brigade will fulfill 150 percent of the plan, no matter what work you give them. Otherwise, they will not work at all."

What could I do? For the boss and foreman of a unit, which I was at that time, work is work, and the main thing was that the prisoners worked and fulfilled the plan. Otherwise, there would be scandal, persecution, and unpleasantness.

I agreed, and with this agreement, we parted. After she left, the labor assistant told me his opinion of how things stood. He said that it would not be worth it to try and take the brigade leader position away from her. Besides that, no matter whom we gave the job to in the brigade, the women would still obey her. We would just be making more problems for ourselves.

After a while, I heard that a group was arriving from a neighboring unit, headed for department headquarters. I arranged for them to stay overnight at our unit. One of the members of this group was a very colorful character: a young, strong, sturdy man who stood a little under two meters high.[4] Although it was winter, he wore no hat, and he had a wide red ribbon tying up his thick, chestnut-colored hair. You could see his bare body, which was covered with hair, because he wore an unbuttoned padded jacket and roomy pants held up by a wide red belt. This was the labor assistant, the "camp husband" of the brigade leader.

I have to add that after that meeting I had with her, the entire brigade immediately began to fulfill the plan by 150–200 percent. But the brigade leader had still not given up on seducing me. Once, we had a little encounter in the bathhouse. Before I got there, the bathhouse had been carefully washed down. I always washed alone. So this time, I undressed, and prepared three tubs of hot water. One was for my feet, another for washing, and the third was a reserve. I had just started washing my head when the door opened up and in came the beautiful brigade leader, who was wearing the smallest of undershirts. Taking little, soft steps toward me, she said, "Citizen Boss, can I rub your back?"

When I saw that she was nearly nude, my "male side" immediately reacted. She noticed this and started walking confidently toward me. The bathhouse was a pretty sizable place, so to get to where I stood was about eight or ten steps.

What to do? On the one hand, I desperately desired a woman, and what's more, right there was my seductress. But on the other hand, I knew that I would never make up for such an act, not in a lifetime. She was already very near me now.

Suddenly I grabbed the tub that I had filled with boiling water, and splashed a bit of it toward her. With a mean look on my face, looking her right in the eye, I said, in a voice that would not allow her to have any doubts: "Get out of here, or I will scald you and destroy your beauty!"

Surprised, she stopped, trying to figure out whether or not I was serious. I then threatened to dump the tub of boiling water right in her face. Obviously, she was afraid of losing her magical charm, so I had gotten the upper hand. With the words "What a fool, what a fool," she left. With this incident, all of her attempts to get closer to me ended.

After a few months, this brigade was sent off to an all-female camp unit.

Civilians entered into intimate relations with prisoners quite frequently. Sometimes these relationships were simply all about satisfying physical needs. Then everything was pretty simple, especially if there were no pregnancies. But once the discovery of the relationship was made on the "civilian side" (and these were not always all men, sometimes there were women), the civilian would be transferred to another camp, far from where the "other party" lived.

It was more complicated when a couple found true love. This happened, as it turns out, quite frequently. Then the "civilian side" by hook or by crook would try to stay near their sweetheart in the camp, or at least near the camp, and wait for their loved one to be freed. A few examples come to mind.

The first one concerns a young female engineer who was sent after graduating from an institute to work in one of the Gulag camps, somewhere in Siberia. There, she fell in love with a prisoner, who was also an engineer. Then they sent that prisoner to work as an engineer at Pechorlag. The female persuaded the leadership to let her also be transferred to Pechorlag. She settled in a job not far from the camp that her loved one was serving time in. I knew both of them. I would ask her, "How long will you wait, living this terrible life?" And she would answer, "Until he is let out." That kind of love merits respect.

In another case, my comrade from the Political Department (I'll call him Boris) and I somehow ended up together on one of the low, open sleds going off for vacation along the tracks. We found ourselves in a horrible snowstorm. The horse could hardly find the road. We decided to stay overnight at a nearby camp unit. This happened to be a punishment unit, whose residents were mostly hardened criminals and gangsters. It would be difficult to describe how surprised we were when we found out that the unit boss was a young, nice-looking woman, who was not even yet thirty years old. She welcomed us warmly, and prepared a tasty, lavish dinner that she served with liquor. We relaxed and started talking to her, and we talked the whole night. I looked at her and was constantly amazed. How could she get on with such out-and-out criminals as her prisoners? And what was the leadership thinking to assign a delicate, soft, young woman to this job? There were plenty of men who could not have done this kind of work.

As we talked, I gradually understood. It turns out that her husband (a crazy risk-taking, cocky sort), was a prisoner serving time in this unit. But he was not simply serving time. The zone's entire criminal riffraff feared him, and was under his command. He forced them to work, which was generally a rarity among this category of men. The camp leaders knew the real situation, closed their eyes to it all, and kept the wife of such a valued cadre with her husband. They even gave her the nominal job of unit boss. In fact, he was the unit boss and he ran everything. This love relationship was also secret, although it had received the blessing of the highest leadership.

For years, neither Boris nor I could get over being surprised at what we had heard that night. A few years later, Boris unexpectedly renewed his friendship with this good-looking camp unit lady, in a way that again stoked the fires of our imaginations.

At the end of the 1940s, after graduating from the Higher Diplomatic School,[5] I was assigned to work at the Ministry of Foreign Affairs in Moscow, which was at that time located on the corner of Kuznetskii Most and Liubianka across from the NKVD (then, the MVD and the KGB). This was still "during Stalin." Since Stalin worked at night, all the ministers worked at night, too. But Stalin slept during the day, and so did the ministers, but we ordinary employees had to work day and night. It was terrible. At that time Boris was working at the MVD (the KGB) and also was incredibly tired. But we were young, and we needed human contact, and the chance to let off some steam. At times, we would phone each other, then take an hour-long walk in the evening, wandering through the neighboring streets and alleys.

On one of these walks, Boris told me how he had been walking late at night along Kuznetskii Most, when he bumped into our female acquaintance from Pechorlag. She was very happy to meet again. She said that her husband had long ago gotten out of prison, and that they were living in a one-room apartment on Liubianka not far from the Ministry of Internal Affairs building (the former NKVD). Her husband was working in Siberia as upper management at the site where they were building the Abakan-Taishet rail line,[6] and she was working as an employee in Railroad Planning. (Both of them worked for the NKVD-MVD.) They had had a son, whom she had sent off for the entire winter to forestry school, and so at that moment, she was living alone. She invited Boris up to her apartment, and he accepted.

Her building had a long center hallway, with one-room apartments lining both sides. The bathroom (one bathroom served all the apartments) and the kitchen were at the end of the hall.[7] She quickly prepared some appetizers, and without intending to, the two of them drank two bottles of vodka while reminiscing. At the time, Boris was single, and had been worrying about not having the time for any romance. So it was very pleasurable to relax in her company.

They had lingered on very late, when she suddenly brought in a washbasin of water, spread out on the bed and said: "Wash your feet and lie down. I'm going to bed now." And she left. Soon she returned, dove under the blanket next to him and they spent the night together. In the morning, she made him breakfast and shocked him with the following words: "I'm going to work. I like you. Here are your keys to the apartment. Here are your sheets. Our day together will be Thursdays. Plan your days so that you will be with me that evening and overnight. And on the other days you can, if you like, hang out here until 8:00 PM. No later. If you like, you can bring other women here. I am not jealous. Here is my telephone number at work. Call me." And she left.

He was glad that he had so easily solved the "female problem" that had worried him, and for several months he enjoyed his life. At the same time, he still wanted to have a family of his own, and he was looking for a suitable candidate. But work took up most of his time and the problem remained unsolved. Then, one day, he met an intelligent young girl, who was naïve and shy. He liked her very much. One evening they went out to the theater (for which he had had to ask for leave from his boss). He took her home around midnight, and when he was walking to the metro, he suddenly remembered: "Today is Thursday. I am supposed to be at my friend's house on Liubianka." But still warm with sweet memories of his evening with the young woman, he decided not to go, nor even to call her the next day. Several days later, even so, he called, and what he heard shocked him. When he asked to speak to her, a male voice with a noticeable amount of compassion said, "You know, she passed away." So he asked, "When?" the man replied, "Sometime between Thursday and Friday."

Boris phoned me saying that he needed to see me immediately. He was depressed and frightened. "You can understand this," he said, "If I had been with her on that Thursday, and she would have died in my arms...What would I have done? The hall is long and the neighbors would all be in the picture, and I would be in my military uniform, with her. What would I have done? Run to the phone booth out on the street to call the emergency squad? Then the doctors would have come and recorded the death. And who am I? The doctors also would have found out that before her death, she had had sexual relations. And her husband also works for the NKVD-MVD. He would have to be called right away, and how would I have explained everything to him? Where had I come from? Plus, I'd have to tell it all to my boss."

Almost every day for the next two weeks or so, Boris wanted me to walk with him around those neighboring alleys. In a million ways he went over and over this theme, thanking God and the girl he had not wanted to leave that night to go to his Thursday night rendezvous.

At the end of the second week, he finally calmed down. And suddenly, again I got a phone call. "We need to meet immediately." We met. And he, who could not be more surprised than he was at the beginning of this story, said, "I was sitting at work, doing my job. A normal phone call. I picked up the receiver and suddenly I hear her muffled voice. 'Where did you go? Why don't you call me?' As if from another world."

The end of this story is sad. After they met again, he went to see her several times. But somehow, something in his body had broken, because no matter how hard they both tried, he could not have sexual relations with her any longer. He had become totally impotent with her.

Soon spring came and she left for the Gulag camp where her husband worked.

CHAPTER 25

A FELLOW TRAVELER FROM ABEZ TO PECHORA

ALTHOUGH MY MEMORIES OF THIS MAN ARE A BIT OFF the topic of my work in the Gulag, still he is a good example of the range of people who ended up as prisoners in the Gulag. In those years, his court case was broadcast across the entire country. Since *Izvestiia* published the name of the convicted man, I will also do so here. His name was Boris Borisovich Tseitlin.

As I mentioned earlier, one day in January 1942, we ended up sharing a sleigh out of the prison camp. When we introduced ourselves, we realized that we had met earlier. When I had been sick in the hospital in the village of Abez (October–December 1941), I used to take walks through the village streets while I was recovering. Once I stepped into a photography workshop at the Camp Administration. Several qualified photographers (who were prisoners free to move around without being under armed guard) were working there. Tseitlin, who was my fellow traveler in the sleigh, had been the boss of this workshop.

I had already heard about him from the other civilian employees at the Camp Administration. They said that aside from being a great master photographer, he was also a famous film director and documentary maker, as well. He had landed in prison for his scandalous "exploits" with women. My acquaintances from the Camp Administration told me that at the end of the 1930s, the newspaper *Izvestiia* had dedicated an entire article to his escapades.

According to my friend, that article began more or less with the following words: "Who would think that in the capital of our Motherland, Moscow, in the center of our cinematography studios, Mosfilm,[1] that there could exist a den where grown men were living with and corrupting under-aged girls." Further, the article gave the details of what took place in the courts after this was discovered. The accused was sentenced to a long prison sentence in the strict regime camps.

When I first met Tseitlin in that photography studio at the Gulag Camp Administration, I had told him that when I was a student, I had loved photography, too. I had taken a lot of pictures, and even learned how develop film and print photos. He showed me around his expensively equipped workshop, and told me that the Gulag camp leadership at Pechorlag and their wives liked his photographs. He also bragged that he (unlike the other unescorted prisoners) was allowed to sleep overnight outside the zone, in the building that housed the photography workshop. He even showed me his cozy bedroom.

Indeed, the several photos that he took for me showed a rare artistry. He was especially talented with lighting. At that time, I sent these photos out to all of my relatives and friends. Remember, that was when I had the doctors' threat hanging over my head that "I wouldn't live to see spring." Today those are our most treasured photographs in my family album.

So that was how I first met this man. And then, out of the blue, we were thrown together again on a long sled trip. We were both traveling to the south of the prison labor camp, and we had to stay overnight at various camp units along the way. In the camp, there were no hotels. As a civilian employee, my choices outside the zone were to spend the night either in the security platoon building or in the foreman's place. (The camp unit bosses at that time had all been sent to the army, so they were not even around.)

Since Tseitlin was a newly freed prisoner, the authorities wanted to put him up overnight in the zone. But I took him along with me. If the foreman did not have a free bed, then we slept somewhere else in his dugout. And we ate together. While we were in the village of Pechora, I helped get him permission to stay in the civilians' dormitory.

Tseitlin had traveled a lot, and in particular, he had been outside of Russia, which at that time was very rare. He spoke brilliantly, and would tell me interesting stories about what he had heard and seen on his travels.

Later, I became convinced that he had the gift of hypnosis. I saw him do this myself. While we were staying in Pechora village, I soon met a

young nurse who lived not far from the men's dormitory, where we had a
tiny room. This nurse was a shapely brunette, serious and reserved for a
young person, but at the same time cheerful and happy. She invited us
over to her place one evening. Before we went, my fellow traveler said: "If
you want me to, I can hypnotize her, and she will do everything that I tell
her to do, absolutely everything. We could both enjoy ourselves." I, of
course, refused.

At that point, I still doubted that he could hypnotize people. On our
way to her place, he told me that of course it was impossible to hypnotize
people who had a strong will, but that with girls, he had never missed. So
I agreed that if no harm were done, he could try an experiment on the
girl we were visiting.

Still it was a shock when, in the middle of visit, he looked into the
girl's eyes and started insisting that water was coming into the room. The
girl immediately became upset. And he said, "The water is rising, higher
and higher," and the girl got onto her feet, on the chair. He said, "The
water is higher, it's almost up to your knees." The girl in fear and confu-
sion began to pull up her skirt above her knees. He said, "The water is
rising," and she pulled her skirt up high enough to show her
underwear.

I said, "That's enough." So he told her, "The water is going down,
down," and the girl started to pull her skirt back down. He said, "The
water is already below the chair," and she pulled her skirt all the way back
down.

When my fellow traveler returned her to normal, she did not remember anything.

On other occasions, we went to the movies together. I remember we
saw the film *Women*. Once he told me that the actress in a film we saw was
very passionate. Then there were times when he would invite several men
over. He would be the one in the middle of them. Later, he began to
extol the "charms" of collective love, where one woman would satisfy the
wishes of two partners at the same time, or even three partners. With my
upbringing at the time, I did not believe him. I was sure that he was just
telling outrageous lies, so I just ended the conversation if he started talking like that.

Once when we were traveling to Pechora, he spotted a deck of cards
in my backpack. In a few quick movements, he began to play tricks with
them. He told me that he had found that card tricks were a sure key to a
woman's heart, if they let him use them. Later, I became convinced that

there was a grain of truth in this, and however strange it is, what the cards say sometimes comes true. He could also read palms, which, in his words, also made women notice him. When I asked about palm reading, he showed me the basics of palmistry (chiromancy).

One day he agreed to show some of his tricks at the village club. He was as good at card tricks as a professional artist, and the public loved him.

During one of our evenings, I asked him if it were true that several years ago the newspaper *Izvestiia* had published a large article about a judicial action against him, in which they described his escapades with women. I wanted to find out if all that had really happened, and how truthfully they had written about him. Without a shadow of embarrassment, he told me that this article had appeared, and that everything in it had been true. Then he himself explained how he had gone about finding fourteen- and fifteen-year-old girls and teaching them to have sex.

The point of his narrative came down to this. He told me that it was well known that young women, especially the pretty ones, dream of becoming actresses and starring in movies. So he and his closest friends at Mosfilm decided to make use of this fact. On a nice day, they would take out an unusual vehicle, a pickup truck that had an open truckbed in the back. There, they would load a large camera on a tripod, and go out to Gorky Street, in the center of Moscow. This is where young people liked to stroll, as they say, "to see and be seen." They would drive slowly along the sidewalk and when they found a seductive girl walking along "to see and be seen," they would slow down the car and start filming her. She, obviously, would notice them.

Sometimes, the filmmakers would turn around after going 100 meters (328 feet) or so, and do another take. Then they would stop the car to approach the object of their attention. They would tell her that they were from Mosfilm and that they were looking for young girls to star in a new movie they were shooting. Tseitlin would mention his name to her, knowing that he was very famous and everyone knew who he was. Then he would invite her to Mosfilm to take a look, with him, at her "first shoot." Generally, the girl they had chosen was overcome with happiness. They would tell her that they were always looking for new talent, but that sometimes, naturally beautiful women could look expressionless and washed out on film. They would say that so much depended on the skill of the filmmaker, on the lighting, on the corner where the shoot had taken place, and on a whole host of things. If all of these things came together, they would say, then the model could "sparkle."

Therefore, he would tell her, they would need more than one shot. In fact, they would need many to get everything right. They would agree on a day and time when she could go to Mosfilm to see her "first shot." But before this, Tseitlin would advise the girl not to tell any of her friends or family about the understanding they had come to. In case nothing came of the shoot, if it just was not very good, then she would not have gotten everyone all excited for nothing. He would add that when they looked for a new model, they always shot and looked at hundreds of clips to get the best one. This was the movies! Tseitlin at this point would say that if the "shoots" were successful, then she, in his opinion, would get the role and star in the film. The Mosfilm coworkers who had come along with him would all agree with him.

At this point, they would part. Tseitlin had created the impression with her that her success depended only on him. When she would show up at the appointed time, Tseitlin's people would meet her at the door of Mosfilm and take her to the viewing room. Tseitlin would be sitting nearby. He would turn out the lights and up on the screen would appear Gorky Street, and then on Gorky Street would appear the girl. Tseitlin would talk out loud as if he were sharing his impressions with his colleagues. He would compliment her figure, discuss separate parts of her body "as objects," criticize something in order to express a little doubt, and in so doing, the girl's head would begin to spin.

Then they would turn on the lights, congratulate her and invite her to have a little drink of champagne with them to celebrate her "first debut." And how could she refuse this? They pumped her full of wine until she was slightly drunk, toasting "to the future actress."

After this, Tseitlin would tell her that they had only a short time in which to pick out the candidate for the role. He would suggest that they immediately do a new "shoot," but this time, not outside, but inside, to see how her figure and her body would look on screen. They would encourage her first to bare her shoulders, and they would film her. Then they would encourage her to bare her chest. The scene would be filmed again. Later they would tell her that she needed to act as if she were at the beach, and that she needed to undress. Again they would film her. And it would go on and on just like this.

By the second or third meeting, Tseitlin would lean on the girl to shack up with him, and as a "reward," he would include her in a scene with a lot of other actors in a film he was making. And he would give her a little money for her participation in the movie. And with this, as a rule, came "the birth of a new actress." But at this point, Tseitlin would hand his new lover over to his friends, so they could play the same role, and he would begin looking for another girl.

However, it turned out that one of the girls he picked up had prominent parents, and she confessed everything to them. A scandal erupted. Tseitlin of course had connections, which were good enough to keep him from getting the maximum punishment and got him out of prison fairly quickly, but they were not good enough to completely stop the scandal from going public.

Tseitlin got the feeling pretty early on that I had not had any experience in relationships with the beautiful opposite sex, and that I was a total zero, as he said "in matters of love." So during those long, boring evenings, my unexpected fellow traveler tried to enlighten me in these matters. I listened to him with a certain interest, since before that, I had never heard anything like what he was saying. But inside, I stayed a little guarded, so that he could not warp me with his cynicism and his feeling that women existed solely as objects of his desire.

At this time in Pechora village, as I said earlier, in the evenings, there was no place to go. In order to discuss such intimate topics, we had to either go to work and look for empty offices, or if the weather permitted, stroll along the snowy roads in the pine forest. Compared to everyone else I had met in Pechora, my fellow traveler from Abez, in his way, was a real find, a "walking book" of all of his moral abnormalities.

One day my fellow traveler left the sleigh at his destination, and our lives never crossed paths again. However, at the end of the 1940s, in Moscow, I once found myself in the company of some young people, and while talking about this and that, someone mentioned chance acquaintances. One of the girls in the group, a Moscow University graduate, a shapely, pretty brunette with a proud bearing and unusually large brown eyes recalled something that had happened to her. Soon after the end of the war, when she was a student, someone in a Moscow University club (which was located across from the Manezh Theater) introduced her to an imposing man from the world of film.

In the beginning, she was interested, and agreed to go out with him. He was very attentive. He brought a beautiful bouquet of flowers with him on every date. He tried to impress her with stories about other countries he'd visited, or other odd things that had happened to him or his friends. He could do card tricks, and read palms. But one time, she said, she felt that he was trying to hypnotize her. She became very frightened, but managed to overcome the sleepy feeling he was causing in her. Then she cut off all contact with him.

That man was the same one I had once known: Boris Borisovich Tseitlin.

PART IV

FINAL WORDS

CHAPTER 26

THE END OF MY STORY

AT THE BEGINNING OF 1946, THE NKVD WAS RENAMED the USSR Ministry of Internal Affairs, or USSR MVD. The Gulag was subsumed into this ministry.[1]

Since Fascist Germany and militarized Japan had capitulated, the necessity to subordinate one's life to the demands of winning the war disappeared. It became possible to follow your heart. I still wanted to continue my studies. In reality, I saw this as my chance to leave the Gulag and return to my former institute, to the Department of Railroad Projecting and Planning, as a graduate student. The head of the department, with whom I met in January immediately after I returned from Orel, was the same one who had been at the institute when I'd studied there and when I had graduated. He remembered me and was totally ready to help me come back to graduate school. But before that, I needed to get discharged from the Gulag. The question was: how to do this?[2]

It turned out that my colleague in the Political Department at Pechorlag, recalled above as Boris, was working in 1946 in the Secretariat as a deputy minister for cadres at the Ministry of Internal Affairs (the NKVD, renamed the MVD). It was this Boris who came to my aid. He and I brainstormed on how to get me out of the Gulag. This is what he came up with. First, I should leave Gulag for the Main Administration of Highways USSR NKVD-MVD, which was doing the planning work on the Baikal-Amur Rail Line. There, I would work as an engineer in the Baikal expedition.

Since the Railroad Planning Department was in the same system as GULAG NKVD-MVD, Boris managed to convince his boss, who was the deputy minister of cadres MVD to meet with me. After the meeting, Boris's boss wrote an order to transfer me. The head of the Political Department of the Gulag was very angry, but he was not going to get into a competition with a deputy minister (who outranked him). So in this way, I was administratively returned to being simply an engineer. Then, the railroad engineering institute from which I had graduated in 1940, agreed that in a half year they would request that the Railroad Planning Department release me to graduate school.

It seemed that everything was clear and shaping up successfully for me at that time.

However, unexpected circumstances arose that would alter these plans drastically. Somewhere in the beginning of that year, 1946, the NKVD/MVD's Communist Party Committee secretary called me in to his office. He said: "I see that you are very eager to go back to school. Why do you have to go back to MIIT? Wouldn't you like to become a diplomat?" I was puzzled by this question, so I asked where he had gotten that idea. Then he explained that the Communist Party Committee had been allotted some slots that they could use to recommend two people to be sent to study at the Higher Diplomatic School of the USSR Ministry of Foreign Affairs. The two people he would nominate for these slots had to already have a degree in higher education, and they had to be able to handle independent work.

"We want to recommend you," said the Party Committee Secretary, "but there is one hitch. Before you can enroll in this school, you have to pass some examinations. These tests require a knowledge at the level of the history faculty at Moscow State University. And you have a technical background. But the exams are in July, so there is still time. Try and get yourself prepared as best you can. Spend your time off on this. Do you agree to do this?"

I had to answer right away, so I decided to try for it. The expeditions to the Baikal-Amur Railroad, I thought, would not miss me. Becoming a professional diplomat was a very enticing idea. So, from this moment on, I began to seriously prepare for the exams. In the end, I passed them successfully and was sent to this school, to the English section.

This is how I left the Gulag and the system of the NKVD-MVD.

As I recall those years in the Gulag, I see that so many things in my life happened by chance. By chance, I became a student of lathe-turning at the factory called "Borets." Since the Komsomol School at this factory was located in the MIIT building, I became a student at this same institute.

No less by chance, I was sent after graduation from MIIT to the NKVD's Gulag. It was by chance that at Pechorlag, I became very ill, and after recovering I was sent to the southern part of the construction site, where I landed in a place where the camp's Political Department head noticed me. He liked me, and that is how I came to change my profession from engineer to Komsomol worker. And it was absolutely by chance that in trying to continue my education by going to graduate school at MIIT, that I ended up at the Higher Diplomatic School of the USSR Ministry of Foreign Affairs (MID).

The series of chances go even further. At the Higher Diplomatic School I was preparing to work in the United States, then I went to China, where I took the path from trainee to diplomat. After twenty years of working at MID, I became the head of the Section on China in the Central Committee of the CPSU. After some time there, they offered me the position of ambassador to Thailand, but instead of this, suddenly the CPSU Central Committee decided to send me to do intelligence work.

The science of philosophy teaches us that chance is a function of necessity. Therefore, my life went along according to science. But it is still not clear, where this "function of necessity" came from. And who calculated and determined this "necessity?" For now, there is no scientific answer to these questions. But the fate of every person belongs only to him—it is inimitable and unique.

CHAPTER 27

THE REAL ESSENCE OF THE GULAG

ON FEBRUARY 21, 1944, A TELEGRAM ARRIVED AT THE Camp Administration from the deputy minister of the NKVD. This telegram stated that I was being reassigned, and that I was to report to the ministry's Department of Cadres. These years of my life had been very difficult ones for me, not only living at the Arctic Circle, but doing so in the conditions of the GULAG NKVD prison camp, witnessing the monstrous inventions of the Stalinist regime. And to get away from a job at the Gulag on one's own during the war years was practically impossible.

Although I had been against being transferred from engineering work to the Komsomol job, actually it was thanks to this that I got my "out" from the North, and from working with prisoners. Although the camp where I was sent to work in the Political Department as the deputy director for Komsomol Affairs was also a part of the vast economy of the Gulag, this camp covered territory that had been only recently liberated from the Fascists. There, I worked only with civilian youth, because they were the biggest part of the collective of workers there.

As I look back on the path I took, I know that I was a completely different person when I left Pechorlag after three and a half years. For one thing, I no longer believed the myth that Soviet propaganda had stubbornly and insistently crafted about our punitive agencies.[1] The myth that the NKVD agencies concerned themselves only with protecting the peaceful labor of all Soviet citizens from intrigues of internal and external enemies had been quickly dispelled. These agencies were supposedly helping out people who had stumbled, or who had committed crimes, by using work to reeducate them. But it wasn't as if they sincerely tried to get people out of prison quickly so they could go back to normal life, to a healthy family of Soviets, who were the builders of a new society.

Little by little I began to see with my own eyes the inhumanity and basic criminal character of the Soviet leadership's policies in this area. As a patriot of our country, for a while I searched for ways to explain away our government's carelessness and incompetence. I looked for reasons why our government seemed unable to put into practice the party's lucid plans for building the first socialist state in the world.

And, as they say, "he who seeks will always find." I thought back on the conversation we three young engineers had in the Gulag Department of Cadres, just before we left for Pechorlag, where we discussed what a noble mission the GULAG NKVD had been given. I remembered the time at Pechorlag when Moscow found out about the huge numbers of prisoner deaths in the camps, and how they immediately fired all the camp bosses and sternly punished them. I have recorded the emergency measures that Pechorlag's new bosses undertook to get the food and clothing off of the barges and ships that had gotten stuck in the river when winter came on earlier than expected. So, I thought, the party and the government not only showed that they cared enough to provide everything the camp needed in good time, but that they were actually able to do it.

Also, I now see how smart it was that the Soviet leadership decided to immediately start building a railroad from Kotlas to Vorkuta and to declare it a site of military significance. This was a far-sighted and wise decision, and totally corresponding with the reality of the approaching war.

But here I must end my quest for facts that would defend my convictions. Because the facts of Pechorlag's harsh reality that are stored in my memory are completely different. As a witness of this reality, I cannot defend my beliefs or provide any good explanations about what went on. I have to ask the following questions.

Question: Why were honest Soviet patriots who volunteered on the Finnish front in the ski battalions for "the campaign at the rear of the enemy" accused in the name of the motherland of being political criminals and given long prison sentences? This was after they had routed the Finns (who were superior fighters in many ways), had encircled them, and had taken them prisoner (many of them injured). The reality is that these Soviet soldiers had been volunteers and they had battled desperately, as long as they could.

Question: Why were enormous numbers of intelligentsia charged as political criminals and sentenced with long prison sentences (and only to hard labor) in the camps? They were only there because their beliefs did not always coincide with the official line of the Soviet government. Moreover, such severe sentences were out of line, since they were often sent to the Gulag for a trivial reason, like for a political anecdote. They were arrested under the special statute No. 58 of our criminal code that charged people "for anti-Soviet behavior." They sentenced a huge number of political prisoners under this statute. For instance, at the 95th camp unit, I met a political prisoner who was a young fellow, a student at a technical school, who at sixteen years old was given seven years in camp for relating an anecdote that someone unthinkingly told him. As a result, his entire life was turned upside down. From that time, he carried the stigma of "counterrevolutionary." Was he really such an "out-and-out criminal" that they needed to isolate him from society and ruin his life?

It's no accident that there was this anecdote from that time: In connection with a purge of the party they called to a committee a CPSU member and asked him if he had ever wavered in following the party line. He answered: "Yes, I have. As the party line moved around, so did I." This is what happens to those who "followed the various party lines"— they could end up banished to prison.

Question: What kind of political criminals could peasants be? These were folks who loved the land, worked it with their families and children, and by dint of working hard, got reasonable results? Why was this a reason to stick them with the stigma of "kulak" and repress them?

Question: Why did they send small-time criminals off to camp for long prison sentences? Was it just to have a huge army of workers who would, with the stroke of a pen, be sent to labor-intensive construction work in far-flung remote regions with terrible climatic conditions?[2] The explanation that the goal of punitive labor was the construction of "the happy socialist future in the conditions of capitalist encirclement" is simply naïve. Who needs this "future" at such a price?

Question: Why did the Camp Administration give the out-and-out criminals (such as thieves, killers, the big-time bribe-takers, and rapists) all kinds of privileges in comparison to the politicals in the camps? As the part of the zek population with nonpolitical status, they were given opportunities to work for the Camp Administration, to get easy jobs, and to receive reduced sentences. Why, when these people were actually the more dangerous elements for society?[3] In the presence of the camp security platoon on the outside, these criminals ran the camp on the inside, by terrorizing, and subordinating the other prisoners to themselves.

The Camp Administration knew this was going on, and instead of putting a stop to it, let it serve its own greedy interests. The recidivists also trained deputies for themselves from among the young fellows (who were often in prison for some minor offence) who were new to the prison. They went after other prisoners whose sentences were longer and obviously did not correspond to the character and seriousness of their crimes, which gave them plenty of time to cultivate their successors.

Question: The maturity of every society is reflected in the attitude toward women, upon whom the continuation of mankind depends. Civilization in every century starts with this. I was convinced (they taught us this from childhood) that we in the Soviet Union, under the leadership of the Communist Party, were building the most advanced society in the world, known as a "socialist" society. But if this were truly so, then why were women treated so barbarically in the camps? And why did they send women to camp for trivial misdemeanors, sometimes for a very long time? In our Gulag camps, the young mothers were sent back to work two months after they gave birth. Often they were still weak because they had not yet recovered their strength, and yet there they were, under threat of punishment if they did not fulfill the plan. They were allowed to see their children only during breast-feeding, and after that, they were allowed to hold their babies in their arms for less than an hour.

Why did we devastate these mothers' souls, even if they were prisoners? For what reason did they deprive these barely developed little creatures from burying themselves in their mothers' breasts? Why do this when it just meant sending these unfortunate women who had been alienated from their children back into our society? And what kind of future awaited the children who were born in our camps, whom the Camp Administration then had to handle according to the rules?

Besides making the lives of women in prison more humane, the authorities could have postponed their punishment, or let them live outside of the camp units, which might have softened their mood and lowered the chances of recidivism. But this was not done—the Soviet leadership did not think about this. Why? "Not enough time?" Or because women in our country were viewed, above all, as being on the same level with men, and were considered as a necessary labor force for the building of "the new society?"

They hid the truth about the Gulag from ordinary citizens, I realized, and these citizens believed the official propaganda. But there was no way that the party and government leaders, along with their closest circles, did not know what was actually going on with the NKVD and the Gulag camps. This policy cannot be explained away as just being mistakes that other people made. If we were building the most advanced, first socialist government in the world, then where did this policy come from? Once they hid it from the population, this meant that the same leaders who came up with it and insisted that they were changing the world, these leaders knew that this policy was at its very core criminal and bad for people. And all the same, they implemented it.

Why? For what? Could it really be for the sake of speeding up the building of "a new socialist society" for future generations, at the cost of many lives and the suffering of the present population? But if it were that, then this is a barbarity that has nothing to do with socialism at all! Socialism is an idea that you may accept, you may repudiate, you may consider it a utopia, or you may fight to have it declared the official course of our country. But why would you torment people in the pursuit of it, when the idea of socialism and communism is for the good of people?

I still to this day have not found any convincing answers to these questions for myself.

Afterword

The Nature of Memoir

As one reads Fyodor Mochulsky's reminiscences, questions may arise about how accurately he describes life in the Gulag in the 1940s, or even about the man himself. What are we to make of a person who recounts his story as if it had taken place in a normal work-place, and not in an unimaginable hell? In some ways, this very question gets at the heart of what a memoir is. It is not always verifiable history; it is one person's selected recollections from a part of his life that he deems significant. It is a window through which readers can experience, with images, recalled conversations, and clear descriptions, places that may no longer exist (such as Pechorlag) or that have changed over time. Mochulsky's memoir is historical, however, in that it captures both a moment in the life of the writer and in the history of a place. At best, a memoir is a personal look at something that can illuminate the telling details of a larger historical moment. Still, some readers may have doubts about the entire genre of memoir, and questions about a memoirist's believability or his memory of events.

The dictionary definition of a memoir is straightforward. A memoir, says the *Oxford English Dictionary*, is a "record of events or history written from personal knowledge or the experience of the writer, or based on special sources of information."[1] Because the Gulag experience was so horrible, was so large, and existed for so many years, many eyewitness accounts have been written. They vary in style, tone, and point of view, but each one is of interest. In the case of the Soviet Gulag, most memoirs were written by former prisoners. Mochulsky was not a convict, so his experience at the same place was markedly different. We can see what an important difference this is by contrasting Mochulsky's Gulag camp boss experience with, for instance, Nadezhda Mandelstam's haunting account of the bogus arrest of her husband, the poet Osip Mandelstam, who died in a transit camp on his way to Kolyma.[2]

Both of these memoirists were caught up in the violent history of the USSR. Because of his young age and circumstances Mochulsky was part of the Soviet war effort in the 1940s. The very year he graduated from training in railroad engineering, the government decided to use convict labor to build a rail line accessing a new coal basin for the war. The camp system in the 1930s had grown exponentially because of the number of arrests during the Great Purges. With the war looming, the Communist Party decided to search out new, talented party members to help run the camps. These young recruits were given the Gulag job as part of their mandatory government service. Their employer would be the notorious NKVD.

Nadezhda Mandelstam documented the terror years that fed the Gulag in the 1930s. Mandelstam's memoir is deeply personal, for she tells the story of her poet husband Osip and their nightmarish encounters with Stalin's NKVD, the very organization that employed Mochulsky in 1940. Instead of viewing the NKVD as an employer that is trying to build a rail line, Mandelstam portrays the terrifying, powerful, often depraved NKVD operatives she and Osip encountered. She views their evil up close, naming names when possible, sparing nobody and leaving no uncertainty as to the insanity of life in the 1930s. Readers easily feel the fear and misery of living under the yoke of this corrupt and degenerate police force that operated outside the law. This was life run by Stalin's NKVD.

While a good memoir requires both art and craft,[3] Mandelstam's memoir emphasizes the art. This is the journey the author takes as she searches for the essence of her past. Along the way, the author discovers more about who she was and who she has become. Mandelstam's descriptions of their hardships, deprivation, mistreatment by guards, the cruelty of NKVD interrogators, dire living conditions, endless interrogations, and senseless deaths all allow the reader to visualize the horrors of the time. The reader feels how difficult it was to survive, and empathizes with the characters. In the very act of survival, tidbits of character and grit are revealed, making the memoir compelling and believable.

The "art" of a memoir is perhaps the major reason people read personal reminiscences. Reading a Gulag memoir, in particular, can fill out the archival record with a more human element, keep scholars connected to the human experience of the Gulag, demonstrate how fluid the Gulag was and how dangerous generalizations are, and make us see that the official record is only part of "the truth."[4]

Mochulsky's account, by contrast, demonstrates the "craft" aspect of memoir. He tells his tale well, he orders events in a way that makes sense, and he chooses the vignettes to highlight his points. His memoir, unlike Mandelstam's, is not deeply personal. It is largely devoid of names and details. He does not rail against the insanity of the Soviet system the way that Mandelstam constantly does, except at the end. Nor does he describe in detail how the prisoners in his workforce were starving, dying of typhus, freezing to death, unfairly punished, killed randomly, and all the rest that we see in many survivor memoirs. He consistently confines himself to the life of a GULAG NKVD boss and the work that was required. In contrast to Mandelstam's tones of anger or disbelief at what she experiences, Mochulsky's tone is relatively flat, an engineer's retelling of events of his life, recounted with little emotion. His perspective of a boss focusing on work issues is illuminating: it demonstrates the government and Communist Party mindset that set priorities on production over human concerns.

No two points of view are the same. It often happens that even two people who worked together in the same job or grew up in the same family will recall the experience differently. In his book *Travels with Herodotus*, Ryszard Kapuscinski notes that the Greek historian encountered this very difficulty in his own quest to record a history of the world.

> Constantly gathering material for his work and interrogating witnesses, and bards, and priests, he finds that each of them remembers something different—different and differently. Moreover, many centuries before us, he discovers an important yet treacherous and complicating trait of human memory: people remember what they want to remember, not what actually happened.[5]

No matter how compelling or evocative a memoir is, it is just one person's recollection. It reflects what that person was most interested in telling. The "real truth" is perpetually elusive, because one can never see the entire canvas of a lifetime, and because memory is always flawed or colored by later events. It is possible for an author to delude a reader by passing off false events as real, but it is equally plausible for an author to delude himself by telling a false story that he believes fervently as the truth.

J. A. Cuddon discusses this problem in his *Dictionary of Literary Terms:* "Everyone tends to remember what he wants to remember. Disagreeable facts are sometimes glossed over or repressed, truth may be distorted for the sake of convenience or harmony, and the occlusions of time may obscure as much as they reveal."[6] Thus, even if one possesses perfect recollection of the past, most people naturally cast their past actions in a more ethically heroic light than might have been the case in reality. Consider, for example, Mochulsky's preoccupation with being the ultimate problem-solver. I have no doubt that he was a good worker and a conscientious employee, but even the best stumble, or at least fail to solve every problem. In his memoir, though, he makes no mistakes.

Was Mochulsky perhaps less heroic or sympathetic than described? Unfortunately, it is nearly impossible to verify the micro events portrayed in any account of events taking place nearly seventy years ago. In the end, all we can do is read Mochulsky's version of events in one Gulag camp for what he tells us, and for what he does not mention.

There are, though, some ways in which scholars can try to verify a memoir. We can read the available survivors' tales, which, of course, are also subject to the same doubts. In searching to authenticate Mochulsky's version of the Gulag, I listened to testimonies at the Shoah Foundation of nearly two dozen people who been prisoners at Pechorlag.[7] The experience of camp life at Pechorlag absolutely corroborated Mochulsky's own experience. (I had naïvely hoped to hear one of the camp survivors mention his name, but it is unrealistic to hope for such a coincidence after so many years.) Mochulsky's memories of camp life, especially its structure and the work regime, although written from the point of view of a unit boss, is largely consistent with the extant prisoner accounts. I also searched the extensive holdings of the Soviet Communist Party archives at Harvard University.[8] Although I read many interesting things about Pechorlag, I found no mention of Mochulsky or of any of the events he describes. That is not surprising, since the camp was extremely large and Mochulsky was a fairly low-level boss. That said, the files I read did not contradict anything in Mochulsky's memoir. Of all the existing scholarly work on the Gulag, Galina Ivanova's book *Labor Camp Socialism* stands out for its emphasis on Gulag staff.[9] Mochulsky's story, checked against her research, corresponds in many ways with the general story of Gulag bosses.

The urge to comprehend and assess a person who worked for GULAG NKVD is understandable. But how do we evaluate a Gulag staff member in the absence of a decent historical record?[10] For in comparison to the immensity of the tragedy, the number of deaths and the extreme trauma to Russian society the Gulag caused, very little progress has been made on constructing an accurate story. Real scholarly work with Russian sources began only in the 1990s, even though the Gulag existed for several decades. The Memorial Society, a nonprofit organization dedicated to preserving the memory of the Gulag and its survivors, with offices in both Moscow and St. Petersburg, has a wonderful collection of articles and materials, but again, the enormity of the task with the resources available means that we still do not have a full picture.[11] As Primo Levi wrote, it is very difficult to understand this "grey zone," which contrasts with simplified images of victims and perpetrators.[12] Can we ever determine whether a particular camp boss or camp guard (no matter how apparently benign) was more or less complicit in the evils of the Gulag? Frequently, GULAG NKVD personnel ended up as convicts in the camps themselves. How responsible are these low-level workers, how responsible are the desk-workers, planners, bystanders, engineers, and civilian employees for what went on? Was an employee who managed the system in fear any less a prisoner of it than his charges?

Joseph Brodsky praised Nadezhda Mandelstam for her honesty, loyalty, and fearlessness, saying that "her piece of reality is unchallengeable."[13] He was able to assess Mandelstam because he knew her personally. He understood the hell she and her husband experienced because he had his own troubles with the Soviet government (although decades later). In assessing Mochulsky's memoir, on the other hand, we have only the words he wrote. I knew Mochulsky for only a few months, so our acquaintance never reached the point of delving "into the soul."

Mochulsky's memoir is unusual in several ways. For one thing, he seems most interested in relating his story as one of "a good man in a bad place." His account is straightforward and work-oriented. The kinds of things he learned are interesting, but not affecting or deeply personal: how lucky he was to be a Communist Party member, how he could play his status as a party member against the powerful NKVD bureaucracy for which he worked, and how he managed to end up through connections and hard work being given a chance for a plum assignment to the USSR Foreign Ministry. Central to his story is his association with both the NKVD/KGB and the Communist Party, but very little on how he felt about this association.

For another thing, he does not focus long and hard on the lives of the prisoners. They are a "labor force" for his tasks, and his problems of too few supplies or bad weather are not human tragedies, merely work details. He mentions that his "labor force" was emaciated and weak, but never does he recall in these pages the deaths that occurred out on the tracks. This is left for the prisoners themselves to recall. One Pechorlag ex-convict, for instance, remembered prisoners dying while they worked building railroad embankments. "If one died, let him lie," was the system, and the convicts were simply urged to move on to the next kilometer.[14] Mochulsky does express remorse that the system he worked for his entire life ruined millions of innocent lives, but missing is that feeling of compassion or sadness at his role in perpetrating the "big Soviet lie" to its citizens. In contrast to Mochulsky, Dmitry Bystrolyotov, a former Soviet spy, reflects on his own role in this "big Soviet lie" in his memoir. He describes how he suffers over the fact that he had served a government whose goals were no different from Fascism and Nazism, the very systems he had fought against. He feels that his career has been "demeaning, self-destructive and immoral." "At night," he writes, "I wake up from burning shame and grief and think: why had we [Soviet spies abroad] endured so many torments and committed so many crimes?"[15]

Instead of expressing a sense of personal responsibility or shame, Mochulsky instead castigates the Soviet government for the "monstrous inventions of the Stalinist regime" and the "inhumanity and basic criminal character of the Soviet leadership's policies" concerning the Gulag. He acknowledges that the Soviet government and the NKVD purposely hid the truth from its citizens about what was taking place in the Gulag. In chapter 27 he writes:

> There was no way that the party and government leaders, along with their closest circles, did not know what was actually going on with the NKVD and the Gulag camps. This policy cannot be explained away as just being mistakes that other people made.... Once they hid it from the population, this meant that the same leaders who came up with it and insisted that they were changing the world, these leaders knew that this policy was at its very core criminal and bad for people. And they implemented it, all the same.

He does not question his own role in that implementation; however, it is impossible not to ask how a perfectly nice, intelligent, seemingly well-meaning man would not make the connection between his work and the leaders' policy that was "criminal and bad for people." He did not shy away from mentioning the violence of the Gulag—any number of times he was told by a superior that he must fulfill his plan or be sent to the Gulag himself. While working at the Gulag, he does not appear to question the reason for its existence. Nor does he, at least in this memoir, express a sense of personal responsibility for the horror of the Gulag. The question is why.

Several personal reasons come to mind. In his talks with me, Mochulsky stressed the importance of patriotism. In the face of a war on Soviet soil, he said, a patriot would do any job the government needed to be done, to win the war. As a lifelong NKVD/KGB employee, he may have been loath to criticize the government or the secret police, out of fear or perhaps even respect.[16] Moreover, he was a believing Communist, prone to statements such as: "I looked for reasons why our government seemed unable to put into practice the party's lucid plans for building the first socialist state in the world." Overall, he seems reluctant to point a finger at the party of which he was member, and that stood for ideals, at least on paper, that he firmly embraced.[17] The problem is, as the director of the Memorial Society Arsenii Roginsky has said, that Stalin somehow had produced millions of victims but no criminals.[18]

In this memoir, Mochulsky writes that he wants to highlight GULAG NKVD's "civilian employees." His point is that people who were assigned to work in the Gulag were unprepared for the reality of it, and made the best of it. Like the German police battalion in Poland that consisted of "ordinary men" who were "singularly unprepared for and surprised by the murderous task that awaited them there in 1942,"[19] Mochulsky was similarly ill-equipped for the reality of the Gulag. But unlike the men in the German police battalion Mochulsky did have an inkling of what awaited him, and he knew what the Gulag was. He might have had some youthful illusions fed by Soviet propaganda, but he no doubt understood that he was being sent to work in a forced labor camp.

For the civilian employees of the forced labor camps, the Gulag had other peculiar features that affected their experience. Unlike the German soldiers, the USSR's citizens were not clear about the real purpose of the Gulag. Was it mainly economic—"everything for the war effort"—as Mochulsky clearly believed? Was it a place to send actual criminals, was it for reeducation purposes, was it to isolate enemies of Soviet power? Thus, while the German police battalion soon learned its genocidal purpose, their Soviet counterparts were not certain why the Gulag existed and had to be maintained.

The Gulag was badly organized and badly run. Prisoners starved to death because the central government allowed only starvation portions. The Soviets also did not manage the task of transporting enough food to these remote camps in a timely fashion, as Mochulsky relates in chapter 6. In addition, there was a huge turnover of bosses, guards, and prisoners, so that at any moment, hundreds of thousands of people were in transit between camps. Mochulsky himself documents his several transfers between units at Pechorlag. Goals changed without explanation; large construction projects were started and then abandoned.

The Gulag was also enormous, and most of it was situated far from Moscow. There was no realistic way for the center to stay in touch and to know what was happening on a daily, weekly, or even monthly basis. There were no telephones, no roads, no rail lines, and barely any radios. This meant that camp administrators had a good deal of autonomy from Moscow and could exercise some ethical choices and even agency. Mochulsky himself demonstrates this freedom time and again as he solves problems without asking for permission. He asks: Whom could I turn to? And he answers: There was no one.

Mochulsky may be no different from the millions of other Russians who feel little personal responsibility for the plight of innocent Gulag victims. This lack of introspective, personal feeling about the Gulag corroborates the general belief that many Russians have yet to come to terms with their past. Responsibility for this massive crime has never been socialized and it remains simple to assign guilt to some nameless others, now conveniently dead. At the same time, and despite all the controversies since Khrushchev's de-Stalinization speech of 1956, Stalin and Stalinism have never been absolutely repudiated. Indeed, at the time this memoir is being published in English, there is a discernable trend toward rehabilitating Stalin.[20] The dictator's present-day supporters focus on the achievements of collectivization and industrialization, the Soviet victory over the Nazis, or the postwar recovery of the economy. Many insist that no matter what crimes were committed or how many people perished in pursuit of his policies, Stalin retains considerable force for Russia. Whatever the achievements, few people who worked for and supported the Soviet regime want to ask the resultant question: At what cost?

What is perhaps most valuable about this memoir is that it offers a view of evil experienced as a daily job.[21] For millions of people the Gulag system was merely a place to work, something to do for a while before a better assignment came along. In showcasing the interactions that Mochulsky had with the prisoners, the guards, and other staff members, the memoir forces us to see that not all the bosses in the Gulag were monsters. Many of them were simply citizens doing their jobs.

This memoir is the story of one man, a Communist Party member and an engineer, whose voice is unique in the Gulag literature. As the translator, I wondered as I labored over the language why Mochulsky wrote this document, and why his family has encouraged me to publish it. I often reflected on Nadezhda Mandelstam's memoir. Her purpose for writing her memoir is clear: She wrote out of deep love for her husband, and a wish to preserve his poems. Mochulsky says he wanted to make clear what the millions of civilian workers did in the Gulag's case, but why? Is it because it reflects the story of millions of Soviets who were forced to participate in their government's crimes? Is it because their stories are complicated sagas of compromise and fear? Or is it simply that Mochulsky was a man who wanted to show us that even in an evil system there were people who tried to do their best?

Mochulsky does not help us to answer these questions. In the end, all we have is this memoir, which affords us another look at an enormous human tragedy. It is valuable as a document of one man's impressions, and gives us a window into that normally closed world of the NKVD. It also allows us a glimpse into the mind of someone who remained a Communist his entire life. There was always the dream of Communism that had yet to be realized. What evils Mochulsky may have perpetrated or justified, or what great acts of kindness and charity he may have committed, we can never truly know.

APPENDIX I

PRETEXTS FOR ARREST UNDER LENIN AND STALIN (BASED ON JACQUES ROSSI, *THE GULAG HANDBOOK*)

Labels used by the USSR government as pretexts to arrest or liquidation during the Lenin and Stalin years:

1917–1918
Speculators (or profiteers), counterrevolutionaries

First mass arrests of Mensheviks and social revolutionaries, as the Bolsheviks attempted to exclude these parties from the newly forming councils

July 1918
Left social revolutionaries, following the Bolshevik suppression of their uprising

Summer 1918
White Guards (in connection with the declaration of the "Red Terror against White Guard Forces")

1918–1922
People called politicals, meaning political prisoners

"Backward elements"

Devout people (who were the ones who were disturbed by the "shaking out of relics," or the confiscation of church utensils)

Saboteurs, who were peasants resisting forced grain requisitioning

1919–1921
Saboteurs

Enemies of the republic

1921
Rebels, or Krondstadt sailors

White Guards

1919–1922
Saboteurs
Kulaks, or peasants opposing forced grain requisition
Priests
People who attended church (including Patriarch Tikhon)

Summer 1922
Mensheviks and social revolutionaries in connection with the open trial of their leaders

1923–1929
Gold hoarders

1922–1931
Central Asian guerrillas

1925
Trotskyites

1925–1928
Nepmen (businessmen who were allowed to do business during NEP, the New Economic Policy)
Speculators, people who worked to earn money in business

1927–1928
Trotskyites
Bolsheviks who spoke out openly in Communist Party discussions
Former anarchists (the intelligentsia)
Saboteurs, or "enemies with a slide rule"

1929
Yakut and Buriat Mongols, following the suppression of their uprising against the Bolshevik takeover
Silver speculators, which was anyone discovered with silver coins worth more than three rubles (in connection with public opposition to Soviet paper money)

1929–1932
Kulaks, the so-called rich peasants
Subkulaks, the so-called lower peasants

1930
Shkraby, or teachers against the officially introduced method of "brigade teaching"

1930–1931
Kazakhs, after their uprising against the Bolsheviks taking power had been suppressed

1932
Plunderers of socialist property

1933–1934
People without a passport

1934–1935
Trotskyites
Enemies of the people
Kirov's murderers (known as the "Kirov flow" into the Gulag)

1935–1936
Komsomol members (Communist Youth League members), for expressing views different from the official line
Caucasian Highlanders, or those who revolted against Russification and Sovietization in their lands
Women who performed abortions

1936–1939
The Great Purge

1939
Poles, Belorussians, and other people from eastern Poland, which was forcibly annexed to the USSR by an agreement with the Nazis

Spring 1940
Soldiers
Traitors to the motherland

July 1940
Barons
Baltic barons, or citizens of the Baltics who were against Soviet annexation

August 1940
Romanians captured in Moldavia and northern Bukovina (which the USSR seized from Romania) and recognized as "anti-Soviet"
All persons related to above persons. If one was to be arrested and was not found, that person's entire family was sent to the Gulag.

June 1941 (Hitler's attack on the USSR)
Defeatists
Rumor-mongers
Agents of Hitler

Fall 1941
"People who were surrounded"; any Soviet citizen, civilian or military, who ended up during World War II in territory that the enemy occupied or threatened to occupy, was considered suspicious.

1940–1942
Slackers

Absentee from a factory

Violators of labor discipline

1942–1947

Traitors to the motherland

Bandits, meaning Ukrainian, Lithuanian, and other partisans who fought during World War II against Soviet or German occupation of their land. Also refers to those who fought only the Germans, but not in detachments subordinate to Moscow.

1943

Deserters

1944–1945

When the Red Army liberated eastern Poland, the Baltic states, and eastern Romania, there were mass arrests of local people. Also arrested were the partisans, who were convicted as bandits.

1944–1946

War criminals from among captured German, Japanese, and others

Traitors to the motherland, which were Soviet citizens the Allies liberated from the German camps and who were handed back to the USSR

Foreigners, or citizens of countries in Europe who were liberated by the Red Army, including White emigrants and White Guards

1945–1946

Samurai (Japanese)

War criminals from Japan

White emigrants and foreigners from northern China, which the Red Army occupied as a result of Japan's capitulation

1947

Ukazniki, or persons arrested according to a specific government decree

The "Four-Fifths," named for the June 4, 1947, decree "On Theft of State and Public Property"

Plunderers

1947–1949

Victims of the "Second Purge"

"Repeater," a person who was reimprisoned or exiled again on a fabricated charge, usually the identical one from the first sentence

Mendelites, so called for the Austrian geneticist. This label was applied to those who opposed the "theories" of approved Soviet geneticist Lysenko.

Cosmopolitans, or adherents of Western culture, mostly Jews

Lower cosmopolitans, or people who were "toadies" of the bourgeois culture of the West

1948–February 1953

Cosmopolitans and "toadies"

Greeks, or Communist partisans in the failed attempt to bring down the Greek government, who escaped to the USSR

1952

Doctors, Jewish doctors who were supposedly involved in the "Doctor's Plot." Also called "murderers in white smocks"

APPENDIX 2

ARTICLE 58, CRIMINAL CODE OF THE RSFSR (1934) (EXCERPTED FROM TRANSLATION BY HUGO S. CUNNINGHAM)

STATE CRIMES

I. COUNTERREVOLUTIONARY CRIME

58–1. "Counterrevolutionary" describes any action directed toward the overthrow, subversion, or weakening of the power of worker-peasant councils or of their chosen (according to the Constitution of the USSR and constitutions of union republics) worker-peasant government of the USSR, union and autonomous republics, or toward the subversion or weakening of the external security of the USSR and the fundamental economic, political, and national gains of the proletarian revolution. In consideration of the international solidarity of interests of all workers, acts are likewise considered "counterrevolutionary" when they are directed at any other workers' government, even if not part of the USSR.

58 1a. Treason to the motherland, i.e., acts done by citizens of the USSR in damage to the military power of the USSR, its national sovereignty, or the inviolability of its territory, such as: espionage, betrayal of military or state secrets, crossing to the side of the enemy, flight (by surface or air) abroad, shall be punishable by—

> the supreme measure of criminal punishment—shooting with confiscation of all property, or with mitigating circumstances—deprivation of liberty for a term of ten years with confiscation of all property [20 July 1934 (SU No. 30, art. 173)].

58–1b. The same crimes, perpetrated by military personnel, are punishable by the supreme measure of criminal punishment—

shooting with confiscation of all property [20 July 1934 (SU No. 30, art. 173)].

58–1c. In case of flight (by surface or air) across the border by a military member, the adult members of his family, if they in any way aided the preparation or carrying-out of treason, or only knew about it and failed to report it to authorities, shall be punishable by—

deprivation of liberty for a term of five to ten years, with confiscation of all property.

Remaining adult members of the family of the traitor, living together with him or as his dependents at the moment of the perpetration of the crime, shall be deprived of voting rights and exiled to remote districts of Siberia for five years. [20 July 1934 (SU No. 30, art. 173)].

58–1d. Failure by a military member to denounce preparations or the carrying-out of treason shall be punishable by—

deprivation of liberty for ten years.

Such failure to denounce by other citizens (not military) shall be punished according to article 58–12. [20 July 1934 (SU No. 30, art. 173)].

58–2. Armed uprising or incursion with counterrevolutionary purposes on Soviet territory by armed bands, seizure of power in the center or areas with the same purposes, or, in particular, with the purpose of forcibly severing from the USSR and an individual union republic, any part of its territory, or of breaking agreements between the USSR and foreign states, shall be punishable by—

the supreme measure of social defense—shooting, or proclamation as an enemy of the workers, with confiscation or property and with deprivation of citizenship of the union republic, and likewise of citizenship of the Soviet Union and perpetual expulsion beyond the borders of the USSR, with the allowance under extenuating circumstances of reduction to deprivation of liberty for a term of no less than three years, with confiscation of all or part of one's property [6 June 1927 (SU No 49, art 330)].

58–3. Dealings for counterrevolutionary purposes with a foreign state or its individual representatives, and likewise aiding by whatever means a foreign state, engaged in war with the USSR, or conducting against the USSR a struggle by means of intervention or blockade, shall be punishable by—

measures of social defense, indicated in article 58–2 of this code. [6 July 1927 (SU No. 49, art. 333)].

58–4. The offering of whatever kind of aid to that part of the international bourgeoisie, which, not recognizing the equal rights of a Communist system replacing a Capitalist system, exerts itself for its overthrow, and likewise to public groups and organizations, being under the influence of or directly organized by that bourgeoisie, in the carrying out of hostile activities toward the USSR, shall be punishable by

—deprivation of liberty for a term not less than three years with confiscation of all or part of one's property, with an increase, in especially aggravating circumstances, up to the supreme measure of social defense

—shooting or declaration to be an enemy of the workers, with deprivation of citizenship of one's union republic, and, likewise, citizenship of the USSR and expulsion beyond the borders of the USSR forever, with confiscation of property. [6 June 1927 (SU No. 49, art. 330)].

58–5. Adherence to a foreign state or any public groups in it, by means of relations with its representatives, use of false documents or other means, toward a declaration of war, armed intervention in the affairs of the USSR, or other unfriendly actions, e.g.: blockade, seizure of state property of the USSR or of union republics, the breaking of diplomatic relations, the breaking of treaties concluded with the USSR, etc., shall be punishable by—

measures of social defense, indicated in article 58–2 of this code. [6 June 1927 (SU No. 49, art. 330)].

58–6. Espionage, i.e., the transmittal, seizure, or collection, with the purpose of transmittal, of information, being a specially kept state secret due to its content, to foreign governments, counterrevolutionary organizations, and private individuals, shall be punishable by—

—deprivation of liberty for a term not less than three years, with confiscation of all or part of one's property, or in those cases where the espionage brought or could bring especially severe consequences for the interests of the USSR— the supreme measure of social defense

—shooting or proclamation as an enemy of the workers with deprivation of citizenship of one's union republic and, likewise, of citizenship of the USSR and expulsion beyond the borders of the USSR forever with confiscation of property.

Transmittal, seizure, or collection for purpose of transmittal of economic information, not consisting by its content of specially preserved state secrets, but not subject to publication either due to direct legal prohibition, or due to the decision of the management of the department, institution, or enterprise, whether for a reward or for free, to organizations and persons listed above, shall be punishable by—

deprivation of liberty for a term up to three years. [6 June 1927 (SU No. 49, art. 330)].

58–7. The undermining of state production, transport, trade, monetary relations, or the credit system, or likewise cooperation, done with counterrevolutionary purposes, by means of corresponding use of state institutions and enterprises or impeding their normal activity, and likewise use of state institutions and enterprises or impeding their activity, done in the interests of former owners or interested capitalist organizations, shall be punishable by—

measures of social defense, indicated in article 58–2 of this code. [6 June 1927 (SU No. 49, art. 330)].

58–8. The perpetration of terrorist acts, directed against representatives of Soviet authority or activists of revolutionary workers' and peasants' organizations, and participation in the performance of such acts, even by persons not belonging to a counterrevolutionary organization, shall be punishable by—

measures of social defense, indicated in article 58–2 of this code. [6 June 1927 (SU No. 49, art. 330)].

58–9. Destruction or damage with a counterrevolutionary purpose by explosion, arson, or other means of railroad or other routes and means of transportation, means of public communication, water conduits, public depots and other structures, or state and community property, shall be punishable by—

measures of social defense, indicated in art. 58–2 of this code. [6 June 1927 (SU No. 49, art. 330)].

58–10. Propaganda or agitation, containing a call for the overthrow, subversion, or weakening of Soviet authority or for the carrying out of other counterrevolutionary crimes (art. 58–2 to 58–9 of this code), and likewise the distribution or preparation or keeping of literature of this nature shall be punishable by—

deprivation of liberty for a term not less than six months.

The same actions during mass disturbances, or with the use of religious or nationalist prejudices of the masses, or in a war situation, or in areas proclaimed to be in a war situation, shall be punishable by—

measures of social defense, indicated in art. 58–2 of this code. [6 June 1927 (SU No. 49, art. 330)].

58–11. Any type of organizational activity, directed toward the preparation or carrying out of crimes indicated in this chapter, and likewise participation in an organization, formed for the preparation or carrying out of one of the crimes indicated in this chapter, shall be punishable by—

measures of social defense, indicated in the corresponding articles of this code. [6 June 1927 (SU No. 49, art. 330)].

58–12. Failure to denounce a counterrevolutionary crime, reliably known to be in preparation or carried out, shall be punishable by—

deprivation of liberty for a term not less than six months. [6 June 1927 (SU No. 49, art. 330)].

58–13. Active participation or active fighting against the working class and revolutionary movement, manifested in a responsible or secret position in the tsarist regime, or with counterrevolutionary governments in a period of civil war, shall be punishable by—

measures of social defense, indicated in art. 58–2 of this code. [6 June 1927 (SU No. 49, art. 330)].

58–14. Counterrevolutionary sabotage, i.e., conscious failure to perform some defined duties or intentionally negligent fulfillment of them, with the special purpose of weakening the authority of the government and functioning of the state apparatus, shall be punishable by—

deprivation of liberty for a term not less than one year, with confiscation of all or part of one's property, with an increase, in especially aggravating circumstances, to the supreme measure of social defense—shooting, with confiscation of property. [6 Jun 1927 (SU No. 49, art. 330)].

APPENDIX 3

GLOSSARY

Apparatchik: a functionary of the Communist Party or Soviet government

Balanda: a thin, watery stew

Cadres Department: Personnel Department

CC CPSU: Central Committee of the Communist Party of the Soviet Union

Cheka/Chekist: All Russian Extraordinary Commission, the official administrative name of the secret police, from 1917 to 1922

Civilian Gulag employee: person employed as staff in the Gulag camps, or anyone who was not a prisoner

Collectivization: Stalin's plan to eliminate family farms and move the peasants to large farms manned by hundreds of people

Dekulakization: word describing the abolition of the peasants as a class, an integral part of Stalin's First Five-Year Plan (1928–1932)

58ers—political prisoners, so called for being sentenced under Article 58 of the RSFSR Criminal Code, as "counterrevolutionaries"

FFYP: First Five-Year Plan, 1928–1932

Great October Socialist Revolution: official name for the Russian Revolution of October 1917

Great Patriotic War: the Russian name for World War II

Great Purge: Stalin's campaign of terror and political repression, 1937–1938, in which 11 million people perished, according to Robert Conquest

GULAG NKVD: Main Administration of Corrective Labor camps, run by the NKVD

ITL: Corrective Labor Camp

Komi ASSR: Komi Autonomous Socialist Republic, a region in the north of Russia, west of the Ural Mountains

Komsomol: Communist Youth League

Kulak: literally "fist" in Russian, a derogatory name given to any peasants who had the means to hire even one person to work on their farms with them

Molotov-Ribbentrop Pact 1939: Also called the Nazi-Soviet Pact, this was the non-aggression treaty that Hitler and Stalin signed in 1939, pledging neutrality in the event either was attacked by a third country

MVD: Ministry of Internal Affairs, or secret police, 1946–1954

NKVD—People's Commissariat of Internal Affairs, or secret police, 1934–1946

Norm: the amount of work a person needed to do daily, weekly, monthly, and yearly, as mandated by the State Planning Agency

Operchekotdel: This was also known as the "third department," and was the main administrative department that supervised all the security platoons and VOKhR officers who worked in the various departments and units of the labor camp

Pechorlag: Gulag camp located in Komi ASSR in northern Russia, on the Pechora River

Pernashor: name of the first unit of convicts Mochulsky heads

Politotdel: Political Department. Each Camp Administration had its own Political Department that exercised party supervision over the entire administration except the security platoon

Politburo: Political Bureau, the highest authority of the Communist Party

RSFSR: Russian Soviet Federative Socialist Republic

Selektor: walkie-talkie device used for communicating in the Gulag

Troika: extra-legal commission for quickly sentencing people to a Gulag term; usually included a member of the NKVD, the judiciary, and the Communist Party

Tufta: cheating on required work norms

Tsingoi: scurvy

Unit of prisoners: the lowest level of work organization in the Gulag, ranging from a few prisoners to several thousand, depending on the camp

Urka: hardened criminal prisoner in the Gulag

VOKhR Guard: armed guards who worked at the Gulag

Zek: convict, comes from the Russian abbreviation z/k for the word *zakliuchenni* (prisoner)

The zone: colloquial name for Gulag camp

ACKNOWLEDGMENTS

I would like to express my profound gratitude to the many people who have helped me during the translation and annotation of *Gulag Boss*. I am incredibly fortunate to have Nancy Toff as my editor. She has made the otherwise long and arduous task of seeing this project through a pleasure. Likewise, Sonia Tycko at Oxford has been a tireless and gracious assistant. I am grateful to Fyodor Mochulsky for giving me the original manuscript and the photographs, the Mochulsky family in Moscow for their support and kind assistance, and to Vitaly Kozyrev for his invaluable help. A special thanks goes to Mark Kramer for his friendship, support, and generosity. Princeton University has supported this project in many ways, in particular the Sociology Department and the Program in Russian and Eurasian Studies. I want to thank Pamela Hersh for her unwavering support at all levels, David Bellos and the Program in Translation and Intercultural Communication, Antoine Kahn of Mathey College at Princeton, as well as Serguei Oukashine, Michael Wachtel, Steve Kotkin, Viviana Zelizer, Paul Starr, Alejandro Portes, Patricia Fernandez-Kelly, Doug Massey, Susan Fiske, Jan Gross, Louise Grafton, Tony Grafton, Michael Gordin, Daria Solodkaia, and of course, my wonderful Princeton students, who all thought about this project with me and added innumerable insights. Tsering Wangyal is my brilliant mapmaker. A big thanks goes to Nina Gorky Shapiro, who was indispensable at guiding me to sources, finding books I needed, giving advice, and helping me with translation questions.

Jay Edson, Larry Parsons, and Miguel Centeno generously converted the little, ancient photographs into the clean copies now in the text. Ksenia Rodionova cheerfully provided much-needed Russian language clarification many times. Several people worked to make the introduction to the text as good as it is, in particular, the three anonymous reviewers for Oxford who all wrote thoughtful, helpful comments. In addition, Lynne Viola, Stephen F. Cohen, Paul R. Gregory, John Major, Dorothy Sue Cobble, and Shelley Kiernan helped me in innumerable ways on the Introduction and the Afterword. Douglas Greenberg and the USC Shoah Foundation Institute were extremely helpful, as were the professors and staff at the Iberian Studies Institute at the University of Salamanca in Spain. John W. Wright provided encouragement and assistance in the early stages. Colleagues and friends all over the place gave their kind support and suggestions, for which I am grateful: Bill Taubman, Vlad Zubok, Jay Lyle, Louis Hutchins, Alan Barenberg, Jeffrey Hass, David Brandenberger, Blair Ruble and the Kennan Institute for Advanced Russian Studies, Sally Paxton, Murray Feshbach, Amy Green, Steve Aron, Father Tim Scully, Jan Vanous, Chuck Movit, Jenny Hartshorne, and finally, the tremendous work of Arsenii Roginsky and the Memorial Society in Moscow.

And finally, thanks to my lovely family, Jack, Pat, and Addie Kaple, Esther Kaple, Kim and Rick Stuck, Dawn Roebuck, Julia and Bob Hare. My profoundest thanks go to my husband, Miguel Angel Centeno, for his unswerving support and love, and our children, Alex and Maya, who have had to endure Gulag discussions far too many times.

NOTES

Introduction

1. Aleksandr I. Solzhenitsyn, *The Gulag Archipelago, 1918–1956: An Experiment in Literary Investigation*, trans. Thomas P. Whitney (Parts I–IV) and Harry Willetts (Parts V–VII) (New York: Harper and Row, 1985). See also his novels: *One Day in the Life of Ivan Denisovich: A Novel* (New York: Farrar, Straus and Giroux, 2005), *The First Circle* (New York: Harper & Row, 1968), and *The Cancer Ward* (New York: Farrar, Straus and Giroux, 1991). Also see Evgeniia Ginsberg, *Journey into the Whirlwind*, trans. Paul Stevenson and Max Hayward (New York: Harcourt, 1995), and *Within the Whirlwind*, trans. Ian Boland (New York: Harcourt Brace Jovanovich, 1981); and Varlam Shalamov, *Kolyma Tales*, trans. John Glad (New York: Penguin, 1994).
2. In other words, he held two jobs: foreman and boss of a unit of prisoners (*prorab y nachalnik kolonny zakliuchennykh*).
3. Since the NKVD administered the Gulag, it is often referred to as GULAG NKVD.
4. An extraordinary book on this topic, concerning the Germans in Poland, is Christopher R. Browning, *Ordinary Men: Reserve Police Battalion 101 and the Final Solution in Poland*, 2001. See this book's afterword for a discussion of this topic.
5. J. Arch Getty, Gabor T. Rittersporn, and Viktor N. Zemskov, "Victims of the Soviet Penal System in the Pre-War Years: A First Approach on the Basis of Archival Evidence," *American Historical Review* 98, no. 4 (October 1993), pp. 1017–49.
6. Current research shows, however, that much of this labor was unproductive, created losses in the long run, and encouraged the leaders to take on (and often abandon) useless projects. See Paul R. Gregory and Valery Lazarev, eds., *The Economics of Forced Labor* (Stanford, Calif.: Hoover Institution Press, 2003), in particular Oleg Khlevniuk, "The Economy of the OGPU, NKVD, and MVD of the USSR, 1930–1953," pp. 43–66.

7. Unfortunately, no single agency kept a "master list" of victims. The archives have thrown light on this, giving data that are often incomplete, or include only some years and not others. Additionally, there was a very high turnover, as prisoners were moved from camp to camp. Many scholars have attempted to address this problem. For a discussion and footnotes about difficulties in counting the victims, see Getty, Rittersporn, and Zemskov, "Victims of the Soviet Penal System," pp. 1020–25. Twenty million victims is Paul Gregory's estimate, in *Terror by Quota: State Security from Lenin to Stalin* (New Haven, Conn.: Yale University Press, 2009), p. 279; and 28.7 million comes from Anne Applebaum, *Gulag: A History* (New York: Doubleday, 2003), p. 582.

8. The estimate of 7 million is from Anton Antonov-Ovseenko, quoted in Getty, Rittersporn, and Zemskov, "Victims of the Soviet Penal System," p. 1022; the 2.7 million is from Applebaum, *Gulag: A History*, p. 583; and the 1.1 million can be found in Binner, Bonwetsch, and Junge, *Massenmord und Lagerhof*, and Werth, *La terreur et le desarroi*. See also Ellman, "Soviet Repression Statistics," pp. 1151–72.

9. Many memoirs and other accounts mention this. Nicolas Werth found archival evidence of several trainloads of prisoners arriving without either documents or a list of names of the prisoners aboard. When prisoners died en route, they remained nameless. Nicolas Werth, *Cannibal Island: Death in a Siberian Gulag* (Princeton, N.J.: Princeton University Press), 2007.

10. Steven A. Barnes, "Researching Daily Life in the Gulag," *Kritika* 1, no. 2 (2000), fn 3.

11. A selected list of Gulag memoirs is included in this book's bibiliography. A more extensive list can be found in Leona Toker's book *Return from the Archipelago: Narratives of Gulag Survivors* (Bloomington: Indiana University Press), 2000. Also see the work of D. J. Dallin and B. P. Nicolaevsky, *Forced Labor in Soviet Russia* (New Haven, Conn.: Yale University Press, 1947); N. Jasny, "Labour and Output in Soviet Concentration Camps," *Journal of Political Economy* 59, no. 5 (October 1951), pp. 405–19, and S. Swianiewicz, *Forced Labour and Economic Development: An Enquiry into the Experience of Soviet Industrialization* (London: Oxford University Press, 1965), among others. Also see Robert Conquest's pathbreaking book, *The Great Terror: A Reassessment* (New York: Oxford University Press, 1991). The first edition came out in 1968.

12. An illuminating new history of the Soviet police is Paul Hagenloh, *Stalin's Police: Public Order and Mass Repression in the USSR, 1926–1941* (Baltimore: Johns Hopkins University Press, 2009).

13. Aleksandr I. Solzhenitsyn, *The Gulag Archipelago*, volume 2, p. 17.

14. An excellent new book on the state security organs is Gregory, *Terror by Quota*.

15. The film is Nikolai Cherkasov's *Solovki* (1928). I am grateful to Cristina Vatulescu for this reference, "Early Cinematic Representations of the Gulag: The Camps as Soviet Exotica in (1928)," paper given at Harvard's Conference on the Soviet Gulag: Its History and Legacy (Cambridge, Mass.: Davis Center for Russian and Eurasian Studies, Harvard University, November 2–5, 2006). This film is used extensively in Marina Goldovskaia's moving documentary *Solovki Power* (1988).

16. Several Illuminating studies have come out from Yale University Press, the Annals of Communism series, at www.yale.edu/annals/books_available/ books_available.htm and the The Yale-Hoover Series on Stalin, Stalinism, and the Cold War, at http://yalepress.yale.edu/yupbooks/SeriesPage. asp?series=147. Two excellent online resources on the Gulag are *Many Days Many Lives*, at http://gulaghistory.org/ and the National Parks Service Online Exhibit "Gulag: Soviet Forced Labor Camps and the Struggle for Freedom," at http://gulaghistory.org/nps/onlineexhibit/stalin/

17. Jacques Rossi, *The Gulag Handbook*, trans. William A. Burhans (New York: Paragon House, 1989), p. 137.

18. V. T. Shalamov, *Vishera: Antiroman*, predislovie Olega Volkova (Moscow, 1989). Quoted in Galina M. Ivanova's study *Labor Camp Socialism: The Gulag in the Soviet Totalitarian System*, trans. Carol Flath (Armonk, N.Y. and London: M.E. Sharpe, 2000), p. xxii.

19. The terror and its effects on Russian society is the subject of several books. See Orlando Figes, *The Whisperers: Private Life in Stalin's Russia* (New York: Picador, 2007); Wendy Z. Goldman, *Terror and Democracy in the Age of Stalin: The Social Dynamics of Repression* (Cambridge: Cambridge University Press, 2007); and Catherine Merridale, *Night of Stone: Death and Memory in Twentieth-Century Russia* (New York: Penguin, 2000).

20. See, for instance Vladimir V. Tchernavin's book *I Speak for the Silent Prisoners of the Soviets*, trans. Nicholas M. Oushakoff (Boston: Hale, Cushman & Flint, 1935). The major exception to the relatively small amount of scholarly interest, of course, is Robert Conquest, who spent years writing of the horrors of Soviet rule in the face of general disinterest and skepticism.

21. As Galina Ivanova notes, the Soviet government based its activity not on law, but on "secret instructions, clarifications, supplements, and commentaries that originated in bodies that did not have any legal rights." Only a select population (judicial practitioners, investigators, NKVD employees, and party officials) knew the procedures for enforcement. Ivanova, *Labor Camp Socialism*, p. 48.

22. Paul Hollander, *Political Pilgrims: Western Intellectuals in Search of the Good Society*, 4th edition (Edison, N.J.: Transaction, 1997).

23. For example, Walter Duranty, the *New York Times*'s Moscow correspondent in the 1930s, was unable or unwilling to report on the extent of the Ukrainian famine in 1932–1933 (millions of people died), even though he no doubt heard about it or even saw evidence of it. See S. J. Taylor, *Stalin's Apologist: Walter Duranty: The New York Times's Man in Moscow* (Oxford and New York: Oxford University Press, 1990).

24. This is not to say that no scholarly work appeared during this time. In 1968, Robert Conquest's *The Great Terror* was published, followed by Solzhenitsyn's *The Gulag Archipelago* in 1973. Both of these works challenged the secrecy of the USSR, thus causing a great sensation both in Russia and in the West.

25. For instance, see Holland Hunter's excellent studies, *Soviet Transportation Policy* (Cambridge, Mass.: Harvard University Press, 1957) and *The Soviet Transport Sector* (Washington, D.C.: The Brookings Institution), 1966.

26. Oleg Khlevniuk, *The History of the Gulag*, trans. Vadim A. Staklo (New Haven, Conn., and London: Yale University Press, 2004), p. 208.

27. One influential, large-scale effort to understand the USSR from outside sources was the Soviet Interview Project, which surveyed Soviet émigrés in the 1980s. See James R. Millar, ed., *Politics, Work and Daily Life in the USSR: A Survey of Former Soviet Citizens* (Cambridge: Cambridge University Press, 1987).

28. This was Stalin's initiative that sent at least ten thousand Soviet citizens to China in the 1950s, to help the new Chinese Communist Party build socialism in their country. My earlier work had already explored how the Chinese sought to emulate the Soviet experience. See Deborah Kaple, *Dream of a Red Factory: The Legacy of High Stalinism in China* (New York: Oxford University Press, 1993).

29. See Deborah Kaple, "Soviet Advisors in China in the 1950s" in Odd Arne Westad, ed., *Brothers in Arms: The Rise and Fall of the Sino-Soviet Alliance, 1945–1963* (Washington, D.C., and Stanford, Calif.: Woodrow Wilson Center Press/ Stanford University Press, 1998), for the details.

30. Mochulsky passed away on November 25, 1999.

31. Stephen F. Cohen and Katrina vanden Heuvel, *Voices of Glasnost* (New York: Norton), 1991.

32. See, for instance, the BBC story of December 28, 2008, "Stalin Voted Third-Best Russian." http://news.bbc.co.uk/2/hi/europe/7802485.stm

33. See Solzhenitsyn, *The Gulag Archipelago*, volume 2, chapter 1, "The Fingers of Aurora."

34. The Bolsheviks distinguished between the acceptable class, the proletariat, which included workers, soldiers, and peasants; and the unacceptable class, the bourgeoisie. In the latter class fell businessmen, landowners, shopkeepers, and intellectuals, all of whom were deemed to be against Soviet power, or "counterrevolutionary." Labeling people by their class turned out to be very useful, for the revolutionaries found that they could label a group of people, and if they were deemed to be anti-Soviet in any way, it was easy to eliminate this class by simply killing them, or throwing them into prisons (later, the Gulag). Labels were given to the streams of arrested, known as "repressed persons." For a list of labels leading to mass arrests, see Appendix 1. For a detailed look at the formation of the Cheka, see Donald Rayfield, *Stalin and His Hangmen: The Tyrant and Those Who Killed for Him* (New York: Random House, 2004), and Hagenloh, *Stalin's Police.*

35. Solzhenitsyn, *The Gulag Archipelago*, volume 2, p. 21. Also, RSFSR refers to the Russian Republic, or Russian Soviet Federative Socialist Republic.

36. Applebaum, *Gulag: A History*, p. 20. See also the 1988 film *Solovki Power* by Marina Goldovskaia.

37. See Khlevniuk, *The History of the Gulag*, p. 9, for details.

38. One of the main goals of Stalin's First Five-Year Plan (1928–1932) was to collectivize agriculture and industrialize the country. In 1928 Stalin announced that the peasants were to "pay a tribute" for industrialization, a program that amounted to a wholesale liquidation of the peasant class. The best description of this state-sponsored tragedy is Lynne Viola's masterful book *The Unknown Gulag: The Lost World of Stalin's Special Settlements* (New York: Oxford University

Press, 2007). Collectivization was so important that many of the Politburo members themselves took part in the bloody violence of grain requisition. See Simon Sebag Montefiore, *Court of the Red Tsar* (New York: Knopf, 2004) for a fascinating account of the lives of the top Soviet leadership.

39. Robert Conquest, *The Harvest of Sorrow: Soviet Collectivization and the Terror-Famine* (New York: Oxford University Press, 1987).

40. See Conquest, *The Great Terror*, for a detailed look at this period.

41. Anne Applebaum, "Inside the Gulag," *New York Review of Books*, June 15, 2000.

42. *Moscow News*, March 4, 1990. Cited by David Hosford, Pamela Kachurin, and Thomas Lamont, "Gulag: Soviet Prison Camps and Their Legacy" (Boston: The National Park Service and Harvard University, 2007).

43. See Gregory, *Terror by Quota*, 2009.

44. The book, *Belomor: An Account of the Construction of the New Canal between the White Sea and the Baltic Sea* (New York: H. Smith and R. Haas, 1935), is an amazing piece of Soviet propaganda.

45. See Cynthia A. Ruder, *Making History for Stalin: The Story of the Belomor Canal*, 1988; and Mikhail Morukov, "The White Sea-Baltic Canal," in Gregory and Lazarev, eds., *The Economics of Forced Labor*.

46. Khlevniuk, "The Economy of the OGPU, NKVD, and MVD of the USSR."

47. Mochulsky does not explain how his father was able to escape his likely fate, but there are many stories of people who successfully fled to avoid arrest. The possibility also exists that the father had to "earn" his escape through some actions that Mochulsky might never have known, or perhaps knew and failed to mention.

48. Khlevniuk, *The History of the Gulag*, p. 236.

49. Two interesting works on the Polish and Finnish convicts are Katharine R. Jolluck's *Exile and Identity: Polish Women in the Soviet Union during World War II* (Pittsburgh: University of Pittsburgh Press, 2002), and Unto Parvilahti's memoir *Beria's Gardens: Ten Years' Captivity in Russia and Siberia*, trans. Alan Blair (London: Hutchinson, 1959).

50. Scholars have long debated whether Stalin thought of the Gulag as a political tool, that is, a place to send real and perceived enemies of Soviet power, or whether he viewed it as another sector of the Soviet economy. See discussion in Khlevniuk, "The Economy of the OGPU, NKVD, and MVD of the USSR "

51. Khlevniuk, "The Economy of the OGPU, NKVD, and MVD of the USSR," p. 64.

52. Mochulsky referred to himself as a civilian, or *volnonaemnii*, in contrast to the NKVD personnel who ran the camps. These civilians worked for the NKVD, but considered themselves temporary employees as opposed to the career-NKVD employees in the Gulag. In an interview in 1992, Mochulsky explained that in light of the German threat of invasion already expected in 1940, the Central Committee of the CPSU decided that the USSR needed to increase the number of party members present at the Gulag camps, to help manage the camps. Unpublished interview, May 3, 1993, in Moscow.

53. Statistics from M. B. Smirnov, ed., *Sistema ispravitelno-trudovykh lagerei v SSSR 1923–1960* [The System of Corrective Labor Camps in the USSR, 1923–1960], (Moscow: Zvenia, 1998), p. 387.

54. Applebaum, *Gulag: A History*, p. 579.

55. The day after Stalin died, Beria suggested streamlining the work of the secret police and moving prisoners from Gulag camps to other ministries. See Amy Knight, *Beria: Stalin's First Lieutenant* (Princeton, NJ: Princeton University Press, 1993), pp. 183–84.

56. For more on the populations of Komi during this time period, see Elena Bole, "The Komi ASSR during the Great Patriotic War: The Demographic Factor in the Development of Strategic Branches of Industry," *Journal of Slavic Military Studies* 22 (2009): 177–94.

57. Applebaum, *Gulag: A History*, p. 78.

58. See Appendix 2 for the famous Article 58 of the RSFSR Criminal Code.

59. Yelena Sidorkina, "Years under Guard," in *Till My Tale Is Told: Women's Memoirs of the Gulag*, ed. Simeon Vilensky, trans. Cathy Porter and John Crowfoot (Bloomington: Indiana University Press, 1999), pp. 15–96.

60. Ginsberg, *Journey into the Whirlwind*, p. 301. See pp. 273–331 for a full description of this hellish trip.

61. Ginsberg, *Journey into the Whirlwind*, p. 301.

62. Janusz Bardach and Kathleen Gleeson, *Man Is Wolf to Man: Surviving the Gulag*, (Berkeley: University of California Press, 1999), p. 103.

63. Bardach and Gleeson, *Man Is Wolf to Man*, p. 105.

64. John Noble, *I Was a Slave in Russia: An American Tells His Story* (New York: Devin-Adair Publishers, 1958), pp. 86–87.

65. Vladimir Petrov, *Escape from the Future* (Bloomington: Indiana University Press, 1973), pp. 188–189.

66. Solzhenitsyn, *The Gulag Archipelago*, volume 2, p. 416.

67. Solzhenitsyn, *The Gulag Archipelago*, volume 2, p. 126.

68. Noble, *I Was a Slave in Russia*, p. 90.

69. Noble, *I Was a Slave in Russia*, pp. 92–93.

70. Lev Kopelev, *No Jail for Thought*, trans. Anthony Austin (New York: Penguin, 1979), p. 190.

71. Nadezhda Surovtseva, "Vladivostok Transit," in Vilensky, *Till My Tale Is Told*, p. 184.

72. Dmitri Panin, *The Notebooks of Sologdin*, trans. John Moore (New York: Harcourt Brace Jovanovich, 1976), p. 84.

73. Ginsberg, *Within the Whirlwind*, p. 20.

74. Shalamov, *Kolyma Tales*, p. 280.

75. Shalamov, *Kolyma Tales*, pp. 280–81.

76. Shalamov, *Kolyma Tales*, p. 282.

77. See, for example, Lynne Viola's presentation "Was the 'Other Archipelago' a Part of the Gulag? The Kulak Special Settlements," and Wim van Meurs' talk, "Siberia's Two Faces: Peripheral Isolation of the Unwanted and Core of Regime Legitimacy," Harvard University, 2006.

78. Galina Mikhailovna Ivanova, *Labor Camp Socialism: The Gulag in the Soviet Totalitarian System*, trans. Carol Flath (Armonk, N.Y., and London: M.E. Sharpe, 2000), p. 184.

1. NKVD USSR, or the People's Commissariat of Internal Affairs of the USSR, was the leading secret police organization for the USSR. Lenin founded the original secret police organization, known as the Cheka (Extraordinary Commission) in 1917. Due to various reorganizations, it has been known as the Cheka, GPU, OGPU, and NKVD. In this book we simply refer to NKVD. Later its name changed to the familiar KGB, then the FSB.

2. A kulak, or "fist" in Russian, was the name the Bolsheviks gave to the farmers during Stalin's deadly collectivization campaign. Starting with forcible grain requisition in 1928, farmers were "dekulakized," which meant the government took away their private farms and forcibly moved them onto government-run collective farms. From the deportations, executions, and resulting famine, Robert Conquest estimates that 14.5 million people died. See Robert Conquest, *The Harvest of Sorrow: Soviet Collectivization and the Terror-Famine* (New York: Oxford University Press, 1987).

3. A norm was a quota the authorities set for how much work a prisoner was expected to do every day, in order to qualify for his ration of food.

4. The most famous being Aleksandr I. Solzhenitsyn's magisterial three-volume set *The Gulag Archipelago, 1918–1956: An Experiment in Literary Investigation*, trans. Thomas P. Whitney (Parts I–IV) and Harry Willetts (Parts V–VII) (New York: Harper and Row, 1985).

5. "Zona," or "the zone," means prison compound. The word "zek" is an abbreviation in Russian for the word for prisoner, which is *zakliuchennii*, and is often written in Russian as *z/k*.

6. From 1928 to 1991, Soviet law required college graduates to accept a two- to three-year assignment to repay the country for their education. Katharine Bliss Eaton, *Daily Life in the Soviet Union* (Westport, Conn.: Greenwood, 2004).

7. It is not clear whether Mochulsky understood at the time that the secret police administered the USSR's railroads. On January 4, 1940, the Chief Administration of Camps for Railroad Construction was formed within the NKVD. See Oleg Khlevniuk, *The History of the Gulag*, trans. Vadim A. Staklo (New Haven, Conn., and London: Yale University Press, 2004), p. 242.

8. Belorussia was incorporated into the USSR in 1919, as the Belorussian Soviet Socialist Republic.

9. Komsomol, or Communist Youth League, which was the Soviet Communist Party's organization for young people. See Ilya Zemtsov, *Encyclopedia of Soviet Life* (New Brunswick, N.J.: Transaction Publishers, 1991).

10. Known as GUSHOSDOR GULAG NKVD, or Main Administration of Highways of GULAG NKVD. This organization was in charge of all road-building in the USSR, and relied on prison and Gulag labor for many of its projects.

11. CPSU is the Communist Party of the Soviet Union.

12. This is tantamount to being sent to the Foreign Service Institute of the State Department. It means the person is being prepared for a career in diplomacy.

13. This is the same Yuri Andropov who later served as general secretary of the CPSU from November 1982 until February 1984.
14. Sometimes called First Chief Directorate in English, its function was foreign intelligence.
15. This was a KGB ranking given him when he was transferred to the Central Committee of the CPSU.
16. This is the Soviet designation for World War II.
17. A unit of prisoners was a group of Gulag prisoners (it can be several hundred) who lived and worked together under the unit boss.
18. Civilians were people who worked at the Gulag camp as a job. Civilians denoted nonprisoners as well as former prisoners who had served their terms and then stayed on to work for GULAG NKVD.

CHAPTER 1

1. He is referring to the arrests and show trials of the 1930s, when thousands of people were sent to the Gulag or simply ordered to be shot.
2. See Aleksandr I. Solzhenitsyn, *The Gulag Archipelago, 1918–1956: An Experiment in Literary Investigation,* trans. Thomas P. Whitney (Parts I–IV) and Harry Willetts (Parts V–VII) (New York: Harper and Row, 1985), and Robert Conquest, *The Great Terror: A Reassessment* (New York: Oxford University Press, 1991), for many such stories.
3. This is a twelfth-century poem by an anonymous writer. See Caryl Emerson, *The Cambridge Introduction to Russian Literature* (Cambridge: Cambridge University Press, 2008).
4. Translator's note: Mochulsky continues with the family's story here. "We left Minsk for Moscow, where my father had friends. In 1917, he had graduated from Moscow State University's Philological Faculty, and several of his classmates had stayed to work in Moscow. For several years, my father worked as a Russian language and literature teacher in the Moscow schools. In 1946, he defended his dissertation, received his Candidate of Philological Sciences and took a job at Moscow State University, where he worked until the end of his life. There he taught a course on nineteenth-century Russian literature. He died in 1973. In the second half of the 1980s, *The Encyclopedia of Belorussian Literature and Art* was published in Minsk, in several volumes (1, 2, 3, 5) in which his name and contribution to the field is mentioned."
5. This blanket denunciation sent thousands of innocent people to the Gulag.
6. This refers to the USSR's first prison labor camp, located at a former monastery on the Solovetsky Islands in the White Sea, which was opened in 1923. It became a notorious Gulag camp under Stalin. See the extraordinary documentary film *Solovki Power* by Marina Goldovskaia (1988).
7. This was a very long canal built by convicts in the 1930s, linking the White Sea and the Baltic Sea. It was Stalin's first large-scale project using slave labor. As impressive as it was, in the end it not very useful because it was so shallow and poorly built. Thousands of people died building it. See Mikhail Morukhov, "The White Sea-Baltic Canal," in *The Economics of Forced Labor: The Soviet Gulag,*

edited by Paul Gregory and Valery Lazarev (Stanford, Calif.: Hoover Institution Press, 2003).

8. Based on a play by Nikolai Pogodin, *Aristocrats: A Comedy in Four Acts*, trans. Anthony Wixley and Robert S. Carr (London: Lawrence & Wishart, 1937[?]).

9. The People's Commissariats later became known as ministries, which are similar to cabinets in the U.S. governmental system.

10. The Molotov-Ribbentrop Pact (formally, the Treaty of Nonaggression between Germany and the Union of Soviet Socialist Republics) of August 24, 1939, pledged neutrality between the two nations. It also included secret protocols giving the USSR portions of Poland, Romania, Finland, and the Baltic States. Once the pact was signed, the Soviets rolled into these countries and "liberated" them by incorporating them into the socialist camp. Richard Overy, *Russia's War: A History of the Soviet War Effort, 1941–1945* (New York: Penguin, 1997).

CHAPTER 2

1. On September 1, 1939, the Germans invaded Poland.

2. Signed on August 24, 1939.

3. Once the Germans invaded Poland, the Soviet Red Army occupied the territories in Eastern Europe that the pact allowed in the secret protocols. The NKVD imprisoned or shot thousands of people in this takeover, including fifteen thousand Polish officers, who were buried in a mass grave at Katyn. Richard Overy, *Russia's War: A History of the Soviet War Effort, 1941–1945* (New York: Penguin, 1997), pp. 82–84; David Glantz and Jonathan House, *When Titans Clashed: How the Red Army Stopped Hitler* (Lawrence: University Press of Kansas, 1995), p. 17.

4. The Donets Basin, known as the Donbas, was the USSR's main source of coal. It is located in present-day Ukraine. Krivoi Rog was the center of the USSR's steel industry, also located in present-day Ukraine.

5. Gnat-like flies, but smaller.

6. He used the word *Instantsiia*, which means the highest authority in the hierarchy of authorities. Mochulsky told me later that *Instantsiia* referred to the Central Committee of the Communist Party of the Soviet Union (CPSU CC), and the government.

7. The word *stroika*, or construction site, was a euphemism for forced labor camp.

8. The camp's formal name was Severo-Pechorski ITL, or the Northern Pechora Corrective Labor Camp. The distinction in the names was made to maintain the fiction that these were actual construction sites, and not forced labor camps. M. B. Smirnov, ed. *Sistema ispravitelno-trudovykh lagerei v SSSR 1923–1960* [The System of Corrective Labor Camps in the USSR, 1923–1960] (Moscow: Zvenia, 1998), pp. 380 and 387.

9. While there was a genuine threat of war at this time, this paranoia about "being surrounded by enemies" had long been a theme of Soviet life. It

began under Lenin, during the civil war, and was still used in the 1930s to justify harsh working conditions at new factories and extraordinary demands on workers to "overfulfill" their work norms. A good example of this is in Stephen Kotkin, *Magnetic Mountain: Stalinism as a Civilization* (Berkeley: University of California Press, 1995), about the building of Magnitagorsk.

10. He uses the word *kharakteristika*, which was not only a record of the courses taken at an institute, but also remarks on the student's community or political activism, membership of student organizations, and CPSU affiliation.

11. Cadres Department refers to the Personnel Department.

CHAPTER 3

1. Mochulsky changed their names in this memoir.

2. It is true that Stalin rarely spoke to crowds or even gave radio addresses. He also assumed a very modest demeanor at meetings among his ministers and staff. Simon Sebag Montefiore, *Stalin: The Court of the Red Tsar* (New York: Knopf, 2004).

CHAPTER 4

1. Jacques Rossi, *The Gulag Handbook*, trans. William A. Burhans (New York: Paragon House, 1989), p. 258.

2. According to the Beaufort Scale of Wind Force, a force 12 wind indicates hurricane conditions with winds blowing at approximately 73–83 miles per hour.

3. Rossi, *The Gulag Handbook*, p. 446.

4. Rossi, *The Gulag Handbook*, p. 239.

5. Some four hundred thousand people who had lived in prewar Poland were deported east to camps and hard labor in three major operations in 1940. One in six of them died in their first year of exile. Donald Rayfield, *Stalin and His Hangmen: The Tyrant and Those Who Killed for Him* (New York: Random House, 2004), p. 373. In all, around two million Polish families were sent to the Gulag via cattle cars. Thousands died of malnutrition, disease, and exposure before even getting to the camps. Richard Overy, *Russia's War: A History of the Soviet War Effort, 1941–1945* (New York: Penguin, 1997).

6. In the Soviet planned economy, every worker had a daily, weekly, and monthly plan of work they had to do. In the Gulag, the government tied their food rations to how much work they actually accomplished every day.

7. Wladislaw Anders was a general in the cavalry and fought the Germans when they attacked Poland in 1939. During the fighting he was injured, and taken prisoner by the Soviets, who took him to the Lubyanka Prison in Moscow, where he was tortured. After the Germans attacked the USSR, he was released and ordered to form a Polish Army that would fight alongside the Red Army. In March 1942, he led his troops out of the USSR. Anne Applebaum, *Gulag: A History* (New York: Doubleday, 2003), p. 453.

8. This was a common charge, usually fabricated, which was a reason to throw people into the Gulag.

CHAPTER 5

1. VOKhR is the Russian acronym for the camp's armed guards. (Literally: Militarized Guards at Places of Confinement.) These were low-level NKVD employees, whose duties included guarding, escorting, and supervising prisoners. I have left the term VOKhR in the text because it is used as a common prison word, pronounced "voxer." See Aleksandr I. Solzhenitsyn, *The Gulag Archipelago, 1918–1956: An Experiment in Literary Investigation*, trans. Thomas P. Whitney (Parts I–IV) and Harry Willetts (Parts V–VII) (New York: Harper and Row, 1985), vol. 2, pp. 557–63, on the role of the VOKhR.
2. Chekist is another name for an NKVD operative. This name dates back to the organization's Leninist origins, when it was called the Cheka. The first head of the Cheka, Feliks Dzerzhinksy, gave the Cheka its romantic aura by calling it the "sword and flame of the revolution."
3. Each Camp Administration had its own Political Department (*Politotdel*), which exercised party supervision over the entire administration except the security platoon. The Political Department was subordinate to the Gulag Political Administration in Moscow. See Jaques Rossi, *The Gulag Handbook*, trans. William A. Burhans (New York: Paragon House, 1989), p. 322.
4. In January 1939, the head of the NKVD, Beria, created the Special Technical Bureau to "make use of the prisoners possessing special technical knowledge and skills" to "construct and produce new armaments for the army and the navy." Oleg Khlevniuk, *The History of the Gulag*, trans. Vadim A. Staklo (New Haven, Conn., and London: Yale University Press, 2004).
5. This is a card game called points.
6. The mass arrests took place during the Great Purges, 1937–1939.
7. A "troika" was a three-man group (an NKVD employee, a party official, and a person from the judiciary) that operated totally outside of the law. These extra-judicial powers allowed them to charge people with crimes (mostly invented ones) and levy sentences, including long Gulag terms or death by shooting.
8. Mochulsky explained that a Selektor was a kind of a telephone with one button. If you pressed the button, the other party could hear you, but when you let go of the button, you could only hear the other party speaking but not speak yourself. Interview May 3, 1993, in Moscow.

CHAPTER 6

1. This was on November 7, 1940.
2. Passes were issued to some prisoners, such as those used as experts on a particular job, so they were able to move about without the presence of the VOKhR guards. These passes were never given to political prisoners or the most dangerous recidivists.

3. The prisoners were not allowed to wear the star on their clothing, since this would be a desecration of a beloved communist symbol. Convicts no longer had the rights of Soviet citizens. Similarly, they could not use the word "comrade," and instead were forced to use the prerevolutionary term "citizen."

4. During the war, a full quarter of all Gulag prisoners died in the camps. Steven A. Barnes, "Researching Daily Life in the Gulag," *Kritika* 1, no. 2 (2000): fn 3.

5. He might have hesitated out of respect for the Communist Party, which was the most important organization in Soviet life at the time. Its policies could not be questioned. Not being a Communist Party member himself, Volodia could feel nervous making policy recommendations to a party member.

6. This was a common charge that landed thousands of people in the Gulag. Throughout the Stalin period, work and managerial errors were treated as serious crimes, often resulting in long prison sentences or death by shooting. Hugo S. Cunningham, "Stalinist Laws to Tighten 'Labor Discipline,' 1938–1940," www.cyberussr.com/rus/labor-discip.html

7. *Tufta* meant forgery, deception, work done only for show, figures purposely inflated, and many other kinds of cheating on results.

8. Finland appeared as one of the "spoils" in the secret protocols to the Molotov-Ribbentrop Pact. When the USSR tried to establish bases in Finland, though, the Finns fought back. Known as the Winter War, because it took place during the winter of 1939–1940, it was a humiliating defeat for the Soviet Union. The Gulag prisoners mentioned here were Soviets who had fought in this war. See Richard Glantz and Jonathan House, *When Titans Clashed: How the Red Army Stopped Hitler* (Lawrence: University Press of Kansas, 1995), pp. 18–23.

9. This was true of all Soviets who were taken prisoner, or ever had any kind of foreign contact. See Aleksandr I. Solzhenitsyn, *The Gulag Archipelago, 1918–1956: An Experiment in Literary Investigation*, trans. Thomas P. Whitney (Parts I–IV) and Harry Willetts (Parts V–VII) (New York: Harper and Row, 1985).

10. Since this security platoon commander arrived at Pernashor later, this seems to be a snide reference to the building of the barracks that had taken place in his absence.

11. He does not say how they kept the work sites lit at nights for these shifts.

12. The massive famine that hit the USSR during and after collectivization affected those in the Central Asian republics, as well. Tens of thousands of Central Asians died of hunger. Uzbekistan was formally incorporated into the USSR in 1919.

13. Traditional Uzbek national dish of rice, meat, and vegetables.

14. According to new Russian research, the numbers of prisoners in this Gulag camp ballooned during these years. In January 1940, there were thirty-eight hundred prisoners; in January 1941, thirty-five thousand prisoners, and in June 1941, there were ninety-two thousand prisoners at Pechorlag. M. B. Smirnov, ed. *Sistema ispravitelno-trudovykh lagerei v SSSR 1923–1960* [The System of Corrective Labor Camps in the USSR, 1923–1960] (Moscow: Zvenia, 1998), p. 386.

15. The prison labor camp was located in the Komi Autonomous Soviet Socialist Republic, a large area in the Far North populated mostly by a nomadic native

population known as the Komi. See L. M. Morozov, *Gulag v Komi krai 1929–1956* [The Gulag in the Komi Region, 1929–1956] (Syktyvkar: Syktyvkarskii gosudarstvennii universitet, 1997).

16. In other words, the highest-ranking bosses from both organizations (the NKVD and the Communist Party) that ran the Gulag camps were in attendance.

17. This refers to the Soviet takeover of territories in 1939, as part of the Nazi-Soviet pact. See Richard Overy, *Russia's War: A History of the Soviet War Effort, 1941–1945* (New York: Penguin, 1997), ch. 3.

CHAPTER 7

1. In the course of the memoir, he is switched from job to job several times. From other camp accounts, this appears to have been common in the Gulag, but it is unclear whether it was a conscious policy or simply based on need.

2. Mochulsky does not say what the man was charged with.

3. Again, there is no mention of the man's crime.

4. Also known as Butyrki, his was the largest prison in Moscow, and was used as an NKVD pretrial investigative center. Jaques Rossi, *The Gulag Handbook*, trans. William A. Burhans (New York: Paragon House, 1989), p. 38. See Robert Conquest, *The Great Terror: A Reassessment* (New York: Oxford University Press, 1991).

5. This is a town in Yaroslavl Oblast, on the Volga River.

CHAPTER 8

1. The 1930s were rife with government-sponsored killings and incarcerations, as Stalin and NKVD head Yezhov went after supposed "enemies of the people" in every sphere of Soviet life. The NKVD was also purged, killing off the best Gulag managers, and mortality at the camps soared. In 1938, Stalin replaced Yezhov with Beria, who set out to make the Gulag more economically viable. Donald Rayfield, *Stalin and His Hangmen: The Tyrant and Those Who Killed for Him* (New York: Random House, 2004).

2. An "absolutely secret" NKVD memo from December 25, 1940, detailing this "criminal behavior" on the part of the leadership can be found in A. I. Kokurin, and Yu. N. Morukov, *Stalinskie stroiki GULAGu, 1930–1953* [Stalin's Gulag, 1930–1953] (Moscow: Materik Publishing House, 2005), pp. 268–70.

3. This is the same director who tried earlier to have him expelled from the Communist Party.

4. Politicals were those who were not criminals, but were serving time for a political sentence. They were known as "58ers," after Article 58 of the Criminal Code. See Appendix 2.

5. Sometimes prisoners who had served their terms were forced to stay on as "civilian employees" by the Gulag. Often, as in the case of a person with needed skills, the job the NKVD offered was good enough to keep them.

CHAPTER 9

1. Taganrog is located on the Azov Sea, which is part of the Black Sea.
2. In the survivor literature, it is usually called the "Isolator."
3. These were hardened professional criminals belonging to the "club." These men observed the rules of the thieves' world only. Jacques Rossi, *The Gulag Handbook*, trans. William A. Burhans (New York: Paragon House, 1989), p. 25.

CHAPTER 11

1. Political prisoners were also called 58ers (sentenced according to the criminal code Article 58, which included all "counterrevolutionary" activities), and they were considered more dangerous than the common criminals. Appendix 2 contains this famous Article 58.
2. This section of the Criminal Code (from 1926–1959) lists the "counterrevolutionary crimes," which included displaying an anti-Soviet attitude, destruction of socialist property, sabotage at work, and so on.
3. An Uzbek word referring to participants in the Central Asian patriotic movements against the Soviets in the 1920s. Jacques Rossi, *The Gulag Handbook*, trans. William A. Burhans (New York: Paragon House, 1989), p. 17.
4. As a way to increase productivity at the workplace all over the Soviet Union, the Communist Party had "competitions" among the workers. The ones who won were lauded in the press, given special attention and sometimes concrete rewards of money or goods.

CHAPTER 12

1. Little biting flies.
2. The *Operchekotdel*, which was also known as the "third department," was the main administrative department that supervised all the security platoons and VOKhR officers who worked in the various departments and units of the labor camp. Jacques Rossi, *The Gulag Handbook*, trans. William A. Burhans (New York: Paragon House, 1989), p. 268.
3. The word here is *chekisti*, or Chekists, a proud reference back to the founding of the Soviet Security Agency in 1917. No matter how many times the agency itself changes its name, the employees still call themselves Chekists.

CHAPTER 13

1. At 3:15 AM on June 22, 1941, the Germans attacked the USSR in Operation Barbarossa.
2. Here he writes *Faterlianda*, which is a Russianization of the German word for fatherland.
3. One prisoner at Pechorlag remembers not knowing anything about the war until the fall of 1941, because the bosses were not allowed to tell the convicts. Testimony of Ernest Vider taken on September 12, 1997, Shoah Foundation Archives.

4. This was because the Soviets had invaded their territory in 1939 as part of the Nazi-Soviet pact.
5. Stalin was caught totally off-guard when the Nazis attacked. The Germans used this to their advantage and made great strides into the territory of the USSR quickly. See the account in Constantine Pleshakov, *Stalin's Folly* (Boston and New York: Mariner Books, 2005).
6. He uses the Soviet name for World War II.
7. In August 1941. It actually was an American program that gave war aid to the USSR and Britain and other countries that were fighting the Axis. The goods that came in through Murmansk came by a rather dangerous convoy from British ports to Murmansk. Richard Overy, *Russia's War: A History of the Soviet War Effort, 1941–1945* (New York: Penguin, 1997), p. 197.
8. Previously the camp bosses had used a document called an "Inclement Weather Graph," conforming to instructions from the Gulag Medical Administration. Before 1936, prisoners had to work outside until the temperature reached −35 degrees C; after 1936, it was −40 C. Jacques Rossi, *The Gulag Handbook*, trans. William A. Burhans (New York: Paragon House, 1989), p. 88.
9. He means with no higher education.

CHAPTER 14

1. Often called the Siege of Leningrad, this blockade by the Germans lasted from September 9, 1941, until January 18, 1941, or about nine hundred days. Over one million inhabitants died from starvation, cold, and disease. See Michael Jones, *Leningrad: State of Siege* (New York: Basic Books, 2008).
2. Altai Krai is a mountainous region in the south of the country, bordering Kazakhstan.
3. Sometimes the camp bosses made special agreements with prisoners when they needed a job done urgently. This was done outside the official norms. Jaques Rossi, *The Gulag Handbook*, trans. William A. Burhans (New York: Paragon House, 1989), p. 471.

CHAPTER 15

1. A Russian city located approximately 360 kilometers (223 miles) southwest of Moscow.
2. A lobar pneumonia is an infection that only involves a single lobe, or section, of the lung.
3. The entire camp, or construction site, was 500 kilometers (310 miles) long. As mentioned earlier, Pechorlag was divided into three regions, each of which had several departments. The departments, in turn, were made up of many smaller camp units.

CHAPTER 16

1. A large number of Gulag bosses and other employees eventually became victims themselves in the Gulag, so it is likely that this boss himself had been threatened in this manner.

2. According to the Geneva Convention, Section III, "The Labor of Prisoners of War officers or persons of equivalent status ask for suitable work, it shall be found for them, so far as possible, but they may in no circumstances be compelled to work."

3. Years later, Mochulsky received two "Red Flag Orders of Labor," one for his work in diplomacy, and the other for his work in the intelligence service. Later, he also received the "Order of the Red Star," and other medals and commendations.

CHAPTER 18

1. The author's name was Aleksandr Evdokimovich Korneichuk. His play *Front* appeared in *Pravda* in 1942, and attracted considerable attention at home and abroad for its sharp criticisms of inefficiencies in the Red Army. Reviewed by F. J. Whitfield in *American Slavic and East European Review*, 5, no. 3/4 (November 1946), pp. 203–4.

2. His point was that the civil war commanders had to be replaced by younger men if the war with Germany was to be won. Charles Moser, *Cambridge History of Russian Literature* (Cambridge and New York: Cambridge University Press, 1992).

3. Komsomol is the abbreviation of Communist Youth Organization, the wing of the Communist Party for young people (ages 14–28), founded in 1918. It was an important source of labor mobilization during the war, as well as, in general, a place where young people could learn the rules and values of the CPSU.

4. The Political Department was part of the CPSU.

5. In other words, the Communist Party could pull rank, and in this case, it did.

6. In the USSR, workers received packets of food or clothing from time to time at work. These were often random assortments of things, but everything was useful to someone. However, if the father was sent to the front and the mother did not work, these packets upon which the family had relied were no longer forthcoming.

7. The Political Department of the Camp Administration exercised party supervision over the entire place, and was not subordinate to the administration or the security platoon. Jacques Rossi, *The Gulag Handbook*, trans. William A. Burhans (New York: Paragon House, 1989), p. 322.

8. This means that he was now an employee of the NKVD, not GULAG NKVD.

CHAPTER 20

1. Orel is a city located approximately 359 kilometers (223 miles) southwest of Moscow. Orel was occupied by the German Wehrmacht in October 1941, and liberated in August 1943, after the Battle of Kursk. The city and its surroundings were devastated.

2. Now he worked for the Main Administration of Highways, which was a part of the NKVD. It was officially called GUSHODOR GULAG NKVD.

3. Kharkov (now Kharkiv) is Ukraine's second-largest city.
4. Sovetskaia Gavan is a town in Khabarovsk Krai, Russia, a port on the Strait of Tartary (part of the Sea of Japan) and the eastern terminus of the Baikal-Amur railway line.
5. This is the capital of Lithuania.
6. In other words, the first truck towed the second one, probably to economize on fuel.
7. Colonel general in the NKVD is a high-ranking officer, whose position would be the equivalent in U.S. military ranking somewhere between and three- and four-star general.
8. Lavrenti Beria headed the NKVD from 1938 to 1953, when he was arrested and shot. Amy Knight, *Beria: Stalin's First Lieutenant* (Princeton, N.J.: Princeton University Press, 1993).
9. In other words, the Communist Party outranked the NKVD.
10. See Kenneth Slepyan, *Stalin's Guerillas: Soviet Partisans in World War II* (Lawrence: University Press of Kansas, 2006).
11. He uses the German word *Polizei*, meaning police, but here *Polizei* refers to the non-Germans such as Belorussians, Lithuanians, Ukrainians, and Russians who had worked for the Germans against the USSR during the war.
12. Germany's capitulation to the USSR was signed late in the evening on May 8, 1945.

Chapter 21

1. A sazhen is 2.13 meters, or almost 7 feet.
2. Nicholas I (Nikolai I in Russian) was the emperor of Russia from 1825 until 1855.
3. In other words, they asked the doctor to measure the emperor's penis. He told them it was 84 millimeters long, or approximately 3.1 inches.

Chapter 22

1. See Lynne Viola, *The Unknown Gulag: The Lost World of Stalin's Special Settlements* (New York: Oxford University Press, 2007), for a close look at this tragedy that befell the peasantry in the USSR.
2. Orlando Figes documents this habit of "learned secrecy" that the Stalin years brought on among Soviet citizens. Orlando Figes, *The Whisperers: Private Life in Stalin's Russia* (New York: Picador, 2007).

Chapter 23

1. Food and goods that were not available anywhere were known as "deficit" in the Soviet planned economy.
2. She thought he was saying "I want to fuck you" in Russian.
3. This is because the major cities in the Komi were built by Gulag labor during Stalin's time.

CHAPTER 24

1. This was the camp unit that housed the hardened criminals.
2. A paddy wagon to transport prisoners around towns; also known as a "Black Maria."
3. Atamansha translates as Cossack leader, and literally means bandit or highway lady. Here it just means the leader of lesbians in her camp unit.
4. This is about 6 feet 7 inches.
5. Chapter 26 discusses in detail how Mochulsky extricated himself from GULAG NKVD and into the Higher Diplomatic School of the USSR Ministry of Foreign Affairs.
6. The Gulag system often promoted convicts to camp management positions. Naftaly Frenkel, arrested in 1923 and sent to Solovki as a prisoner, worked his way up to a management job in which he is credited with linking the inmates' food rations to their rate of production. It is thought that this innovation led Stalin to believe that prison labor could be efficient, and the practice was adopted in all Gulag camps. Frenkel became the production chief at the White Sea Canal, then went on to head Bamlag (the camp set up to build the Baikal-Amur Rail line) in 1937.
7. This describes a typical "communal apartment" built in the Stalin period in many Soviet cities.

CHAPTER 25

1. Mosfilm is one of the largest and oldest film studios in the Soviet Union and Russia. Founded in 1923, it has always been a very influential and prestigious organization.

CHAPTER 26

1. On March 15, 1946, the new name for USSR NKVD was now USSR Ministry of Internal Affairs, known as MVD. Jacques Rossi, *The Gulag Handbook*, trans. William A. Burhans (New York: Paragon House, 1989), p. 231.
2. Once a person had worked for the secret services, it was nearly impossible to leave the organization.

CHAPTER 27

1. He means here the secret services, the NKVD and MVD.
2. There is an ongoing debate among scholars about the real purpose of this extensive Gulag. Some argue that Stalin needed the camps to absorb his perceived enemies, and others argue that the government believed that slave labor could be economically feasible.
3. The Bolsheviks felt that most criminals were in the correct class, namely, part of the proletarian class, and not the bourgeois class, and therefore were natural allies to the revolution once they were reeducated. The political prisoners, in their eyes, were not reformable.

AFTERWORD

1. The *Oxford English Dictionary*, http://www.oed.com/
2. Nadezhda Mandelstam, *Hope against Hope*, trans. Max Hayword (New York: Modern Library, 1999).
3. William Zinsser, *Inventing the Truth: The Art and Craft of Memoir* (New York: Mariner Books, 1998), pp. 14–15.
4. Leona Toker, *Return from the Archipelago: Narratives of Gulag Survivors* (Bloomington: Indiana University Press, 2000).
5. Ryszard Kapuscinski, *Travels with Herodotus*, trans. Klara Glowczewska (New York: Knopf, 2007), p. 262.
6. J. A. Cuddon, *A Dictionary of Literary Terms and Literary Theory*, 4th edition (Oxford and Malden, Mass.: Blackwell, 1998), p. 63.
7. The Shoah Foundation, http://college.usc.edu/vhi/
8. State Archive of the Russian Federation (Gosudarstvennyi arkhiv Rossiiskoi Federatsii), Fond r-9414.
9. Ivanova, *Labor Camp Socialism: The Gulag in the Soviet Totalitarian System*, trans. Carol Flath (Armonk, N.Y., and London: M.E. Sharpe, 2000), ch. 3.
10. See Lev Razgon, *True Stories*, trans. John Crowfoot (Ann Arbor, Mich.: Ardis, 1997).
11. www.memo.ru/eng/index.htm.
12. See Primo Levi, *The Drowned and the Saved* (New York: Vintage, 1989).
13. See Brodsky's "Afterword" in Mandelstam's *Hope against Hope*.
14. Testimony of Ernest Vider taken on September 12, 1997, Shoah Foundation Archives.
15. Emil Draitser, "A Life Cut in Half: The Case of Dmitry Bystrolyotov," in *Gulag Studies*, 1 (2008), pp. 35–55. For a full biography of Bystrolyotov, see Draitser's *Stalin's Romeo Spy: The Remarkable Rise and Fall of the KGB's Most Daring Operative* (Evanston, Ill.: Northwestern University Press, 2010).
16. To wit, Vladimir Putin, the current de facto leader of Russia, proudly calls himself a Chekist even today.
17. In this way, he was part of his generation. For a beautiful description of the intelligentsia of Mochulsky's generation, see Vladislav Zubok, *Zhivago's Children: The Last Russian Intelligentsia* (Cambridge, Mass.: Harvard University Press, 2009).
18. See Paul Gregory's blog posting "Stalin's Reach from the Grave: The Moscow Stalin Conference." http://whatpaulgregoryisthinkingabout.blogspot.com/2009/02/stalins-reach-from-grave-moscow-stalin.html.
19. Christopher R. Browning, *Ordinary Men: Reserve Police Battalion 101 and the Final Solution in Poland* (New York: Penguin, 2001).
20. The Russian government now and then calls for more Gulag museums and memorials, as President Medvedev did on October 30, 2009. At the same time, a new Russian history textbook for school children, published in 2007, glosses over Stalin's crimes and heralds his economic achievements. www.timesonline.co.uk/tol/news/world/europe/article2163481.ece
21. See Leona Toker, *Return from the Archipelago*, on the use of memoirs by Gulag scholars.

SELECTED BIBLIOGRAPHY

Gulag Memoirs in English

Bardach, Janusz, and Kathleen Gleeson. *Man Is Wolf to Man: Surviving the Gulag.* Berkeley: University of California Press, 1999.

Ginsberg, Evgeniia. *Journey into the Whirlwind.* Translated by Paul Stevenson and Max Hayward. New York: Harcourt, 1995.

———. *Within the Whirlwind.* Translated by Ian Boland. New York: Harcourt Brace Jovanovich, 1981.

Herling, Gustav. *A World Apart.* Translated by by Andrzej Ciozkosz. New York: Arbor House, 1986.

Kopelev, Lev. *No Jail for Thought.* Translated by Anthony Austin. New York: Penguin, 1979.

Mandelstam, Nadezhda. *Hope against Hope.* Translated by Max Hayword. New York: Modern Library, 1999.

Noble, John. *I Was a Slave in Russia: An American Tells His Story.* New York: Devin-Adair Publishers, 1958.

Panin, Dmitri. *The Notebooks of Sologdin.* Translated by John Moore. New York: Harcourt Brace Jovanovich, 1976.

Parvilahti, Unto. *Beria's Gardens: Ten Years' Captivity in Russia and Siberia.* Translated by Alan Blair. London: Hutchinson, 1959.

Petrov, Vladimir. *Escape from the Future.* Bloomington: Indiana University Press, 1973.

Razgon, Lev. *True Stories.* Translated by John Crowfoot. Ann Arbor, Mich.: Ardis, 1997.

Scholmer, Joseph. *Vorkuta.* Translated by Robert Kee. New York: Henry Holt, 1955.

Tchernavin, Vladimir V. *I Speak for the Silent Prisoners of the Soviets.* Translated by Nicholas M. Oushakoff. Boston: Hale, Cushman & Flint, 1935.

Vilensky, Simeon, ed. *Till My Tale is Told: Women's Memoirs of the Gulag.* Translated by Cathy Porter and John Crowfoot. Bloomington: Indiana University Press, 1999.

Scholarly Books and Articles

Adler, Nanci. *The Gulag Survivor: Beyond the Soviet System.* New Brunswick, N.J.: Transaction, 2004.

Alexopoulos, Golfo. *Stalin's Outcasts: Aliens, Citizens, and the Soviet State, 1926–1936.* Ithaca, N.Y.: Cornell University Press, 2003.

Amis, Martin. *Koba the Dread: Laughter and the Twenty Million.* New York: Vintage, 2002.

Applebaum, Anne. *Gulag: A History.* New York: Doubleday, 2003.

———. "Inside the Gulag." *The New York Review of Books,* June 15, 2000.

Arendt, Hannah. *Eichmann in Jerusalem: A Report on the Banality of Evil.* New York: Penguin, 1994.

Barnes, Steven A. "In a Manner Befitting Soviet Citizens." *Slavic Review* 64, no. 4 (Winter, 2005): 823–50.

———. "Researching Daily Life in the Gulag." *Kritika* 1, no. 2 (2000): 377–90.

Binner, Rolf, Bernd Bonwetsch, and Marc Junge. *Massenmord und Lagerhaft: Die andere Geschichte des Grossen Terrors.* Berlin: Akademie Verlag, 2009.

Bole, Elena N. "The Komi ASSR during the Great Patriotic War: The Demographic Factor in the Development of Strategic Branches of Industry." *Journal of Slavic Military Studies* 22 (2009): 177–94.

Browning, Christopher R. *Ordinary Men: Reserve Police Battalion 101 and the Final Solution in Poland.* New York: Penguin, 2001.

Cohen, Stephen F., and Katrina vanden Heuvel. *Voices of Glasnost.* New York: Norton, 1991.

Conquest, Robert. *The Great Terror: A Reassessment.* New York: Oxford University Press, 1991.

———. *Harvest of Sorrow: Soviet Collectivization and the Terror-Famine.* New York: Oxford University Press, 1987.

Cuddon, J. A., ed. *A Dictionary of Literary Terms and Literary Theory.* 4th edition. Oxford and Malden, MA: Blackwell, 1998.

Cunningham, Hugo S. Article 58, Criminal Code of the USSR (1934.) Translated by Hugo S. Cunningham. http://www.cyberussr.com/rus/uk58-e.html

———. "Stalinist Laws to Tighten 'Labor Discipline,' 1938–1940." www.cyberussr.com/rus/labor-discip.html

Dallin, David J., and Boris P. Nicolaevsky. *Forced Labor in Soviet Russia.* New Haven, Conn.: Yale University Press, 1947.

Draitser, Emil. "A Life Cut in Half: The Case of Dmitry Bystrolyotov." *Gulag Studies* 1 (2008): 35–55.

———. *Stalin's Romeo Spy: The Remarkable Rise and Fall of the KGB's Most Daring Operative.* Evanston, Ill.: Northwestern University Press, 2010.

Eaton, Katherine Bliss. *Daily Life in the Soviet Union.* Westport, Conn.: Greenwood, 2004.

Ellman, Michael. "Soviet Repression Statistics: Some Comments." *Europe-Asia Studies* 54, no. 7 (2002): 1151–72.

Emerson, Caryl. *The Cambridge Introduction to Russian Literature*. Cambridge: Cambridge University Press, 2008.

Ertz, Simon. "Making Sense of the Gulag: Analyzing and Interpreting the Function of the Stalinist Camp System." PERSA Working Paper No. 50. Revised version received 4 March 2008. Original version received 17 August 2007. University of Warwick, Department of Economics. URL: www.warwick .ac.uk/go/persa

Figes, Orlando. *The Whisperers: Private Life in Stalin's Russia*. New York: Picador, 2007.

Getty, J. Arch, and Oleg V. Naumov. *The Road to Terror: Stalin and the Self-Destruction of the Bolsheviks, 1932–1939*. New Haven, Conn.: Yale University Press, 1999.

Getty, J. Arch, Gabor T. Rittersporn, and Viktor N. Zemskov. "Victims of the Soviet Penal System in the Pre-War Years: A First Approach on the Basis of Archival Evidence." *American Historical Review* 98, no. 4 (October 1993): 1017–49.

Glantz, David M., and Jonathan House. *When Titans Clashed: How the Red Army Stopped Hitler*. Lawrence: University Press of Kansas, 1995.

Goldman, Wendy Z. *Terror and Democracy in the Age of Stalin: The Social Dynamics of Repression*. Cambridge: Cambridge University Press, 2007.

Gorky, Maxim, ed. *Belomor: An Account of the Construction of the New Canal between the White Sea and the Baltic Sea*. New York: H. Smith and R. Haas, 1935.

Gregory, Paul. *Behind the Façade of Stalin's Command Economy*. Stanford, Calif.: Hoover Institution Press, 2001.

———. *The Political Economy of Stalinism: Evidence from the Soviet Secret Archives*. Cambridge: Cambridge University Press, 2004.

———. *Terror by Quota: State Security from Lenin to Stalin*. New Haven, Conn.: Yale University Press, 2009.

Gregory, Paul R., and Valery Lazarev, eds. *The Economics of Forced Labor: The Soviet Gulag*. Stanford, Calif.: Hoover Institution Press, 2003.

Hagenloh, Paul. *Stalin's Police: Public Order and Mass Repression in the USSR, 1926–1941*. Baltimore: Johns Hopkins University Press, 2009.

Hochschild, Adam. *The Unquiet Ghost: Russians Remember Stalin*. Boston and New York: Mariner Books, 2003.

Hoffmann, David. Editor. *Stalinism: The Essential Readings*. Malden, Mass.: Blackwell, 2003.

Hollander, Paul, ed. *From the Gulag to the Killing Fields*. Wilmington, Del.: ISI Books, 2006.

———. *Political Pilgrims: Western Intellectuals in Search of the Good Society*. 4th edition. Edison, N.J.: Transaction, 1997.

Hosford, David, Pamela Kachurin, and Thomas Lamont. "Gulag: Soviet Prison Camps and Their Legacy." Boston: The National Park Service and Harvard University, 2007.

Hunter, Holland. *The Soviet Transport Sector*. Washington, D.C.: The Brookings Institution, 1966.

———. *Soviet Transportation Policy*. Cambridge, Mass.: Harvard University Press, 1957.

Ivanova, Galina M. *Labor Camp Socialism: The Gulag in the Soviet Totalitarian System*. Translated by Carol Flath. Armonk, N.Y., and London: M.E. Sharpe, 2000.

Jakobson, Michael. *The Soviet Prison Camp System, 1917–1935*. Lexington: University Press of Kentucky, 1992.

Jasny, Naum. "Labor and Output in Soviet Concentration Camps." *The Journal of Political Economy* 59, no. 5 (October 1951): 405–19.

Jolluck, Katharine R. *Exile and Identity: Polish Women in the Soviet Union during World War II*. Pittsburgh: University of Pittsburgh Press, 2002.

Jones, Michael. *Leningrad: State of Siege*. New York: Basic Books, 2008.

Kaple, Deborah. "The BAM: Labor, Migration, and Prospects for Settlement." *Soviet Geography* 27, no. 10 (1986): 716–40.

———. *Dream of a Red Factory: The Legacy of High Stalinism in China*. New York: Oxford University Press, 1993.

———. "Soviet Advisors in China in the 1950s." In *Brothers in Arms: The Rise and Fall of the Sino-Soviet Alliance, 1945–1963*, edited by Odd Arne Westad. Washington, D.C., and Stanford, Calif.: Woodrow Wilson Center Press/ Stanford University Press, 1998.

———, with Holland Hunter. "Transport in Trouble." *Soviet Economy in the 1980s: Problems and Prospects*. Part 1. Selected papers submitted to the Joint Economic Committee, U.S. Congress, 1982, pp. 216–41.

Kapuscinski, Ryszard. *Travels with Herodotus*. Translated by Klara Glowczewska. New York: Knopf, 2007.

Khlevniuk, Oleg. "The Economy of the OGPU, NKVD, and MVD of the USSR, 1930–1953." In *The Economics of Forced Labor: The Soviet Gulag*, edited by Paul Gregory and Valery Lazarev, pp. 43–66. Stanford, Calif.: Hoover Institution Press, 2003.

———. *The History of the Gulag*. Translated by by Vadim A. Staklo. New Haven, Conn., and London: Yale University Press, 2004.

Klimkova, Oxana. "The 'Great Terror' in the GULAG: A Case Study of the White-Sea Baltic Combine and Camp of the NKVD." PERSA Working Paper no. 47. Original version received 9 August 2006. University of Warwick, Department of Economics. http://search.warwick.ac.uk/website?indexSection=sitebuilder &q=klimkova&x=0&y=0

Knight, Amy. *Beria: Stalin's First Lieutenant*. Princeton, N.J.: Princeton University Press, 1993.

Kotkin, Stephen. *Magnetic Mountain: Stalinism as a Civilization*. Berkeley: University of California Press, 1995.

Kuromiya, Hiroaki. *The Voices of the Dead: Stalin's Great Terror in the 1930s*. New Haven, Conn.: Yale University Press, 2007.

Levi, Primo. *The Drowned and the Saved.* New York: Vintage, 1989.

Merridale, Catherine. *Night of Stone: Death and Memory in Twentieth-Century Russia.* New York: Penguin, 2000.

Millar, James R., ed. *Politics, Work and Daily Life in the USSR: A Survey of Former Soviet Citizens.* Cambridge: Cambridge University Press, 1987.

Montefiore, Simon Sebag. *Court of the Red Tsar.* New York: Knopf, 2004.

Morukhov, Mikhail. "The White Sea-Baltic Canal." In *The Economics of Forced Labor: The Soviet Gulag,* edited by Paul Gregory. Stanford, Calif.: Hoover Institution Press, 2003.

Moser, Charles A., ed. *The Cambridge History of Russian Literature.* Cambridge and New York: Cambridge University Press, 1992.

Overy, Richard. *Russia's War: A History of the Soviet War Effort, 1941–1945.* New York: Penguin, 1997.

Pleshakov, Constantine. *Stalin's Folly.* Boston and New York: Mariner Books, 2005.

Pogodin, Nikolai. *Aristocrats: A Comedy in Four Acts.* Translated by Anthony Wixley and Robert S. Carr. London: Lawrence & Wishart, 1937 [?].

Rayfield, Donald. *Stalin and His Hangmen: The Tyrant and Those Who Killed for Him.* New York: Random House, 2004.

Rossi, Jacques. *The Gulag Handbook.* Translated by William A. Burhans. New York: Paragon House, 1989.

Ruder, Cynthia A. *Making History for Stalin: The Story of the Belomor Canal.* Gainesville: University Press of Florida, 1998.

The Shoah Foundation. Oral Testimony Archive, USC Shoah Foundation Institute for Visual History and Education, Leavey Library, 650 W. 35th Street, Suite 114 Los Angeles, CA 90089–2571.

Slepyan, Kenneth. *Stalin's Guerillas: Soviet Partisans in World War II.* Lawrence: University Press of Kansas, 2006.

Smith, Kathleen E. *Remembering Stalin's Victims: Popular Memory and the End of the USSR.* Ithaca, N.Y.: Cornell University Press, 1996.

Solzhenitsyn, Aleksandr I. *The Gulag Archipelago, 1918–1956: An Experiment in Literary Investigation.* Translated by Thomas P. Whitney (Parts I–IV) and Harry Willetts (Parts V–VII). New York: Harper and Row, 1985.

Swianiewicz, Stanislaw. *Forced Labour and Economic Development: An Enquiry into the Experience of Soviet Industrialization.* London: Oxford University Press, 1965.

Taylor, S. J. *Stalin's Apologist: Walter Duranty: The New York Times's Man in Moscow.* Oxford and New York: Oxford University Press, 1990.

Toker, Leona. *Return from the Archipelago: Narratives of Gulag Survivors.* Bloomington: Indiana University Press, 2000.

Vatulescu, Cristina. "Early Cinematic Representations of the Gulag: The Camps as Soviet Exotica in (1928)." Paper given at Harvard's Conference on the Soviet Gulag: Its History and Legacy. Davis Center for Russian and Eurasian Studies, Harvard University. November 2–5, 2006.

Vider, Ernest. Interview taken on September 12, 1997, in the city of Mukachevo. Oral testimony can be found at the Shoah Foundation. Archives Code 35817–48.

Vilensky, Simeon, ed. *Till My Tale Is Told: Women's Memoirs of the Gulag.* Translated by Cathy Porter and John Crowfoot. Bloomington: Indiana University Press, 1999.

Viola, Lynne. *The Unknown Gulag: The Lost World of Stalin's Special Settlements.* New York: Oxford University Press, 2007.

Werth, Nicolas. *Cannibal Island: Death in a Siberian Gulag.* Princeton, N.J.: Princeton University Press, 2007.

———. *La terreur et le desarroi: Staline et son systeme.* Paris: Perrin, 2007.

Whitfield, F. J. Review of H.W.L Dana, ed., *Seven Soviet Plays* (New York: The Macmillan Company, 1946). *American Slavic and East European Review* 5, no. 3/4 (Nov., 1946), pp. 203–4.

Zemtsov, Ilya. *Encyclopedia of Soviet Life.* New Brunswick, N.J.: Transaction Publishers, 1991.

Zinsser, William. *Inventing the Truth: The Art and Craft of Memoir.* New York: Mariner Books, 1998.

Zubok, Vladslav. *Zhivago's Children: The Last Russian Intelligentsia.* Cambridge, Mass.: Harvard University Press, 2009.

FICTION

Amis, Martin. *House of Meetings.* New York: Vintage, 2008.

Shalamov, Varlam. *Kolyma Tales.* Translated by John Glad. New York: Penguin, 1994.

Solzhenitsyn, Aleksandr I. *The Cancer Ward.* New York: Farrar, Straus and Giroux, 1991.

———. *The First Circle.* Translated by Thomas P. Whitney. New York: Harper & Row, 1968.

———. *One Day in the Life of Ivan Denisovich.* New York: Farrar, Straus and Giroux, 2005.

INTERNET RESOURCES

Gulag: Many Days, Many Lives http://gulaghistory.org/ Life in the Gulag presented through archival documents, photographs, art, film, and a bibliography, a project of The Center for New History and Media, George Mason University.

The Stalin Project www.stalinproject.com/ A multimedia, interactive resource about Stalin and Stalinism.

The Memorial Society www.memo.ru/eng/index.htm Memorial is dedicated to the memory of Stalin's Gulag. It is a library, a repository for documents and books, a home for researchers, and an advocacy organization in Moscow and several other cities in Russia.

Gulag: Soviet Forced Labor Camps and the Struggle for Freedom http://gulaghistory.org/nps/onlineexhibit/museum/beyond.php Formed by the Gulag Museum of Perm, Russia, and the National Park Service, this site features photos, drawings, explanations, and the history of the USSR's Gulag camp system.

DOCUMENTARY

Solovki Power, Marina Goldovskaia. Documentary, USSR, 1988.

RESOURCES IN RUSSIAN

Afanasev, Yu. N., editor. *Istoriia stalinskogo Gulaga: Konets 1920-pervaia polovina 1950 godov: sobranie dokumentov v semi tomakh* [History of Stalin's Gulag: From the end of the 1920s until the first half of the 1950s in 7 volumes]. Moscow: Rosspen, 2004–2005.

Berdinskikh, Viktor. *Viatlag*. Kirov: Kirovskaia oblastnaia tipografiia, 1998.

Borodkin, L. I., P. Gregory, and O. V. Khlevniuk, eds. *Gulag: Ekonomika prinuditelnogo truda [Gulag: The Economics of Forced Labor]*. Moscow: Rosspen, 2008.

Gvozdkova, L. I. *Stalinskie lagerii na territorii Kuzbassa, 30–40-e gg* [Stalin's Camps in Kuzbass, 1930–1940]. Kemerovo: Kemerovskii gosudarstvennii universitet, 1994.

Khlusov, M. I., compiler. *Ekonomika Gulaga i ee rol v razvitii strany, 1930-e gody* [The Economics of the Gulag and Its Role in the Development of the Country in the 1930s]. Moscow: Rossiiskaia akademiia nauk, 1998.

Kokurin, A. I., and Yu. N. Morukov. *Stalinskie stroiki GULAGa, 1930–1953* [Stalin's Gulag, 1930–1953]. Moscow: Materik Publishing House, 2005.

Kokurin, A. I., and N.V. Petrov. *GULAG: 1918–1960*. Moscow: Materik Publishing House, 2002.

Kolpikova, E. F., *My iz gulaga* [We Are from the Gulag]. Moscow: Ripol klassik, 2009.

Morozov, L. M. *Gulag v Komi krai, 1929–1956* [The Gulag in the Komi Region, 1929–1956]. Syktyvkar: Syktyvkarskii gosudarstvennii universitet, 1997.

Smirnov, M. B., ed. *Sistema ispravitelno-trudovykh lagerei v SSSR 1923–1960* [The System of Corrective Labor Camps in the USSR, 1923–1960]. Moscow: Zvenia, 1998.

Triakhov, V. N. *Gulag y voina: zhestokaia pravda dokumentov* [Gulag and War: The Terrible Truth of the Documents]. Perm: Pushka, 2004.

INDEX